"This winning history of a recent revolution in product design—making objects that are easy to use and which people actually need—includes fascinating case studies and anecdotes drawn from the authors' careers in the field."

—*The New York Times Book Review* (Editors' Choice)

"*User Friendly* weaves a stirring and unexpected story of how the machine age gave way to the iPhone era. Monolithic tools of war became chipper assistants, but at a price. Passionate and poised, Cliff Kuang and Robert Fabricant show us how user-friendliness took command, mapping a new root structure for the simmering chaos of the recent internet."

—Alexis Madrigal, author of *Powering the Dream*

"In this epic work, Cliff Kuang and Robert Fabricant offer us a compulsively readable successor to *The Design of Everyday Things*. They have crafted a definitive narrative that is as well designed as the products that grace its pages."

—Brian Merchant, author of *The One Device*

"[An] engrossing history of how the design of commercial products and technological innovations came to be singularly focused on the user experience . . . An erudite and insightful exploration of a revolution in human thinking that most people have probably never considered."

—*Publishers Weekly*

"A readable, instructive study of the role of design in making our lives easier to live . . . Of a piece with the work of Henry Petroski or Donald Norman, Kuang and Fabricant's book serves up plenty of useful examples and offers a few rules for would-be designers, the very first of which is 'start with the user.' A book that belongs on every designer's shelf—and that consumers of design will enjoy, too." —*Kirkus Reviews*

"Digital-era design has striven to eliminate the user manual: to make and sell us things that 'just work.' But this leaves us uncertain of how things do work—or why they've been made to work the way they do. *User Friendly* gives us answers. It's the missing manual to the designed world, and that's just what we need."

—Rob Walker, author of *The Art of Noticing*

"Happy, shiny, smiley gadgets! They're everywhere, and they're watching us. User-friendliness is the cognitive lubricant that makes us love the stuff we use. This fascinating book unveils how—and why—everyday products try so hard to be likeable and friction-free." —Ellen Lupton, author of *Beautiful Users*

"*User Friendly* is essential reading for anyone who seeks to understand why business and society have turned to design in pursuit of growth and change. Simply put, empathy is good business in today's world. The case for placing design at the center of human enterprise is stronger than ever, thanks to this insightful work."

—Tim Brown, chair of IDEO and author of *Change by Design*

"*User Friendly* illuminates our current age, in which our devices strive to know us better than we know ourselves. Anyone who cares about the fraught but increasingly urgent role that design plays in our lives owes it to themselves to read this hugely compelling book."

—Scott Dadich, former editor in chief of *Wired*
and creator of *Abstract: The Art of Design*

Cliff Kuang with Robert Fabricant

User Friendly

Cliff Kuang is an award-winning journalist and UX designer. He was previously the head of UX at *Fast Company*, as well as its design editor. In that role, he founded Co.Design, one of the world's leading design publications.

Robert Fabricant is the former vice president of creative for Frog Design, one of the leading industrial design studios of the past fifty years, and is an award-winning cofounder and partner at Dalberg Design.

User Friendly

How the hidden
rules of design
are changing
the way we live,
work, and play

Cliff Kuang with
Robert Fabricant

PICADOR

MCD

Farrar, Straus and Giroux
New York

Picador
120 Broadway, New York 10271

The Library of Congress has cataloged the MCD hardcover edition as follows:
Names: Kuang, Cliff, 1978– author. | Fabricant, Robert, 1966–
Title: User friendly : how the hidden rules of design are changing the way we
    live, work, and play / Cliff Kuang with Robert Fabricant.
Description: First edition. | New York : MCD/Farrar, Straus and Giroux, 2019. |
    Includes bibliographical references and index.
Identifiers: LCCN 2019022184 | ISBN 9780374279752 (hardcover)
Subjects: LCSH: Product design—Social aspects.
Classification: LCC TS171.4 .K83 2019 | DDC 658.5—dc23
LC record available at https://lccn.loc.gov/2019022184

Picador Paperback ISBN: 978-1-250-75820-0

Designed by Richard Oriolo
Illustrations by Chris Allen

Our books may be purchased in bulk for promotional, educational, or
business use. Please contact your local bookseller or the Macmillan
Corporate and Premium Sales Department at 1-800-221-7945, extension 5442,
or by e-mail at MacmillanSpecialMarkets@macmillan.com.

Picador® is a U.S. registered trademark and is used by Macmillan Publishing
Group, LLC, under license from Pan Books Limited.

picadorusa.com • instagram.com/picador
twitter.com/picadorusa • facebook.com/picadorusa

10 9 8 7 6 5 4 3 2 1

For my wife and daughter

—CLIFF

To my family and friends
Hopefully this will explain once and for all
what I do every day, and why it matters

—ROBERT

Contents

User Friendly

Apple Macintosh (1984)

Introduction:

The Empire of User-

Friendliness

User Friendly
1. Computing. Of hardware or software: easy to use or understand, esp. by an inexperienced user; designed with the needs of a user in mind.
2. In extended use: easy to use; accessible, manageable.

At only four stories tall, the world's largest office building sits low to the ground but commands a footprint worthy of a UFO that could blot out the sun: a perfect doughnut shape, a mile around its edge. In the middle lies a grove meant to recall the time, just fifty years ago, when Silicon Valley wasn't Silicon Valley, but rather the Valley of Heart's Delight, covered in 10 million fruit trees—apricot, cherry, peach, pear, and apple. It took Apple, the computing giant, years to buy up all that land in secret, assembling some sixteen different plots across fifty acres in a $5 billion jigsaw. If the building looks like a spaceship, then it's one that lifted off directly from Steve Jobs's imagination to land in the heart of an otherwise sleepy suburb. It was one of the last undertakings that the great man signed off on before he died.

Every morning during the construction of Jobs's last dream, Harlan Crowder woke up to the dull roar of heavy trucks on their way to the site, their alarms bleating as they nudged their loads into place. When we met, Crowder was seventy-three years old with three grown children. He wore a white goatee and a retiree's wardrobe of rumpled pants and floral shirts. In Crowder's neighborhood, the hubbub attending Apple Campus 2's arrival had unleashed a swarm of real estate agents trawling door-to-door and offering to make people rich.

These agents were mostly women buffed to a high gloss, and they came adorned in big brass jewelry that served as armor against holdouts like Crowder. "There was one, she said it just like that: 'I have ten people waiting to start a bidding war for your house,'" Crowder said in his Texas drawl as we sat talking on his back patio. Houses like his had originally been built in the 1960s for the population boom incited by the nascent transistor industry. When I visited, modest three-bedroom ranch houses like Crowder's were easily fetching $2.5 million. In a year, he assumed it could be 10 percent higher, maybe more. It was all some strange dream.

Crowder isn't a famous person—there are untold thousands like him, spread out in the Valley: people of technical ability who built the place but whose names are lost to history. But Crowder is one of the first people in the annals of history to use the term "user friendly" to refer to a computer. Every week or so, Crowder fends off the real estate agents and their offers of a multimillion-dollar payday. Apple fuels it all—Apple, the company that made "user friendly" into an idea that we live with every day.

Crowder looks on at the new Apple Park during his daily walks past the campus, the crown jewel in an empire built upon trillions of dollars in iPods and iMacs and iPads and Apple Watches and iPhones—devices that, despite being some of the most advanced computers ever made, can still be operated by toddlers. Their power dwarfs that of the "supercomputers" Crowder once worked with at IBM. That he'd come to IBM at all seemed like another kind of dream. He'd failed eighth-grade algebra. After high school, he bummed around until enlisting in the Army, where he trained as a medic: a year and a half of doctor's training with all the theory stripped out, so that you simply knew the essentials required to save a life. The practicality and the pressure lit into him. The one-time layabout graduated first in his class. After service came college at East Texas State University, in Commerce. "It wasn't the edge of nowhere, but you could see the edge," he told me.

Crowder had seen an IBM recruitment flyer on a bulletin board at college, calling for science majors to enter a newfangled training program. He replied, and they called him back. He flew up to Yorktown, New York, without much idea of what to expect. IBM's research center was a crescent-shaped architectural landmark designed by the great Finnish American designer Eero Saarinen—the original corporate-campus-as-spaceship. Its facade was a gleaming curved-glass curtain wall, and the walls inside were hewn from New York's native granite. The building's design was a statement about the modern workplace from the world's smartest company, with as many Ph.D.s on staff as a university.

Crowder walked to his job interview in awe. The building resembled nothing so much as the spaceship from *2001*, a bright techno future that was big news in 1968. Here was a place where the water-cooler conversations were about scientific breakthroughs. "I'd have done anything to work there. I didn't care if I had to clean the toilets," Crowder said, his voice still shimmering with glee. IBM had run out of computer programmers, and the company wanted to make more of them. Crowder got the job, and he took to the pragmatic nature of the work, using computers to solve real-world problems that you could measure by the ton, such as mapping shipping routes and calculating trucking loads. He found that he had a mind for visualizing the complex equations his job required.

The field where Crowder worked, operations research, began with World War II and the Marshall Plan. Rebuilding Europe meant shipping a mind-boggling amount of matériel across the Atlantic, but also shipping back a mind-boggling amount of matériel that had accumulated in dozens of countries during a war effort of unprecedented scale. Loading ships efficiently on the way over, then loading them up efficiently for the return home, was a math problem whose unruly complexity demanded computing power.

Crowder was working on these sorts of operational problems for IBM's clients in the 1960s. To create a computer program, he had to use a machine to punch intricate holes in cards the size of an airplane boarding pass. When he was done, he couldn't just walk up to the computer himself. The computer was a $5 million machine—about $35 million in today's money—patrolled by two security guards and a perky-eared German shepherd. Crowder would spend all day programming and then take his stack of cards to the computer attendant behind a window, who fed the cards into the machine. The computer would spend all night calculating, and the results would usually be ready for Crowder by the morning—if he hadn't made a mistake. This was a big "if." A mistake would be as simple as a misplaced character that gummed up the processing, or a poorly defined equation that divided by zero and sent the computer into looping infinities. (Shades of Apple again: The address of its former campus is One Infinite Loop.)

Faced with fitfully waiting overnight to see if all the days they'd spent programming had been wasted by a typo, a cultish group of programmers at IBM found a way out. Working at a minicomputer tied to a mainframe down the hall and using a simplified programming language called APL—literally, A Programming Language—you could simply write a program and run it. You just typed up your program, saw whether the computer spat out meaningful results, and immediately knew whether your program was heading in the right direction. This was magic. Simply seeing the fruits of your work right away let you shape new ideas in your head just as soon as you had them. Years later, Steve Jobs would describe a computer as a bicycle for the mind—a fabulous machine that could turn the muscle power of a single person into the ability to traverse a mountain in a day. Crowder and his colleagues were among the very first to experience that ideal firsthand. The machine, once it was capable of *immediate feedback*, was actually augmenting what your mind could do. An insight might flash before you, and you could test that idea out right away. Seeing how well it worked would spur new ideas, and on and on. Thanks to these feedback loops, computer programming, which had once had the stately pace of chamber music, entered its own improvisational Jazz Age.

These "jazz musicians" traded their ideas in academic journals. The only thing was, it was awful trying to re-create the music someone had made on their machines. You couldn't tell how easy it would be to test another person's work or replicate it. The programs simply didn't consider what *someone else* might do with them. To Crowder, they weren't *user friendly*. And so Crowder proposed that a computer program be gauged not just on how well it solved a problem but on how easy it made the lives of the people trying to solve it. To be clear, he didn't actually invent the term. As far as he knows, it had been floating around in the air, and it was there when he needed it. Which tends to prove how powerful it was—how it encapsulated something that people had started to feel.

And yet IBM didn't go on to invent the user-friendly world—even though it hired some of the best designers in the world, such as Paul Rand, who created its logo; Eero Saarinen, who created its campus; and even Eliot Noyes, who designed its Selectric type-writer. Instead, that accomplishment is typically credited to Apple, which adapted ideas seeded at Xerox PARC to create the Macin-tosh. Just a decade after Crowder first wrote his paper describing user-friendly algorithms, Apple was making ads for user-friendly machines:

In the olden days, before 1984, not very many
people used computers—for a very good reason.
    Not very many people knew how.
    And not very many people wanted to learn . . .
    Then, on a particularly bright day in
California, some particularly bright engineers
had a brilliant idea: since computers are so
smart, wouldn't it make sense to teach computers
about people, instead of teaching people about
computers?
    So it was that those very engineers worked
long days and late nights—and a few legal
holidays—teaching tiny silicon chips all about
people. How they make mistakes and change their
minds. How they label their file folders and save
old phone numbers. How they labor for
their livelihoods. And doodle in their spare
time . . .
    And when the engineers were finally finished,
they introduced us to a personal computer so
personable it can practically shake hands.

There's a certain magic in how a few words can elide so many stories and so many ideas. This book is an attempt to paint a picture that's gone missing in plain sight.

It began as an idea first broached with me by Robert Fabricant, who at the time was vice president of creative at the firm Frog Design. We'd known each other for a couple of years, and Robert's pitch, which mirrored a decade of my own work as a writer and an editor, was simply that user-experience design, which had been the province of computer geeks and futurists, wasn't a niche anymore. In an era in which 2.5 billion people own smartphones, user experience now occupies the center of modern life, remaking not just our digital lives but also business, society, even philanthropy. It was Robert's idea to call this book *User Friendly*—a term whose very familiarity proves the thesis. And yet the history of the term, the meaning it conveys, the mechanics of how it works—these all remain, outside of a few professional circles, either untold or known only in pieces. What we first conceived over a period of a few months—and assumed would take six months to complete—eventually took me six years to write and report. That is the book you're reading now, one that tries to show how "user friendly" was invented, how it shapes our everyday rhythms, and where it will go next.

There is a certain generation of designers who quarrel with the term "user friendly." They disagree with the premise that gadgets should always presume a chipper familiarity to their users; they quibble about whether "friendliness" is the right relationship between a device and its user; they consider the idea condescending in how it implies that users must be treated like children. These critiques are sometimes reasonable. They also fail to undermine the term itself while missing a larger point.

Today, alluringly designed gadgetry has remade the texture of everyday life, from how we make money to how we make friends to how we make babies. We now expect that the tools we use to diagnose cancer or to identify a problem with an airplane engine will be as simple to use as *Angry Birds*. We aren't wrong to do so. Technology should become simpler over time. Then it should become simpler still, so that it disappears from notice. This has already happened with stunning speed, and that transformation is one of the greatest cultural achievements of the last fifty years. But even as the designed world shapes us, its inner logic remains almost totally absent from daily conversation. Instead, whether we're speaking to our kids or speaking to our grandparents, the only words we have are "user friendly." We hardly examine them at all—and yet they're the standard by which we judge the designed world.

"User friendly" rolls off the tongue unconsciously because we know what it means, or we think we know what it means. It means something like "Did this thing do what I want?" But even that simplified formulation raises a litany of questions: Why should some product defer to our desires? How does the person who created that object come to understand what I want to begin with? What can go wrong in translating our desires into artifacts? It took more than a century of progress and peril to answer those questions. This book is about how the idea of user-friendliness was born and how it works. We travel backward and forward in time, from the paradigm shifts that made user-friendliness into something people cared about at all to the present day, when user-friendliness has redefined nearly every minute of our waking lives.

Many of the ideas in this book will be familiar to user-experience designers—the people who observe our lives so that they might invent new products. Still, this story should be new. User-experience design, which has come to encompass everything from theme parks to chatbots, simply hasn't had a narrative thread comprehensible to both laymen and experts. The great chain of ideas that spawned it typically hasn't been appreciated as a tapestry of personalities, happenstance, and ideological struggle. If user experience is foreign to you, I hope you'll come away from this book understanding how the world is being remade every day—the ideals, principles, and assumptions that lie behind the taps and swipes you take for granted. If you're a designer, I hope you'll better understand the origin of the ideas you swim among, so that you might better examine—and even challenge—the values you put into the things you make. At the very least, I hope you'll be able to offer this book to the people you know and say, "This is why user experience matters."

Part I

Easy to Use

Three Mile Island cooling towers (1978)

1

Confusion

Wednesday, March 28, 1979: The worst nuclear accident in American history begins with a clog in the basement at a lonely hour. One of the specialists, Fred Scheimann, huffs from the control room down eight flights of stairs into the sprawling guts of the Three Mile Island facility. Scheimann knows every pump and pipe and gauge that he passes while crossing the basement's central walkway, which stretches nearly the length of a football field. He finds his way to Tank 7, where his night shift workers have been gathered since before midnight. Then he clambers on a giant pipe running along its flank so that he can peer in through the tank's sight glass. It's jungle hot, noisy with clanking pumps and sighing valves. Far down on the other side of the complex, the plant's five-hundred-ton turbine—a block long and spinning thirty times a second—issues a piercing squeal.[1] Scheimann takes his glasses off to get a better look, then mops his brow. *This goddamn clog.* "Hey, Miller . . ." he calls out. But before Miller can answer, the entire assembly begins to shudder. The gathered men all feel a surge of water, "like a freight train,"[2] barreling through the giant pipe Scheimann is standing on. Scheimann hurls himself off just before the pipe bursts from its moorings, then cracks, showering the spot where he'd just been standing with a geyser that would have stripped off his skin.

Still, this is a tiny leak. A plant like this has been designed to protect itself, and the men can hear the plant's thousands of subsystems shudder into action. Hundreds of yards away in the heart of the complex, the reactor core begins an automatic shutdown. High above them all, the cooling towers, thirty stories tall, release a million pounds of steam into the predawn skies above the slow-moving Susquehanna River. A farmer across the river in Goldsboro later recalls stopping short under the light of his barn, listening to what sounded like the whoosh of a jet engine.[3]

Scheimann picks himself up off the ground and then runs back to the control room at a dead sprint. The place is laid out like the bridge of a ship. In fact, almost everyone in the room is ex-Navy, having served stints aboard nuclear submarines or aircraft carriers. In the center of the room is a massive console; behind that, there's another wall of control panels arrayed in an arc ninety feet long and reaching up to the ceiling.[4] All told, there are eleven hundred dials, gauges, and switch indicators, and more than six hundred warning lights. At this moment, it seems like every one of them is wailing. The room is buried in noise. Here, at a critical moment, the machine is generating not just noise but chaos in the minds of its operators. The taint of that chaos will linger for hours.[5]

What on earth does any of it mean? How do you find the one thing wrong when the system is telling you there are hundreds? Scheimann starts riffling through the emergency manuals, making sure that every procedure is followed to a T. Reactor trips are a pain, but they aren't uncommon. With hundreds of fail-safes layered atop one another, the chances of a meltdown seem vanishingly small. Barring human intervention, the plant will shut itself down at any hint of danger. But you shut down one light and another goes off; the way it's all designed—or isn't designed—makes it impossible to imagine how it's all linked, or how one missed signal can cascade.

Every single one of the reactor's systems is designed to serve two abiding purposes: to either create heat or contain it. The core itself is made of thousands of uranium pellets the size of a finger. The heat flows from the uranium as its atoms split apart, spewing heat and neutrons. The neutrons cause more uranium to split, powering a chain reaction that grows upon itself exponentially—the power of that chain reaction is such that each pellet can produce as much heat as a ton of coal.[6] While all that happens, the heat must be controlled, and that requires massive amounts of cool water, flowing over and past the reactor, carrying heat from the core, driven by pumps two stories tall that are powerful enough to reverse the flow of the Colorado River. The water flows over the core, transferring the heat and carrying it away. That water, now hot, is used to make steam; the steam spins a giant turbine, which generates enough electricity for a small city.

The men up in the control room first make sure that the core has all the water it needs by switching on pumps and monitoring boilers and turbines. Then something strange happens—a critical slippage between what the men understand and what the machine is telling them. Even though the emergency pumps are on at full blast, the water pressure in the reactor core is somehow going *down*. Scheimann is still at the manuals, shouting out every protocol one step at a time, then nodding as someone shouts back that it's been done. Then the water level stops sliding. It starts to hold. The emergency pumps seem to finally be filling the system back up with water. Relief washes across the room. Minutes later, that relief evaporates. There has to be pressure in the system. That's what tells you there's enough water. But there's a Goldilocks range, and the reactor loop seems to be shooting past it. The pressure begins to rise slowly at first, then quicker. *What the hell is happening?* To 160 inches, 180 inches, 190, 200. And then a spike: 350, higher than they'd ever seen. Worry starts creeping through the room's cool professionalism.[7]

"Okay, we're going solid!"

This is everyone's greatest fear. "Going solid" means that the reactor loop is filling completely with water, so the pressure will just build until the pipes burst, draining the reactor and causing a meltdown. Hurriedly, the men switch off the emergency pumps, to keep them from adding more water to the core.[8] It will turn out to be the day's single worst decision.

While all this is happening, the temperature in the core is continuing to rise. That shouldn't be possible. If there's so much water in the system, why isn't the reactor cooling down? *Maybe there's a valve open somewhere, and all the water is simply leaking out?* There's a gauge in the control room that should have the answer. It's hard to find, squirreled away out of sight on the back of a control panel on the other side of the room. The man sent to check the gauge finds it, and sees that it looks fine. But he's looked at the wrong one. So he walks away and tells everyone else that the valves are closed: the system's not leaking water, and it's time for everyone to start over again and look for another answer. No one knows the core is beginning to destroy itself.[9]

Just a few hours later, at 6:00 a.m., the catastrophe has taken on a sickening momentum, though no one seems close to figuring out what's really happening. Pete Velez walks into the control room of Reactor 2 to begin his usual shift. There's typically only a couple of men there, gliding about among the institutional-green control panels and thousands of placidly glowing lights, enjoying the special silence of supreme order. But today Velez can see that something terrible is in motion. People are everywhere amid the telltale signs of swallowed panic: coffee cups strewn about, stacks of safety manuals piled high, men tearing at them while sweat stains spread under their arms. Velez has encountered some of the bigwigs now milling around only as names atop a memo—regional managers and their managers, in from headquarters in Ohio, all of them trying to decipher what the hell has gone wrong. He plucks a fresh green notebook from his pocket and jots down his first entry of the day: *Aw shit.*[10]

Velez and everyone here knew the dangers that came with working in a nuclear plant. It's what they trained for until the dangers were familiar enough to feel routine. But Velez was also uniquely intimate with a gruesome kind of calculation: As the radiation-protection foreman, it was his job to know exactly how much nuclear exposure a worker could handle. Typically, he shouldn't be exposed to more than 3 rem of radiation in three months. (This being 1979, at a nuclear plant, the workers are almost all men.) Emergencies were different. Say you had to send a man to save some critical piece of equipment. In a month, he'd probably be fine if he'd soaked up 25 rem. No lasting effects. You could justify that tiny personal risk against the chance of a great catastrophe. Any more radiation than that, things got complicated. The rule of thumb was that saving another man's life was worth the risk at no more than 100 rem. Any higher—say 120 rem—and it became a decision no one else could make but you. Could you let someone just suffer there alone?

None of this is abstract anymore when the next day, March 29, Velez finds himself cracking a door to steal a peek inside a room that could kill him. He huddles with Ed Hauser, the chemistry foreman in charge of monitoring the water that constantly cools the reactor, saving it from its own ferocious heat. They're both covered head to toe in coveralls, wet suits, gloves, boots, and masks, with every seam taped up. In that split second, he can see that when the hazard klaxons had started screaming, the men on duty had literally dropped what they were doing and ran: hats and coats still on the rack, telephones off the hook, a pot of coffee scalding the table.[11] At the back of the room there are about twenty-five faucets above a hooded sink. That's what Velez and Hauser are here for: to understand just what's happening in the reactor, to understand how bad the situation has become, because instruments in the control room aren't making sense.

No one knows how much radiation is leaking from the reactor core. These twenty-five valves connect to twenty-five pipes running thousands of feet through the building's unseen creases. There is one pipe in particular, no bigger around than a man's finger, connecting to the next building. It is a live wire to the nuclear core, which might already be melting.

Working like this, the men share the exposure and share the risk. Each man does his part, and no one gets more radiation than the other. Hauser is glad for it. Just yesterday, running a test elsewhere in the plant as everything turned to shit, he'd soaked up 600 rem within minutes. Yet he's still here, on duty again, planning with Velez. It becomes clear that Velez doesn't know how all the valves are ordered. Hauser does. So despite his prior exposure, he's the first man in, 600 rem and counting.

Velez looks to Hauser, checks his watch, and marks the time. *Go!* Hauser races into the room, straight for the valves at the sink, tearing open fifteen of them in exactly the right sequence. He's barely got his hand on the last one before he's turning heel, bursting back into the hallway. Now they wait. It takes an agonizing forty minutes for the water from Reactor 2 to travel the thousands of feet to this place and then sputter into the sink. There's still more valves to be turned. Velez has every excuse not to rush in—he doesn't know which ones. But instead, he presses Hauser for a description of the room so that he can take a dose of the exposure, so that Hauser doesn't get any more than necessary. Velez rushes in to turn the last valve. Now it's Hauser's turn to finish up the job. He rushes into the room, up to the sink, and catches a water sample in a vial. It seethes like a witches' brew, yellowed with chemicals engineered to soak up radioactive isotopes. Hauser raises his dosimeter to the sample. It spikes to 1,250 rem: so high that if you touched that vial with a bare hand, your fingertips would tingle.[12]

Miraculously, both Hauser and Velez survived the ordeal. It would be tempting to say that neither would have had to risk his life, but for one misread light on the back of some poorly laid out control panel—or, preceding that, a chain of misunderstanding which simply didn't go as it should have. But when we step back to see what went wrong—when we step back to imagine those eleven hundred dials and six hundred alarms, blaring at once—it's not merely that a machine broke down, or that a human failed to do what he was supposed to. The machine might have been made differently, with some greater awareness of how too much information and too little meaning can overwhelm the humans who are supposed to be in control. Instead, the machine and the human couldn't speak to each other in a language that each could understand. They were opposed in ways that no one in the moment could appreciate. The story of that opposition carries on today.

The only reason I'd ever thought to delve into the history of Three Mile Island was a hunch: that when you look hard enough at monumental machine disasters, you can usually find a design problem. It's almost always the case when planes crash. In fact, a misread signal at the worst possible time was responsible for the burning of Notre-Dame in 2019: A state-of-the-art fire system with inscrutable controls led to a bungled inspection while the blaze grew unchecked for thirty minutes.[13] Disasters always mirror the way things *should* work. So what would Three Mile Island reveal about the ways in which humans and machines should interact?

I expected to tell that story and why it mattered through analogies and metaphor—rhetorical sleight of hand, if I'm honest. But then, buried in a report about the disaster, I found a passing reference to another investigation into what had gone wrong, commissioned by Congress and coauthored by one Donald A. Norman. Could it be *that* Don Norman, the guy who'd actually invented the term "user experience" in the 1990s?[14] Seeing Norman's name mentioned in that report suddenly made it seem that the tenuous thread connecting Three Mile Island to the problems of the present day was instead a steel cable, buried but already in place.

In the era before user experience came to define digital life in the twenty-first century, Norman was the Moses of product design: In 1988, he published perhaps the only mainstream bestseller about the field, *The Design of Everyday Things*, which documented all the ways in which the fodder of everyday life failed us, from door handles to thermostats. His books became desk references for a generation of interaction designers. He'd tried to retire in the early 1990s, before Apple lured him there. He started by creating a panel of usability gurus, whom he dubbed "user-experience professionals" and who were meant to track every product as it was developed; in doing so, he became an early champion of the recently hired Jony Ive, who would go on to design the iPod, the iMac, and the iPhone.[15] Yet when I thumbed through Norman's books and all their footnotes, I found only passing references to nuclear reactor design—and none of them seemed to mention Three Mile Island at all. How had that catastrophe shaped the godfather of modern design?

Norman is slight, around five foot three, with stooped shoulders and a thin waist and a daily uniform of black turtleneck, jeans, and a gray newsboy cap. He stays fit by walking from his home to his office, up and over the steep hills that run across the UC San Diego campus, which straddles a series of scenic gorges. I visited him at the Design Lab, which he'd founded, on a typically warm, sunny December afternoon when the air was bright with the scent of eucalyptus and wild rosemary.

We were sequestered in a tiny meeting room with self-consciously kooky green shag carpeting. I was seated in a low-slung patio chair as Norman stood above me, pacing as he warmed up to the rhythm of a lecture. He began to describe the project that was to be his last great work, begun just six months prior. It was his second time coming out of retirement, and he would soon turn seventy-nine, on Christmas Day. "The university, you see, is filled with people who analyze in great depth," he said in his high, gnomish voice. "Designers don't analyze, they put together. This lab is an opportunity to put together all the knowledge at this university to solve problems in the environment, aging, health care. These are the kinds of problems we want to solve."[16]

I looked out into the lab beyond: just a few desks so far, filled by a handful of graduate students tapping at lines of code. The Design Lab held a prime location on campus, at the corner of a shiny new postmodern building. Like a lot of newer college campuses, UCSD is an open-air timeline of modern architectural fads, beginning with the library, done in the brutalist style popular in the 1960s, when the university was established, and continuing through a few ironic studies in classical forms that marked 1980s postmodernism. This building, composed of jagged bands of steel and glass, was the newest wave.

Norman's sprawling vision for design's power doesn't belong to him alone—it has, in fact, spread among the designers themselves. "I was in Shanghai visiting Frog, where they were very proud to tell me that their firm owned product design," Norman says. "Then I visited IDEO and told them what their competitor had said. And they said, 'We don't care. Singapore came and asked us to design their whole city.'" That wasn't a boast: Today, "design thinking"—the processes that inform modern design—has spread far beyond the design firm IDEO, which was a pioneer in marketing the movement. Design thinking is now marshaled to solve myriad problems at every scale. What was once a niche profession more commonly associated with chairs is now talked of as a solution to the world's ills, simply because of a shift in perspective.

Norman has a tendency to insert long pauses between thoughts or before answering questions—the kind of thing you grow comfortable doing only after many decades of people hanging on your every word. When I finally had the opening, I asked him, What do you remember about Three Mile Island? He described it as a break in his career, between the wonky academic research he'd been doing and the wider world. Early in his career, Norman spent years classifying the many ways people err when a task is set before them. What he discovered at Three Mile Island was notable in that it revealed just how little *other* people seemed to know about what he'd been working on. "The problem was that they spent so much time designing the technical parts, and none on understanding what it was like to work there, what was going on for people," Norman recalled. "The control room was done last, almost an afterthought when there wasn't time or money left."

He told a terrifying story of just how ingrained that myopia was: Reactors were almost always built in pairs; at some point, someone had realized that rather than customize two separate control rooms, it was cheaper to build one and then build its mirror image. Thus, the staff would have to work one day in one control room, and the next in a literal bizarro world, where everything was reversed. Those examples and others made Norman "realize that there wasn't any understanding of technology combined with psychology. We were building technology for people, but the technologists didn't understand people."

That myopia was reflected in the culture at large—a fracture between academics like him, who'd been studying how humans used the machines around them, and the people who created those machines. "The really good work in human error started in the Second World War, but it didn't become a major item for everyday people. Researchers like me didn't know who else was doing the same work," recalled Norman. And meanwhile, the designers "used to come from art schools or advertising, so it was all about style without any substance." Norman didn't know any designers himself at the time; he was an outsider to a profession that had leaped ahead, stumbling into a new world without a compass or a guide. Norman's books thus adopt an abiding tone of bemusement: *Dear God, will these people please listen to me?*

Norman's grand emphasis on such complex problems—the environment, period—belied the fact that he was famous, in large part, for the modesty of his insights as a design guru, thinking about doorknobs and teakettles. In his books, Norman is like Job, always being tested by some uncaring design god. He pushes on doors when they should be pulled, he has a hard time turning on the lights in his house, he's constantly being scalded in the shower. But in his thoroughgoing confusion, he's us.

The most consequential assumption behind all his work is that even if human error is to blame, it is hard to imagine any human not making these errors. Humans might fail—but they are not wrong. And if you try to mirror their thinking a little, even the stupidest and strangest things that people do have their own indelible logic. You have to know why people behave as they do—and design around their foibles and limitations, rather than some ideal. His great insight was that no matter how complex the technology, or how familiar, our expectations for it remain the same. Norman's discipline, cognitive psychology, wasn't so much about the nuances of buttons and control panels—though there's plenty of that, if you want to look—but rather the ways in which humans *assume* their environment should work, how they learn about it, how they make sense of it. This is what you have to understand if you are to design an app that people can use the first time they try it, or a plane that humans won't crash, or a nuclear reactor that humans can't cause to melt through the continental shelf.

All these lessons might have remained the obscure province of professors and anonymous designers and engineers if not for a coming wave of technological change: the profusion of computers and electrical gadgets in our everyday lives, driven by the rise of cheap transistors and silicon. Starting in the 1980s, the complex problems you might have found at Three Mile Island became consumer problems, having to do with making buttons work on gadgets such as VCRs and computers; the nuances of designing such devices went on to be expressed in the smartphone. It's no surprise then that the reasons a bad app drives you crazy have a direct relationship to the reasons that Three Mile Island almost melted into the earth. The problems that caused Three Mile Island are similar to the ones that frustrate you when you're trying to turn off the notifications on your smartphone; the inscrutability of a poorly designed light switch shares the same cause as your inscrutable cable box: a button that seems misplaced, a pop-up message that vanishes before you can figure out what it means, the sense that you did something but you don't know what. The presiding notion that you don't know how something works.

It was perhaps only natural that as the smartphone came to take over our everyday lives, the principles that had created it would come to seem like the answers not just to problems of the moment (How do I get people to understand this app?) but to problems of the era (How do I get people to understand their health care?). It made perfect sense if you believed that all these problems came down to the way that the machines failed the people who used them—and knowing that those failures revealed a truth about how people made sense of the world around them, and how they expected the artifacts of everyday life to behave.

Back to March 28, 1979. The graveyard shift was nearly over and the sun just starting to rise when the men finally solved what they thought was the biggest problem—too much water flooding the system, going solid. To stop that, they had made a fateful choice: to shut off the emergency water pumps. Once those pumps were off, they watched as the water levels fell in the pressurizer that fed the reactor's circulatory loop. Relief once again filled the room. Once again, it didn't last. Even though there seemed to be so much water in the system that it threatened to burst—so much water that the reactor should have been cooling down—the temperature just kept creeping up with a sickening steadiness.

As you watch this disaster movie unfold in your mind's eye, let the camera open upon the reactor control room, tracking slowly to the control panel at the center. Then let the camera pan across all those blazing warning lights. And then let it stop upon just one of the lights, a great big red one with a tag taped below it, saying exactly how to read it. It's one of the few lights along the panel that isn't lit, and that's a good thing. The men must have glanced over at it hundreds of times just to make sure. But that light was lying.

Its importance came from what it was supposed to be connected to—a manual release valve at the top of the reactor. The valve works like the whistling spout of a teakettle, venting steam whenever the pressure inside the reactor gets too high. If it was open, then that would mean the reactor had a massive leak at the top. Yet, as investigators later learned, the so-called PORV (pilot-operated release valve) light was designed around a deep conceptual error: it turned off when someone flipped the switch controlling the valve—not when the valve *actually closed*. Put another way, the light was merely marking intent, not action. If the light was off, that might mean the operator had done the right thing, closing the valve—or it might mean that the operator had done the right thing, but the switch wasn't working.[17] The misdesigned light could only ever say things were just fine.

In fact, the reactor's circulatory system had a huge hole in it, and no one could know, simply because the switch's feedback was meaningless. As the men called for help from more and more people across the country, and as the country began learning that something was going wrong at Three Mile Island, the temperature in the core kept rising. The machines had reached a limit to what they could reveal. The computer readouts, relaying the core temperature, stopped at 700 degrees. Now all they were saying was "???"[18] The systems were mute about what was actually happening. In fact, the core had reached an astounding 4,300 degrees. At just 700 degrees more, the 150-ton uranium core would have melted, searing though the eight-inch-thick steel containment vessel, then the twenty-foot-thick concrete foundation, not stopping until it hit bedrock beneath the Susquehanna River, blowing radioactive geysers straight into the sky.

It was nearly three hours after the clog in the basement caused the reactor's systems to lurch into a shutdown that the hole was finally plugged, by a man on the next shift who came on with fresh eyes and a hunch about what might have been missed. He'd shut the backup to the PORV, just to make sure. Then, hours after that, one of the system's original engineers finally commanded that the emergency cooling system be turned back on, ending the disaster. It was only later that anyone discovered that a complete meltdown of the reactor core had been as little as thirty minutes away.[19]

The Three Mile Island disaster happened less than two weeks after the release of *The China Syndrome*, a Jane Fonda blockbuster about a cover-up at a nuclear power plant. The movie's title came from the urban legend that an American reactor meltdown could bore a path through the earth's core, to China. Pop-culture fantasy and a real-world disaster together killed the growth of America's nuclear energy industry.[20] Plans for around eighty plants were scrapped; not a single new reactor was approved until 2012.[21] Today, what some experts argue is the safest, cheapest, and most reliable source of renewable energy remains clouded by fear. So, measured by what might have been, it's reasonable to call Three Mile Island the biggest design failure in American history. It's also the most instructive. The failures at TMI are a mirror image of the user-friendly age we live in, a tally of all the underlying principles that allow smartphones and touch-screens and apps to blend into our lives.

What Norman and the investigative team discovered at Three Mile Island was terrifying because it all seemed so obvious. The catastrophe unfolded over two days. In that time, hundreds of eyes pored over the system. If someone had closed the right valve sooner, or if, at any time, someone had thought to turn the emergency pumps back on, the place would have been saved. These men were not stupid. And yet even today, the few reports on TMI still blame "equipment failures and operator errors."[22] That's not it at all. At Three Mile Island, there were no grand equipment failures. The staff were some of the industry's best, and, incredibly, they never panicked.

In fact, the plant mostly behaved like the beautifully engineered machine it was meant to be. It would have saved itself if the men had left it alone.[23] What happened instead was that the men, thanks to catastrophically bad control-room design, were unable to understand what was going wrong. Swaddled in a fog of misdirection, they made catastrophic choices. The plant and the men were talking past each other: The plant hadn't been designed to anticipate the imaginations of men; the men couldn't imagine the workings of a machine.

Begin with the lights of the control panel. Despite every appearance of industrial precision, they had no abiding logic that a user could understand. Yes, a lit-up red bulb meant that a valve was presumably open. But not every valve was meant to be open or closed. Thus, normal operation was a hodgepodge of conflicting indicators, instead of them all being just one color when things were fine. The investigators who descended upon TMI in the wake of the accident reported that there were *fourteen* different meanings for red, and *eleven* for green. The consistency we now expect in countless rounded buttons and red warning lights was totally absent at Three Mile Island.

Sometimes the lights were above the control they corresponded to, sometimes off to the side. They weren't even grouped in a way that made sense: On the very same panel that would warn of water leaking from the reactor were alarm lights indicating elevator trouble. It was as if someone had taken a map of the reactor, cut it up into pieces, thrown it into the air, then taped it all back together. With such a map, you'd never be able to navigate. One reason we find apps easy to understand even if we've never used them before is that *navigability* and *consistency* are so ingrained into the patterns of app design today. Menus all largely behave the same way; so do swipes and taps.

There was also no indicator that would tell the men that the circulatory system was empty, like the gas gauge on your car. They were so fixated on the first panic—of filling the whole thing with too much water—that their imaginations simply failed. This, too, was a design failing that we now consider a given. When something works well enough for you to predict what it'll do next, you eventually form a *mental model* of it. That mental model can be deep or shallow—it might vary from just a sense that this button does that, to a picture in your head about how your hybrid car charges its battery. But those mental models are knowingly crafted by the designers who put interfaces in front of you.

Meaningless alarms, information clustered nonsensically, no consistency anywhere—these things translated to no mapping, no navigability, no mental models. These are tenets that everyone who owns a smartphone today takes for granted. These are the principles that make the user-friendly world work. You need all these principles in place to master a machine, whether that machine is a nuclear reactor or a child's toy. For you to master how a machine works, it needs to adhere to a pattern language.

But there was one essential thing whose failure loomed largest at TMI, one essential thing that we demand of any gadget in our lives: feedback. When the light was lying, when the temperature readouts were printing "???," and when there was no indicator telling anyone the system's total water levels, the machine just wasn't telling the men what they needed to know. With every little thing they tried, they grabbed on to the wrong feedback, focusing on the wrong things.

Feedback that works surrounds us every day, so we rarely think about it. It's feedback that defines how a product behaves in response to what you want. It's feedback that allows designers to communicate to their users in a language without words. Feedback is the keystone of the user-friendly world. In fact, the importance of feedback for both mankind and machines was a founding insight of both neuroscience and artificial intelligence. It was pioneered in 1940 by Norbert Wiener, a mathematical genius teaching at MIT. At the height of World War II, the German Luftwaffe had unveiled new warplanes faster than anything that had come before; they bombed British cities with impunity, banking too fast for any gunner to react—retaliatory artillery shells exploded in empty skies. Wiener thought to invent an algorithm that might automatically take radar data about a warplane's position, add in the flight time of an artillery shell, and spit out an anticipated vector where a gun could be pointed. The idea was to identify a brief window in time and space where an attacking plane would probably be, given the incoming radar signals. As new radar signals came in, that window would shift, creating a feedback loop.

Wiener and his collaborator, Julian Bigelow, realized that they'd stumbled onto something bigger. Imagine picking up a pencil: You form the idea in your head. You start to move your arm. And as you do, your brain must make an infinity of tiny corrections, using your eyes, muscles, and fingertips. Wiener knew, from a neuroscientist friend, that this was precisely what went wrong in certain hand tremors: The brain, having overshot its mark, would get stuck in a ricochet of overcorrections—just as Wiener's equations predicted. Wiener and Bigelow realized that feedback was "required by *any* voluntary action."[24] Feedback is what links the ineffable stuff in our minds—the things we want—with the machinery of our bodies and the information from our environment. As the anthropologist Gregory Bateson later marveled, "The central problem of Greek philosophy—the problem of purpose, unsolved for twenty-five hundred years—came within range of rigorous analysis." Feedback is what allows information to become action—and not just at the level of data, neurons, and nerves.

When you swing an ax to chop a piece of wood, the wood either splits or it doesn't. If it doesn't, you set the wood upright and swing again. When you put your bread in the toaster, you push the lever, and it clicks when you've pressed it far enough to turn the toaster on. Then you hear the filaments start to hum with electric current, a sign that the toaster has in fact turned on. You're getting feedback all along the way that the toaster has done what you'd wanted it to do. There was the click of the button, which had to be designed and engineered. And there was the sound of the wires heating up, which is simply a useful by-product of the toaster's physics. Without all those signals along the way, you'd just be endlessly fiddling, trying to understand whether the toaster was working.

The natural world is filled with feedback; in the man-made world, that feedback has to be designed. When you push a button, does the button actually affect the thing it's supposed to? The world of everyday life is so densely layered with information that it can be hard to realize how much information—how much feedback—we have to re-create in the world of design. And yet feedback is what turns any man-made creation into an object that you relate to, one that might evoke feelings of ease or ire, satisfaction or frustration. These are the bones of our relationship with the world around us.

Is there any problem in which our behavior doesn't match how we'd like to live that isn't a feedback problem? When we eat too much or eat the wrong things, it's a problem of not realizing in the moment how that tiny choice might affect our future. In the United States, doctors rarely track what happens *after* they've prescribed a drug or procedure, and so they just keep prescribing both to new patients, aiming to try everything since they can't see if any one thing actually works. And so we spend more and more each year on medical costs. Even climate change can be seen as a feedback problem. We cannot see our everyday contributions to carbon emissions, and the timeline is too long for us to see their effects. Imagine if carbon emissions had no other effects than they do now, but that carbon accumulation turned the sky from blue to green. In a world like that, it's hard to believe that we'd still be arguing about whether mankind was having an effect on the climate. We might instead be arguing about what to do about it. These are all problems of not feeling the stakes. Until the worst has happened, there is no feedback about what the effects of our actions are, and by then it's too late.[25] There may be no greater design challenge for the twenty-first century than creating better, tighter feedback loops in places where they don't exist, be they in the environment, health care, or government.

Feedback already defines the world we live in today. For example, we tend to assume that the internet's great revolution was connecting people. That's partly true. But consider the birth of buyer/seller feedback. eBay was an unknown startup until it rolled out a feature in which buyers and sellers could rate one another. Today, buyer/seller feedback is what has made us comfortable with the online economy—from buying products that we've never seen before on Amazon to staying in the homes of people we've never met, through Airbnb. In a previous era, we used brands to create trust—when you saw a toothpaste stamped with Colgate, you knew it was the product of a big, stable company whose long-term success depended on good products. Today, we have feedback from people who've tried out something we might like; even if you don't know them, you put your faith in there being a lot of them. As the economist Tim Harford has mused, without feedback, internet commerce might not be like it is now, with strangers trusting one another. It might be more like hitchhiking, something done only by people willing to take a risk.[26] Even the biggest startup of the last fifteen years, Facebook, was a company formed because of feedback. The Like button offered nothing less than a new way to send and receive affirmation, and in so doing, it rewired the social fabric of one-third of the world. (We'll see more of what that world has wrought in chapter 9.)

New technology improves the kind of feedback we can get, and how fast, allowing us to be more efficient and to act on new types of information. When you think about futuristic new technologies, you're often thinking about feedback that doesn't exist yet. From slickly designed custom nutrition regimens tailored to your metabolism, to public buses that are rerouted in real time, according to demand—these are all products predicated on bringing new feedback to the market. One of the most significant technologies of the twenty-first century, artificial intelligence, rests on feedback: Put simply, AI and machine learning are a collection of methods that allow algorithms to gauge how well they've performed, and then tweak their own parameters until they perform better. AI's chief breakthrough was in allowing algorithms to process feedback. (The very first "neural networks" were proposed by Warren McCulloch and Walter Pitts; McCulloch was inspired during one of Norbert Wiener's first lectures on feedback.)[27]

While the goal of most feedback is just to reassure us that something has gone as we expected, there are higher values and needs that feedback can address, whether they be soothing us or making us anxious or spurring our competitive instincts. For example, the Facebook Like button allowed us to attach a number to the loose uncertainty of our social bonds; it created a lighter, more fleeting definition of what counted as a relationship. And differing approaches to feedback lie behind two of the most successful startups in recent history: Instagram and Snapchat.

Instagram came first, in 2010. The app initially just let you share photos and see the photos of friends to whom you were linked. Soon after it launched came the commonsense policy, popularized by Facebook, of letting your friends like your posts (and, of course, seeing how many likes your friends' posts had gotten). That was the simple act of affirmation that the app revolved around. How many likes had you gotten? How many had your friends? Snapchat was built differently. It, too, was meant as a basic photo-sharing app. But it differed in two crucial ways: For one, photos you posted would disappear after twenty-four hours. And two, the photos did not earn likes. If you saw the photos your friend had posted, the only option available was to message your friend in response. Put another way, the only feedback you might get from a photo you posted was a direct conversation with a friend. The idea was that you could share without consequences—that sending a message of yourself looking sad and writing "BAD DAY" was enough, that you wouldn't be judged for it. That it would just be for the people you cared about. That it would just be *you*.

By 2016, Instagram had noticed that its users were talking differently about the product. It had been intended as a service for sharing photos in the moment—but users didn't talk that way about it anymore. They talked about the worry of wanting to curate what they showed other people. They talked about wanting to present the best possible picture. A feedback loop had set in, and reinforced itself: Likes made users more self-conscious about what they were posting, at the same time as improving cameras and Instagram stars were steadily raising the bar of what counted as a great Instagram post. "It started feeling like Instagram was for highlights rather than what was going on now," said Robby Stein, a product manager at Instagram.[28] This might sound innocuous, but it was potentially disastrous. The fear was that self-conscious users, because they posted less and less, would drift ever so slightly away from the app. If you were Instagram, that was a mechanism that could end your business altogether. And so Instagram ruthlessly adopted Snapchat's feedback philosophy, inserting a strip of "stories" at the top of the app, which let users share photos without the possibility of getting likes, and with the only way of replying being to send a direct message. It worked. Instagram Stories was wildly successful, used by 400 million people a day within a year of launch, helping Instagram nudge its average user time ever upward.

You could talk about Snapchat and Instagram as the story of two billion-dollar apps that gave people new ways to entertain themselves, and one another. Instagram had started to become the equivalent of an art gallery. Snapchat had become a spontaneous goof for your friends. The difference between those two businesses was really the story of the differing experiences that feedback could produce. Forty years after Three Mile Island, feedback is more than just what makes machines intelligible. When feedback is tied not merely to the way machines work but instead to the things we value most—our social circles, our self-image—it can become the map by which we chart our lives. It can determine how the experiences around us *feel*. In an era when how a product feels to use is the measure of how much we'll use it, this is everything.

The scariest things are often the easiest to forget. Sometimes, the forgetting is a reflex meant to keep us safe in our routines. Other times, it's a more willful erasure that carries an agenda. In the case of Three Mile Island, both seemed to be true. Three decades after the accident that nearly ended America's investment in nuclear energy, the industry has been utterly quiet, apparently afraid to draw any attention to itself whatsoever.

In the wake of the accident in 1979, Reactor 2 at Three Mile Island was shuttered and sealed. Meanwhile, Reactor 1 quietly continued to operate for another forty years. After Norman's commission suggested a number of changes to the design of all American reactors, it was retrofitted to be easier to operate. You might think that the very fact of Reactor 1's continued operation would be a success to celebrate, and yet that isn't the case for an industry covered fearfully in the press and misunderstood by the public. I wanted to learn exactly how it had been redesigned—what had been done to prevent the fog of confusion seen at Reactor 2. It took me months to convince the power plant's PR minders that I wanted to visit not to see what remained dangerous but to see what had been *fixed*. Finally, I went—not long before it would finally close, in September 2019.

I approached the Three Mile Island power plant on a wooded two-lane road, where the trees would briefly open up to offer flickers of a riverbank. Then, finally, I saw two gargantuan cooling towers on a tiny island of their own. They were three hundred feet tall, out of scale with everything around. Steam rose from just Reactor 1, in cottony plumes at the shambling tempo of a work song. Next to it, the tower of Reactor 2 stood quiet and streaked with rust, a dead sentry. It produced an eerie, strangely beautiful effect. Impossibly expensive to tear down, Reactor 2 loomed like a monumental post-modern sculpture. It was the commentary shadowing the reality.

Across the road was the ho-hum, squat brick building where workers trained so that the remaining reactor at Three Mile Island would never again come close to failing. Inside, it was appointed in institutional drab: orange-brown-gray carpet, public-school-style furniture made from chrome and chipboard.

The only reason this plant came to Pennsylvania at all was because of organized crime. In the 1970s, Metropolitan Edison had at first tried to build it in New Jersey. The Mob, which ran thick in the local unions, threatened to sabotage the work site unless it got the customary 1 percent kickback on the total building cost—which amounted to $7 million against $700 million. The power company pressed ahead anyway and began laying the foundations. Then, while a crane was lowering the 700-ton reactor core into the ground, some unknown construction worker dropped a literal wrench into the crane's workings. The message was clear: Pay up, or else the plant would be sabotaged in ways no one would ever know until it was too late. The power company promptly abandoned the site and decamped for a little spit of land in Pennsylvania. As a result, Reactor 2 was re-configured at Three Mile Island within a mere ninety days, for a site it was never meant to occupy. For those who worked there, Reactor 1 always performed beautifully. Reactor 2 remained a tetchy, temperamental beast.[29] Indirectly, the Mob truly had sabotaged the thing.

The simulated control room inside the training facility—with control panels painted an industrial green and rows of lights shrouded in protective cowls—resembled a movie set for Apollo Mission Control. My tour guide that day was the man who ran the room, a friendly, slightly built engineer with wire-rim glasses and decades on the job. He wore sturdy brown walking shoes and clothes that were scrupulously beige, making him look like an extra from a period movie about the Space Race. He was in charge of simulating the beginning of the end of the world, to see how the workers would respond. The room was an exact replica, down to the switch, of everything within the control room at Reactor 1.

In the wake of the accident at Reactor 2, a slew of subtle but powerful changes have worked their way across the industry. Standing in the facsimile control room, I could see them all. For one, from the back of the control room, everything was visible—there were no hidden indicator lights to be forgotten behind a panel. The room was easily navigable. The lights here were consistent: When everything checked out, they would all glow blue.

Normal wasn't why we were there, though, and it wasn't why this room was designed. The engineer stole away into an observation room at the back, and then came out to announce that the reactor had shut itself down. Just like it would have when the clog happened at Reactor 2.[30] A bank of lights went off, but the effect was muted. Contained. I pushed the button to quiet everything so that we could isolate what was happening.

For the people who were assembled in the control room at Three Mile Island in 1979, all these problems—erroneous feedback, controls that were inconsistent and impossible to navigate—added up to a greater problem. The men on duty literally couldn't imagine what was going wrong, because the machines wouldn't let them. They had no mental model showing how all these disparate and strange events might be connected, which would have helped them deduce what was going on.[31]

Mental models are nothing more and nothing less than the intuitions we have about how something works—how its pieces and functions fit together. They're based on the things we've used before; you might describe the entire task of user experience as the challenge of fitting a new product to our mental models of how things *should* work. To take one simple example, we have expectations of how a book "works": It has pages of information, laid out one after the other in a sequence; to get more information, you turn the page. One key to the enduring success of the touchscreen Amazon Kindle lies in how well it has remapped that mental model; just as you turn a page in a book, you "turn" a page by swiping at an e-book.[32]

When we can't assume how a gadget works, we use feedback—in the form of trial and error—to form a hazy mental model of its logic. But the most literal way to develop a mental model is to draw a picture. Looking around the Reactor 1 control room, I could see how it had been remade to create a mental model of the entire reactor. Even for a neophyte like myself, the major pieces of the system were easy to imagine. The room simply mirrored the reactor's design. Each control panel represented a discrete system—for example, the secondary circulation system or the reactor core—so that when I surveyed the room, I could see how those systems linked up, each flowing from one to the next. The reactor had been mapped to the room—just the same way you find the burners on your stove mapped to their corresponding dials, or the controls on your car's driver's seat mapped to buttons that resemble the seat's parts.[33] All of it was meant to create a durable picture in the minds of its operators, one whose steadiness could keep confusion at bay.

But the most curious thing I noticed was the way that workers were trained to interact inside this little bubble of precision. When workers would go to confirm some crucial reading, they went in pairs:

One would do an action, the next one would confirm the action; the first one would confirm the action had been done right, then the second one would as well. This process was meant to eliminate the kind of error that happened in 1979, when one worker went to the back of a control panel and misidentified the gauge that might have revealed an open valve. Instead, the workers would now follow the same steps built into any working button: After it's been pushed, the button issues feedback to confirm what's been done. In the reactor control room, that feedback came verbally, from the second worker. It's the same idea.

It is a strange kind of world we live in, where to make sure that men make no mayhem with a machine, they're made to behave like buttons. But then, it's maybe not surprising on deeper reflection: As Norbert Wiener discovered in his pioneering work designing feedback algorithms for shooting down German bombers, feedback is what turns information into action. Buttons, in turn, have become the connection point between our will and the user-friendly world. Embedded in them is a fundamental truth about how our minds make sense of the world. As banal as buttons may seem, properly viewed they can also seem like everything. The point arrives from surprising places, all the time. For me, the strangest was when my wife told me that her psychologist had said that the secret to having a productive argument with your spouse is to listen to what she has to say, *repeat* what you just heard, then finally have your spouse *confirm* that's what she meant. Push the button, provide feedback, confirm the action. Like a button. The creation of a shared understanding precedes any influence we might wield upon the world. Design is nothing more—and nothing less—than creating artifacts imbued with such shared understanding, legible to their users.

What happened at Three Mile Island was a transition between

two eras: from one in which machines doomed their operators to make mistakes, to one that is the user-friendly world we live in today. Consider that Three Mile Island was designed in complete ignorance of the ways in which man and machine interact, which had been studied with excruciating care in a thirty-year period beginning after World War II. Whatever lessons should have been learned were instead squirreled away. And yet just five years after the Three Mile Island accident, the first Mac ads began to appear, touting a machine made to be utterly intuitive. It would be too much to say that without Three Mile Island, you'd never have the iPhone, but the two are bound together in a great chain of influence. The lights that didn't work, the gauges placed in baffling places—their opposite lives on in gadgets that get these ideas right, so that we never have to bother about figuring it out. You tap a button on the screen, it depresses just a little to show it's been pushed, then a new screen pops up in response—success. You encounter some new screen filled with new buttons on a menu in your phone, yet you can still figure out what to do, because the options are all laid out right before you. In all these cases, the opposite example—important because it illustrates how things go wrong without some shared understanding—is Reactor 2, with its lights and dials hidden from view and its fateful buttons that never confirmed what they were meant to.

Not long after I spent the afternoon with Harlan Crowder, the retired engineer living near Apple's new campus, I took a walk around downtown Palo Alto, trying out Google Lens. It was hard not to feel as if I were holding the future in my hand. Simply by using the camera on my smartphone, I could glean information about what was around me. I could train the camera on the marquee outside a theater and, at the bottom of the screen, buttons would appear for finding out showtimes, booking tickets, or reading reviews about the movie. I could hold my phone up to a tree and be told its species.

It was as if the internet had been seamlessly superimposed on the real world. Or, more precisely: Google Lens is what you get when you transform the company's familiar search box into a spyglass. What powers it is some of the most advanced artificial intelligence on the planet, capable of recognizing words and objects, then guessing what you are wondering about based solely on what your phone is seeing. It represents billions of dollars in research, reaching all the way from neural networks—simulated clusters of neurons, dwelling in an algorithm—that can distinguish cats from dogs, and Korean from Japanese, to the very servers that house those calculations, whose circuitry has been custom-engineered for the computations required. Yet the end product of all that technology is not much more complicated to use than a magnifying glass. Here is one of the most advanced technologies in the world and it needs no instruction manual.

To be clear, there's a difference between a nuclear reactor and a smartphone. One is meant to be used by specialists, the other meant to be used by everyone. But there is a broad trend in our culture driving the most specialized things to become easier to use.[34] You can spy it from many angles at once. We expect everything from our washing machines to our deodorant to be "professional grade"—powerful enough for the most extreme application, even if we're not running a laundromat or an NFL team. Meanwhile, our economy is increasingly built upon systems in which the human professional is interchangeable—transient, contract workers whose value doesn't lie in their training or specialization but in their "hustle." Uber drivers don't need to know the city they drive in; factory workers, if they still have jobs at all, have a precarious hold on the tasks that machines cannot do yet.

We now expect almost every aspect of our lives to work as simply as something on our smartphones—and it has to, for a rapidly changing workforce that often can't catch up to the pace of technological change. Indeed, because of the smartphone's ubiquity and immediacy, heavy work is now done on the move. Via smartphone, we can diagnose fleets of jet engines, exotic forms of cancer, and tetchy wind turbines. The user-friendly world is encroaching into successively tinier niches—and the nature of human expertise is shifting. Today, we take it for granted that the most advanced technologies ever created should never need any explaining whatsoever. How is that possible? How are we able to understand what something should do without ever being told?

Before I left Donald Norman at his fancy office, I remarked to him that it seemed like a kind of magic that some insight about the way we use a nuclear reactor control panel, or reach for a doorknob, might tell us so much about the shape of tools we haven't yet dreamed up. I meant to open a crack so that Norman might reflect a little about all the connections he'd seen. Wasn't it like a kind of magic? "But it's not!" Norman exclaimed. "It's science! That's what science does. You try to find general principles that hold true." Norman said that it seemed to him obvious that people weren't to blame for the errors they made. He believed that minds were knowable by science—that the frailties he was discovering weren't a feature of things going wrong, but were an essential facet of us, and what we expect of the world, whether we're swinging an ax at a log or pushing a button. We just expect things to work. Almost all of design stems from making sure that a user can figure out what to do, and can tell what's going on. The beauty and difficulty lie in what happens when the object at hand is new, but needs to feel familiar so that its newness isn't baffling.

I asked if he had any designs that he lived with that he admired. Norman looked around, and then his gaze settled on his watch: a black Braun, whose clean lines and haute-utilitarian face were descended from the famous models designed by Dieter Rams and Dietrich Lubs in the 1960s. Except the watch face was marred by one detail: In addition to the analog hands, there was a honking LCD readout. It told the time twice in two different ways, for no apparent reason at all. For a long time, Norman said, he hated that watch; when he ordered it, he hadn't known it would come with a double readout. It was a silliness that was remarkable insofar as it was unique: You don't see telephones with two sets of keypads, or cars with two dashboards. But it grew on him, the way the watch seemed at war with itself. The way it seemed designed by two competing minds. "I love the conflict of my watch between beauty and function," Norman said. "I love that tension. This beautiful elegant dial that's ruined by this ugly LCD." There are many ways to make something work—deciding which one is right is another thing entirely. There's a psychology to design, but there's also art in it, and a culture, too. Design presumes that we can make objects humane, but doing so requires a different way of seeing the world. Three Mile Island showed us how machines should behave; by itself, this explains only part of the user-friendly world. Left unsaid are the motivations we bring to the things we make.

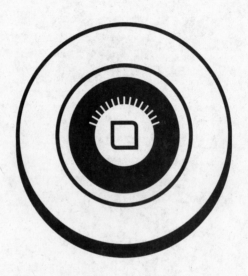

Honeywell Round thermostat (1953)

2

Industry

Mladen Barbaric is a collector of strange problems. Barbaric packs these away like a naturalist, thinking: Maybe there's something here worth figuring out later. He grew up in Sarajevo, a teenager in 1992 when the Serbian politician Slobodan Milošević, after a career spent stoking ancient hatreds between Orthodox Serbs, Catholic Croats, and Muslim Bosniaks, finally sparked a three-way genocide. After a restive peace, the Bosnian War exploded with terrifying fury. Barbaric was always a meticulous planner, self-assured and intense even as a kid. His mother thought it was weird how he could sit in a corner for hours, concentrating on a drawing or disassembling a radio one tiny screw at a time. When the shelling started, his father soberly laid out the dangers for him: A grenade could decimate perhaps one wall in their high-rise apartment building; an RPG could take down two. This wasn't to scare the boy. Rather, it was practical advice about what shelter to take, depending on the explosions he was hearing and how close they were. And so Barbaric lay awake at night for weeks tallying the explosions he heard, then carrying that data to its logical end. Grenades were the most common thing, followed distantly by RPGs. Rockets, which could destroy three walls, were rare. Barbaric concluded that he simply had to make sure at least two walls surrounded him at all times. He lived for a year winding through alleys and basements, surrounding himself with walls within walls.

Soon after, Barbaric's mother managed to get seats aboard two rescue buses out of Sarajevo for herself, Barbaric, and his younger brother. Eight months later, the three were in Canada and reunited with Barbaric's father. His mother was lucky enough to become a blackjack dealer at a casino, which just barely supported the family. Barbaric tore through high school, then design school, with an immigrant's fear of having nothing. When big class projects were due, Barbaric would work for eight or ten hours, sleep an hour, wake up, and do it again for ten days at a stretch.

Today, Barbaric is CEO of a small but prosperous design studio called Pearl, located in Montreal. I asked him what, if anything, his childhood taught him about being a designer. He remembered how people changed during the war: how an adult neighbor stole a bunch of strawberries from a child, and a quiet boy who'd joined the Bosnian resistance transformed into a hot-tempered thug. "I assess people with a grain of salt," Barbaric said. "I don't know that I do it consciously. I just assume there's more. There's only one type of person I can't understand, and it's people who are dismissive." Later, as we were finishing our dinner, Barbaric started talking about the product he was working on now, admitting that it was a big bet—a bet that a button might breed a new sort of Good Samaritan. This was a designer's way of looking at the world: the sense that if our better selves are within easier reach, then of course we'll be better people.[1]

Barbaric often fielded wild calls from people in the grip of their own great ideas. Bo Gillespie would have been an easy person to ignore. Freshly graduated from a mid-tier college, he had a Southern twang, old-fashioned manners, and none of the swaggering self-assurance of a startup bro. But, on the other hand, Gillespie was fully, naively committed to solving a problem that his mother had encountered. After her kids were out of the house, Gillespie's mother wanted to start working again. Real estate seemed like a reasonable career, given that she was in South Florida, where housing speculation was the state's unofficial pastime. Still, she worried. Her girlfriends would tell stories of men who'd cruise new neighborhoods, collecting open-house brochures. They'd make an appointment to see a house. If you were a woman, you'd take the call, set up a meeting with this pleasant-sounding man—*a fresh lead!*—gather up all the keys to the houses you were showing that day, get to your appointment fifteen minutes early, unlock the door, and sweep up after the contractors who'd walked through the kitchen once again in their dusty boots. When the fresh prospect arrived, you'd usher him in and shake hands with a great big smile. The door would click shut, and the two of you would be alone.

When Gillespie's mother would go out on house showings, she'd call her son, tell him where she was going, and say, "If I don't call you back in twenty minutes, then you call the police." Gillespie would nod and silently wonder what on earth he'd tell 911 to convince them that his mother was in trouble at the twenty-first minute of waiting. Then Gillespie thought, "What if there were a button she could push herself, that would tell the police exactly where she was and who she was?"[2] Gillespie called on Barbaric to design it. But Barbaric was hesitant because he was used to inventors who were giddy about a half-baked idea. He delicately told Gillespie not to be too wedded to their concept sketches. After all, what did a bunch of young men really know about being a woman who felt threatened?

Barbaric had prepared for this moment by inviting Dr. Dusty Johnstone into the process soon after he took the job. She was a friend of his wife's who'd spent her career studying sexual assault, and when Barbaric had first invited her to consult on the project, she quickly told him that the idea for an emergency-call button was hopelessly wrong. After months of working together, the time came for Barbaric and Johnstone to show Gillespie what all that work had yielded. During a presentation at Barbaric's office, I watched from the back of the room as Barbaric summarized all the technical details of what they'd invented and all the nuances of the product they were trying to create. Then Dr. Johnstone stood up with a scene-stealing confidence that snapped the room to attention. It was all a bit of self-conscious stagecraft that Barbaric had orchestrated—leading with the things Gillespie was expecting to hear, then throwing in a curveball of a guest to take the conversation in an entirely new direction. The point was to help Dr. Johnstone's insights land with a declamatory thud.[3] The chief provocation she had to offer was that the scenario Gillespie had imagined, an attack from a stranger lying in wait, is so extraordinarily rare that it clouds the truth: 80 percent of all assaults are by someone the victim knows.

"It occurs at house parties and bars, around people you know and people you've seen before, in the bedroom of the friend you've known for twelve years," Johnstone told the room. In such circumstances, dialing 911 is absurd, because the very act means escalating a precarious, uncertain situation into an outright confrontation.

You'd never think to dial 911 if you're unsure that you're actually being attacked, or if you're afraid of embarrassing yourself. Johnstone's message to Barbaric and Gillespie was that creating a new way to dial 911 wasn't enough. You instead had to create an alternative to it. Johnstone finished her presentation, and the room shifted uncomfortably. "Any questions?" Gillespie politely raised his hand: "Can you make this any more complicated?" Everyone laughed.

When Johnstone and Barbaric had first started talking, Johnstone had told him that keeping someone safe was sometimes as simple as a bystander butting in at the right time to ask, "Hey, are you okay? Do you want me to call one of your friends?" or a woman being savvy enough to say, "Oh, look! My friend is texting and I have to go!"[4] *That's all it takes.* The idea had rung in Barbaric's ears.[5] It was clear enough that this wouldn't ever work in some cases—for example, the darkest scenarios of outright assault. But in so many others, what if a woman had a plausible excuse within reach, anytime she actually thought, *Hey, I wish someone were here to help me out*? A way of asking someone else to intercede? As Johnstone finished her presentation, Barbaric got up to take over. "We have to decide what problem we're trying to solve," he announced. "So let's dive into the rest."

When Barbaric is trying to sell a new idea, his eyebrows lift up in a soothing, wide-open expression. Presently, his eyebrows went to work. The gadget would be a button the size of a dime that a person could pin anywhere—on a bra strap, a key fob. It would call the police if you tapped the button three times. But the more interesting thing is what would happen when you pressed it once. Rather than calling 911, a single press would beckon a network of friends or bystanders, whoever was closest, asking them to come find you and check in to see if you were okay. That's what gave the product its name: Ripple. It was the equivalent of making an excuse available at the press of a button—while simultaneously ensuring that help was on the way. "We need to recognize that if we don't consider these psychological issues, we're not going to get the right effect," said Barbaric. The wrong effect would be a button that escalated a problem, when all a woman wanted was an easy pretext to get out of a difficult situation.

The striking idea of creating an ad hoc, on-demand network of guardian angels didn't quite make it through the next two years of product refinement, owing to fears about legal headaches. But the central insight did. When Ripple made its debut on the Home Shopping Network in 2017, it had become a reinvention of the very idea of 911: At the push of a button, you could demand a call from a specialist, trained to figure out what kind of help you'd need. When you pushed the button, it would ping a concierge to call or text you. You might be in the midst of an uncomfortable closing time at a bar, or car problems, or any other chancy situation. The concierge would call to ask what was happening—providing a plausible excuse to dip out of whatever situation you were in, if needed—and figure out what help to lend. But thanks to Johnstone's urging, Ripple had remained more than a user-friendly version of 911. It was a service for the great many times when you knew you needed help but simply didn't know what *kind* of help you needed.

Ripple was ingenious insofar as it showed how you might solve a problem hiding in plain sight—and useful insofar as it illustrated how obvious problems aren't obvious at all once they're scrutinized. Bo Gillespie had wanted to solve a problem inspired by his mother's fears; Dr. Johnstone had spurred a deeper understanding of the social context that superseded those fears; and Barbaric, the war refugee from Sarajevo, and been primed to invent something built upon the social capital he'd seen fall apart in his childhood. Each brought some kind of assumption to the process. And yet every one of the people involved had held on to an unspoken faith that stands behind the products surrounding us. The designers who create them assume that better product design can be wielded to solve almost any problem, even those on a societal scale. Ripple was an extreme case, embodying the idea that a literal button—and redesigned feedback—could address the sprawling challenge of finding just enough help at just the right time. It was, of course, a wildly ambitious aim; nearly every startup fails, never mind one aiming to remake the way we seek aid. Yet in smaller doses every day, we assume that we can usher in a better world by inventing new and better *things*. This is such a pervasive ideal that it seems self-evident. But it wasn't always. You can trace it to the dawn of the twentieth century, when an abiding faith in consumption as social progress birthed a new profession: the industrial designer.

It was 1925 and Henry Dreyfuss, wearing his trademark brown suit, stood vigil in front of the sparkling new RKO theater. He was there to solve a problem that had bedeviled the theater's owners back in New York: They'd invested a tidy sum in this new showplace and no one was coming in. The location was good. This was a prosperous stretch of downtown Sioux City, Iowa, and the RKO theater hosted popular traveling vaudeville shows and newer, better movies. Yet the happy families and farmers mostly scuttled past the theater's twinkling new marquee and the plush red carpet blanketing the sidewalk on their way to the shabby competitor down the street. Dreyfuss was standing around so that he could just watch them, and see if he might understand them.

In an era before marketing consultants or business strategists, Dreyfuss had gotten the job simply because he seemed to know something about theater design. He was, at the time, just twenty-one, but already known as a wunderkind designer of Broadway shows. His success had allowed him to start styling himself more as an engineer of consumer demand. When Dreyfuss first arrived at the theater in Sioux City, he lowered prices, ran triple features, and gave away free food—still, none of it worked. After spending three days just observing, he ventured into the theater lobby to eavesdrop on what customers there were saying. Then he overhead someone say how afraid they were of messing up such rich carpet with their muddy shoes. Dreyfuss looked back at the slick tongue of carpet lolling in the theater's glossy maw and saw how intimidating it must have been to the "farmers and workmen."[6] The problem he'd been sent to fix—a theater design that wasn't drawing crowds—ended up not being the problem at all. It wasn't that the theater wasn't nice enough. It was rather that, having been conceived on some drawing board in New York City, the theater was too nice for the practical and unassuming Iowans.

The next day, Dreyfuss had the carpet ripped out and replaced with a plain rubber mat. Then Dreyfuss returned to the theater and waited. First a couple of people came, then a few more, then a few more and a few more, until it was filled. His trick had worked. It seems strange that a floor mat could really make people feel like they belonged. But it was Dreyfuss's myth, which he elevated because it captures an ideal about design: By understanding someone else's life—abashed, prideful, confused, curious—you could make their life better. By understanding how he or she thought, you could reach past the obvious problem and into the problem that they couldn't quite articulate, the one that they might not even think to solve. Dreyfuss turned the question from *what* to make and how to make it, into *whom* to make it for. A designer, Dreyfuss would later say, was "a man of vision who is not a visionary."[7] Design meant a certain kind of deference. The brown suit he wore was, in fact, a statement of purpose. The only color Henry Dreyfuss ever wore was brown: brown pajamas, brown bathing suit, and, especially, a brown suit, which he wore every day, all of it fastidiously tailored. Today, brown seems like a drab choice, but in an era of gray and black, it marked a certain suave polish: distinguished but not foppish. It was a uniform meant to place him as a man of business, rather than a man of art.

Dreyfuss traveled an unlikely path to get there. He'd grown up quickly after both his grandfather and father died within a few months of each other. At sixteen, his talent for drawing had landed him a scholarship to a tony private school, which planted a seed in his mind.[8] The Society for Ethical Culture, founded in 1876 by Felix Adler, was both resolutely progressive and radically secular. Inspired by Kant, Adler didn't believe that morality was God-given. Instead, it resided in people choosing for themselves. The ethos was a revelation to young Dreyfuss. How many times had his neighbors, who'd heard about his dead father and knew how he worked to support his mother and brother, wished God's grace upon them all? Here was a school that told young Henry not to wait for God. That it was his responsibility to raise up everyone else, the people just like him.

It wasn't but a few years after graduating that Dreyfuss became a stage designer. He badgered his way into his first real job—in a way so storybook as to suggest a self-conscious reenactment of the 1920s American fable. Eighteen years old, Dreyfuss went to see a show on Broadway and despised the set. Afterward, he strode up to the stage door, asking the doorman if he could speak with the director. Johnny, the doorman, turned him back. So Dreyfuss returned again every day for a month, getting to know Johnny, sharing Johnny's pipe. Johnny, eventually, got Dreyfuss an audience with the director, Joseph Plunkett: "There's a fine young designer downstairs, Mr. Plunkett." Plunkett asked Johnny what made him so sure about this young man's talents. "He told me so himself," said Johnny. Dreyfuss stepped in and promptly told Plunkett his sets were "rotten." Plunkett was stunned. Dreyfuss said he could do better, for twenty-five dollars a week. Plunkett, eager not to be outdone in showmanship, made it fifty.[9] Years later, it was Plunkett who would dispatch Dreyfuss to Sioux City.[10]

Dreyfuss was an almost immediate success on Broadway, designing lavish sets, such as a giant piano case, thirty feet long and twenty feet high, that would fit four pianos inside it, their keyboards side by side, to be played by four glittering showgirls, elbow to elbow. He was always watching the audience to see what drew them. "I got to the point where I could guarantee with almost mathematical certainty that certain combinations of color, light, and line would bring a wave of applause when the curtain rose," he later told a reporter.[11] It was a telling quote. Dreyfuss built his career on the faith that there was an underlying logic to what people wanted.

Maybe because of his quick success, Dreyfuss viewed his work with a mix of pride and disdain, the latter thanks to smarmy clients who didn't pay their bills.[12] Just as he was registering his dissatisfaction, Dreyfuss began hearing about "industrial design," a new profession invented by ad men such as Walter Dorwin Teague. Dreyfuss had heard that Norman Bel Geddes, who'd given him his first theater apprenticeship, was diving into this new profession, and he knew that Teague had announced in 1926 that he was quitting advertising altogether.[13] Teague came up designing magazine ads for housewares, and, as those ads become more and more commonplace, he realized that for the product to sell, it had to sell itself. These sinks and irons and latches and kettles and washboards and door locks had to be more beautiful and more useful than what a person already had. So while the profession of industrial design started literally with how good a product looked on the printed page, it began to reach into questions of what a product should be about—what kind of story it should tell to the consumer.

Industrial design, and the very idea that the stuff of everyday life could be remade, helped transmute Dreyfuss's gnawing pickiness into something purposeful—into an abiding idealism that things should be better. He saw a great landscape of terrible junk that no one had ever tried to dignify through thoughtfulness.[14] Having complained his way onto Broadway, he tried complaining his way into a new profession. He'd peer at a lock and find the maker's name or kick at a bathmat in the shower to find the imprint, then look them up. *Don't you know how lousy this is?* He'd write a letter describing his burgeoning approach to design, with his signature taking up half the page. *Your product would be much improved if . . .* He'd even ginned up a slogan: "Design is the silent salesman."[15] The lure never drew many bites. Discouraged and burned out, Dreyfuss bought himself a ticket to Paris, and eventually found himself in Tunis, where, the night of his arrival, he lost all his money playing roulette.[16] Dashing, well-dressed, and suddenly in desperate need of a job, he became a tour guide for American Express. His place was the markets, full of hawkers touting rugs and fabric and spices, birds squawking from reed cages, and meat hissing as it roasted over ashy coals. The labyrinthine bazaar would force casual visitors to buy their way out or else stay lost. Dreyfuss knew whom to indulge and what to hustle past in the maze of consumer temptation.[17] But he was still waiting for his chance to be not just the guide in that maze but the designer of the maze itself.

Dreyfuss had a talent for timing: Even while he was trying to bull his way into a nascent American design profession, America itself was on the verge of a transformation that flowered in the wake of World War I. America had entered the war in 1917, just two years after Henry Ford had first unveiled his idea for an assembly line, at the Panama-Pacific Exposition in San Francisco. Wiry and energetic, self-aggrandizing and monomaniacal, Ford was inspired by the slaughterhouses of Chicago, in which the carcasses of cows were hung from the ceiling and conveyed across the room as workers broke them down in stages. His own factory lines initially broke down the car's manufacture into eighty-four discrete, repeatable steps. Before, workers buzzed around the skeleton of a car, and it grew in place. Now the workers would stay still as the car arrived in front of them—thus eliminating all the extraneous milling about, and whittling the time it took to build a car from twelve hours to a mere ninety minutes. It was so fast that visitors to the expo could order a car and pick it up by the time they left. Ford lent his expertise to the war effort, personally helping other manufacturers retool themselves on the assembly-line model, and helping America imagine war at an unprecedented scale. Machine-gun production climbed from 20,000 a year to 225,000; using Ford's techniques, rifle production swelled to 500,000 a year, along with more than a billion bullets.[18]

But the revving war machine also paused the globe's biggest economies. Every finance minister in the world knew that when the war ended, their economies would restart all at once, producing a race for industrial supremacy. In this, the United States had an edge. Its factories, which had swung the war, would now be tasked with delivering prosperity for its citizens. Americans naturally shaded the promise of machine-made goods with a moralizing gloss. Richard Bach, the curator of industrial art at the Metropolitan Museum of Art in New York, neatly summarized that ethos in a lecture before his peers: "If all products were hand-made few of us could afford them. Therefore it is left for us to give the machine its proper place. If good designs are not available for the man in the street, the system which produces these designs must be undemocratic and wrong." That speech is like the X-ray of a primitive fish crawling onto land: its bones hint at the mechanisms that will propel countless descendants to come in the user-friendly world. Bach equates mass production with democracy; he implies that good design is a kind of manifest destiny for market societies.

The war had come on the heels of the Machine Age. Yet America still betrayed an odd anxiety about its own ability to *create* that seems almost incomprehensible today. The anxiety sprang from how heavily American manufacturers leaned on Europe to tell them what they should be making. By comparison, the French saw themselves as the pioneers of a new aesthetic, suited to the times, with clean lines and radically pared-down decoration. To bring that point home, France's cultural grandees passive-aggressively resolved to finally hold an exhibition in 1925, the Exposition International des Arts Décoratifs et Industriels Modernes, which had been delayed a decade by the war. The exhibition would implicitly place France as the leader in this new age of "industrial art," while also bringing all the countries of the world together to show their own achievements and—here's the passive-aggressive part—be diminished by comparison. Every country was invited but one: Germany, which had become a pariah after the Great War, despite the fact that the Bauhaus was already recognized as a leader in the industrial arts. And every country that was invited showed up, save two: China, which was facing the prospect of civil war, and the United States.[19]

That decision had been made at the top. Herbert Hoover—fat-cheeked, self-assured, infinitely practical, and, at the time, America's secretary of commerce—had gotten the invitation to Paris. The preparations would have to begin soon to put on the show. He asked around, wondering if the United States should venture its own pavilion in Paris. After the answers came, he shrugged and shook his head: "The advice which I received from our manufacturers was that while we produced a vast volume of goods of much artistic value, they did not consider that we could contribute sufficiently varied design of unique character or of special expression in American artistry to warrant such participation."[20] This was a breathtaking humiliation, made more stunning by how public it was.

It was indeed a pivotal event to have skipped out on: An obscure young architect calling himself Le Corbusier debuted on the international scene with a design for the French pavilion, dedicated to "L'Esprit Nouveau."[21] The "machine for habitation" was made up of clean white planes of concrete and filled with radically austere furniture, stripped of any decoration. "Decorative art, as opposed to the machine phenomenon, is the final twitch of the old manual modes, a dying thing," Le Corbusier explained. "Our pavilion will contain only standard things created by industry in factories and mass-produced, truly the objects of today." His ideas dovetailed with those of Peter Behrens, the grandfather of the Bauhaus and widely considered the first modern industrial designer. Within a few years, the Bauhaus would grow to dominate the era's design ideology, advocating radically spare designs that would reflect the new ways that goods were made and, as Behrens said, "invite use." By contrast, America had no grand theorists, no guiding principle for its creations. Even her biggest boosters didn't believe in the originality of American design. The self-doubt stemmed from a self-awareness that American markets had always understood "taste" as something to be imported. All this would change in the short span of a few years, as mass-manufactured goods became less about familiar, decorative objects driven by fashion and more about new gadgetry for the home. The idea that America could only copy the heritage of the Old World was overthrown by a powerful new voice in the markets: women.

In the United States after the Great War, low-income immigrants were transforming into the new middle class. That rising tide of better prospects brought with it a profound sense of displacement that was unevenly distributed across the sexes; where men were finding new jobs and new professions, women had to reconcile two competing threads of American promise. On the one hand, women were more powerful than ever: They'd gained the right to vote and were marching for access to contraception, the power to control their family planning. Yet they were still yoked to the household—an all-consuming endeavor in the time before electrical appliances. How could women square those greater opportunities outside the home with the constant obligations within it?

That dilemma birthed the field of home economics, led by a new generation of women writers like Christine Frederick, who was a journalist for *Ladies' Home Journal*. Frederick and her peers, such as Mary Pattison, had an ingenious answer to the problem of resolving the persistent drudgery of maintaining a home, and the promise of greater freedoms: Create more free time. For those first-wave feminists, home economics was about fostering more efficient housework so that women could pursue more "individuality and independence"—the chance to be more fulfilled, more influential. The era's undisputed master of time-saving was Frederick Winslow Taylor, whose school of "scientific management" advocated watching every action on a factory floor for wasted seconds. Henry Ford was one of his early devotees; Christine Frederick was another. In Taylor's ideas, Frederick saw a way to connect women's work to broader notions about modern progress—and a way to boost how society valued a woman's labor. After first hearing Taylor's gospel at a three-hour speech, Frederick called on her readers to "eliminate lost motion" and standardize how long each chore took—from mixing a layer cake (ten minutes) to cleaning a bathroom (twenty minutes).[22] Dozens of other writers and columnists took up the same cause; Mary Pattison offered a novel expansion of it, emphasizing the value of the tools women bought and the power they wielded through those purchases. She called it a "moral responsibility" for women to demand improvements in their tools, for the betterment of all—"molding the future conditions under which purchasing must be done."[23] Women were on the leading edge of consumers *using* things they bought, using their dollars to demand that products be more thoughtful.

Even as American women were cottoning to the idea that their purchasing power was an invisible hand for the greater good, businessmen were realizing that they had been missing a greater opportunity. In 1929, the American Management Association held its annual conference at which the keynote speaker, a merchandising consultant, declared, "There was a time when our best things were hand-made, our poorest made in mass production. Cheap, nasty poor-taste things were turned out by the machine. The reverse seems to be beginning to be true." The speaker went on to urge attendees to "sell beauty to the public." At that same conference, a typewriter executive said that in 1926, all his wares had been black. By 1929, three years after introducing a few other colors, only 2 percent were. E. B. French reported that at KitchenAid, a redesign of the mixer had cut its weight in half, cut the price, and made the mixer better looking, too. Sales had jumped by 100 percent.[24] There was a burgeoning sense that it wasn't enough to merely make things cheaper than they had been—rather, things had to be made to be more desirable as well.

That dawning awareness was perhaps best exemplified in Henry Ford, and the myopia that nearly sunk his business. For eighteen years, the Model T never changed, because Ford assumed that customer tastes were static—that the only way to improve the Model T was to make it more efficient every year, and thus cheaper to buy. He famously groused that his cars came in any color "so long as it's black." This worked, for a time: In 1921, Ford owned two-thirds of the American car market; by 1926, it was half that, thanks to General Motors, which offered a wealth of models in a range of colors and configurations. By 1927, Ford's alarming decline couldn't be ignored any longer.[25] The company shut down nearly all its factory lines, spending $18 million to retool them around a new car, the Model A, which came as a sedan or a convertible in a profusion of colors with myriad options such as a rearview mirror and a heater. It was a hit; while the Model T launched Ford, the Model A saved it.

Yet these new ideas—of consumption as social progress, and aesthetic appeal as an engine for consumer demand—sprang up beneath a looming cloud. On the very same day that those manufacturing leaders were meeting to discuss how beauty could be used to mold consumer demand, October 29, 1929, the Dow Jones Industrial Average fell by 12 percent, ringing in the Great Depression.[26] This should have ended the nascent field of industrial design before it began. In fact, the opposite happened: Industrial design came to be seen as a cure for flagging markets, thanks in no small part to people like Henry Dreyfuss.

After a month working as a tour guide in the bazaar of Tunis, still stung by his lack of success haranguing manufacturers about how bad their wares were, Dreyfuss made his way back to Paris, where a stack of correspondence lay waiting for him at his hotel. There was one series of telegrams whose message had stayed constant: Would Dreyfuss please come work at Macy's, to redesign anything that he wished? This was a jaw-dropping opportunity. Dreyfuss was broke, and despite his epistolary bluster he had no real qualifications for the job. Macy's wanted him, it seemed, because it had heard about the design practice that Dreyfuss had been trying to start; there weren't many others purporting to do that job at all. Macy's, at the head of a new retailing boom, was offering him a ticket home.[27]

When he finally arrived back in New York, Dreyfuss's first priority was a tour of Macy's one-hundred-plus departments. Its giant building represented a new way of shopping, which was a revelation for consumers raised in the era of mom-and-pop general stores. Macy's, much like the Sears catalog, was built upon the new wealth of choices that consumers now had: There were aisles and aisles of the same thing, made by different companies, competing on the shelf. Dreyfuss ran his hands across hundreds of items, from pocket-knives to electric stoves. True to form, he hated them all.[28]

This prickliness belied something more than just distaste. Dreyfuss realized that fixing any of them required an intimate knowledge of how they were produced, the ability to know enough detail about the process so that he could actually catch a decision as it was being made, with an eye to something greater than simply manufacturing products cheaply. It wasn't enough to just add a pleasing shape to an essentially finished product.[29] Broke from a string of debts owed by his Broadway clients, and on the doorstep of a brand-new profession, Dreyfuss turned down the job, later explaining to a reporter that the Macy's executive had "the cart before the horse."[30] Without talking with the manufacturers, without knowing how something was made, how much a change might cost, what to sacrifice and what to save, Dreyfuss couldn't do anything at all. He was perhaps the first American designer to articulate and then act on the idea that design wasn't just styling—it sprang from a knowledge about how things were made and what was possible.

After refusing the Macy's job, Dreyfuss set up an office on Fifth Avenue with nothing more inside than a borrowed card table, two folding chairs, a telephone, and a twenty-five-cent philodendron, and nothing to do other than look out the window and make watercolors of the things he hoped to redesign.[31] He put out a request for a business manager. Then, while he was still waiting at the window, a black limousine pulled up on the street below. An elegant woman stepped out onto the sidewalk and came to the door. The buzzer rang, and after a few moments he ushered her in, sitting her down for a brief interview. When she left, Dreyfuss told his secretary, "That's the girl I'm going to marry." A few months later Dreyfuss and the woman, Doris Marks, bought a ring at a pawnshop and tumbled into a cab, rushing downtown to City Hall to say their vows while the cabbie whistled the "Wedding March."[32]

In founding a business together, Doris and Henry played the roles that fit within the era's expectations. Henry was the genius and Doris was the hard-nosed business manager. But Doris, a stern and elegant daughter of New York's recent aristocracy, helped craft Henry Dreyfuss's vision.[33] She abhorred ostentation, and that aversion worked its way into the studio's workmanlike ideology. Dreyfuss bootstrapped their business, designing an avalanche of anonymous stuff that spoke to the new plentitude of daily life in the 1930s: pens, egg beaters, waffle irons, dental chairs, rubber mats, playpens, school desks, razor boxes, cold-cream labels, a piano.[34] By the early 1930s, he had worked himself up to interiors for airplanes—and managed to become one of the poster children for this odd new profession called industrial design. "Dreyfuss brings to his work no special aptitude for mechanics and only a moderate gift in the handling of materials," noted *The New Yorker* in 1931, in one of the first glossy profiles anywhere of an industrial designer. But "he has to a high degree a sense of the ultimate use to which commodities will be put, *a feeling for the comfort of the man* who is going to use the fountain pen for writing more than as a decorative adjunct to his desk." (Emphasis mine.) This is the spine of the user-friendly world, unchanged whether you're talking about smartphones or toothbrushes or driverless cars: a deference to the complexity of understanding people as they live.

Dreyfuss was gleeful when describing what miracles might come from a life made easier at the edges: a peanut butter jar with sloped shoulders so that every last bit could be scooped out with a spoon; a shaving brush with a handle of the right proportions so as not to mess your hand with lather; and a stove with cleverly shielded handles so that the users never burned their hands. And while these examples might sound banal to our ears, they were a revelation in their time. It was stunning to hear that someone actually spent their days applying creativity to details that had always been overlooked. Dreyfuss was sketching a vision of life as the sum of innumerable details, irritations, and fixes—arguing that leisure, gained by a few seconds here and there, contributed to social progress. He had fully internalized the tenets articulated by home economists, in which the products people bought were the link between the individual pursuit of happiness and the steady growth of industry.

Dreyfuss wasn't just selling the idea that product design was tantamount to social progress. He was also trying to convince American businesses why they should care. What he had to offer was the elixir of sales growth. In the progressively lean years of the Great Depression, manufacturers battled one another over decreasing demand and became more desperate to find novel ways to spark consumer lust.[35] Christine Frederick herself was one of the loudest advocates for "consumption engineering." As the historian Jeffrey L. Meikle wrote in his sweeping survey *Design in the USA*, "This new expert would anticipate 'changes in buying habits' and create 'artificial obsolescence' by convincing people that 'prosperity lies in spending, not saving.'"[36] But no one would spend more on the same things they already had—manufacturers had to convince people that what they were offering was something new and better. This was the milieu Henry Dreyfuss was stepping into: a new era infused with the idea that sparking the urge to buy might well save the country from ruin; that the only way to make people buy was to make things better than they'd ever been.

Industrial design seemed like a miracle cure in Depression-era America. In one of his first press interviews, Dreyfuss told a magazine reporter about a man who'd been pestering him to design a better flyswatter. Dreyfuss refused to see him at first, but eventually admitted the man to his office and sketched him a flyswatter for free: The paddle had concentric rings like a pistol target, which made swatting flies into a game. Months later, Dreyfuss got a thousand-dollar check in the mail, a royalty offered in gratitude. Sales had gone wild.[37] Dreyfuss's first great hit from the era, the Toperator washing machine, sold through Sears, looked a little bit like a robot from Fritz Lang's *Metropolis*. There are ideas in it that you can recognize in objects all around us today. He avoided any joints that would be hard to clean—which happens to be one of the chief design concerns in modern medical appliances. And, in a nod to the consumer's psychology that is now ubiquitous in modern apps and gadget interfaces, Dreyfuss bunched all the controls together so that the user could readily understand all its functions. Sears sold twenty thousand of them in six months. Other designers had similar successes, and there were enough of them for manufacturers to begin to believe that designers could conjure demand from thin air. In

February 1934, near the peak of the Depression, *Fortune* ran an article on Dreyfuss, "New Product Designs Start Stampede," in which the reporter claimed that a Dreyfuss-designed check-writing machine caused a salesman to weep and a repairman to faint.

These visions of success brought forth two intertwined goals: modernizing how products looked, and rethinking how they worked. Overseas, in Europe, the Bauhaus stewarded that ethos, summarized in the old saw that form follows function. Yet that design movement had a shortcoming, insofar as the Bauhaus's most iconic products were all geared toward an elite consumer who could understand and appreciate its aesthetic. In America, the lens was more practical and market-oriented. It was coarser. Goods had to look different for a consumer to know they were indeed better. Thus, the men who roosted over the newfound profession of industrial design leaned heavily toward looks. If you're familiar with design from that era, then you probably picture an airplane in polished steel, or a radio looking much the same, covered in chrome. These echoes were intentional; they were, at one point, dogma. Charismatic, silver-tongued designers such as Raymond Loewy and Norman Bel Geddes wanted to imbue their designs with a palpable ethos of progress. So they stripped away the heavy, historical flourishes of the Victorian era in favor of "streamlined" metallic forms meant to evoke the speed and efficiency of the era's symbols of forward progress: the airplane, the locomotive, and the automobile. The application of these forms was indiscriminate and universal, encompassing everything from refrigerators to pencil sharpeners, all of them meant to look as if they had been tested in a wind tunnel. The new streamlined aesthetic clothed every product in the same metaphor. Where streamlining made airplanes slip through the air with less wind resistance, streamlined household goods eliminated "sales resistance."[38]

Dreyfuss, thanks in no small part to his wife's influence, held a more sober view that presaged how the user-friendly world would develop; his instinctual deference toward everyday life is still recognizable in how the discipline of user experience is practiced today. Not only that, Dreyfuss's belief in the market foretold a future in which businesses would see their fortunes bound up in how well they understood their products' users. For him, styling was secondary to both finding better solutions to problems people had taken for granted and the ceaseless pressures on the businesses that made those goods. As the historian Russell Flinchum wrote in his seminal book about Henry Dreyfuss, "He was beginning to define an approach that was friendly to big business but still allowed him to criticize the status quo, that was protective of the consumer without being patronizing." Dreyfuss described design as an act of translation between the companies that made things and the consumers who used them.[39] "The strength of the designer's influence on industry and the public rests in this double role," he wrote. "He is in the happy position of making both the producer and the consumer happy with the same egg beater or the same electric refrigerator."[40] Designers, by aligning consumer design with business incentives, thus became high priests of the faith that better goods meant better lives all around. Such faith remains the unspoken message embedded in how new products are invented today. Consider the story that opened this chapter, that of Mladen Barbaric and Bo Gillespie, and how they tried, after years of testing and reworking, to create a new alternative to 911. The two of them weren't just interested in solving a problem for its own sake, nor were they merely trying to exploit a business opportunity. They presumed that business, product design, and social progress were all so intermingled that you couldn't separate one from another.

The timbre of Barbaric's process was coolly professional, rational, and ordered. Things were different ninety years ago, when the newfangled idea of industrial design was imbued with a kind of mania. Dreyfuss himself approached his work with a showy, gonzo dedication to understanding whom he was designing for. To create tractors for John Deere, he learned to drive a combine and played at being a farmer; to create a sewing machine, he took sewing classes alongside the ladies. The method was a precursor to modern design research—a sprawling industry that would eventually capitalize on the talents of anthropologists, psychologists, and social scientists. But Dreyfuss's enthusiasm had its limitations. What he didn't have was a full-blown process that could embody his motivations, which were clear enough and defined around humans rather than machines. Decades later, that ethos would be known as "human-centered design." Yet centering things around human beings wasn't as obvious as it seems. The precondition was a new ethos of how machines should fit into everyday life. The catalyst was World War II.

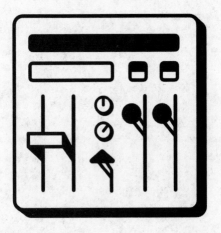

B-17 Flying Fortress control panel (1936)

3

Error

World War II is at its height, but there's a profound ease that comes from floating in friendly waters in the South Pacific, with American steel in every direction for three hundred miles, cradled by the routines of ship life. Thunderclouds scroll across the horizon, but the sun's still shining. The tropical air is thick. Except, in the nerve center where the officers monitor the planes they've sent out, there's a crack opening up: a lost pilot, somewhere close but low on fuel and overdue to return.

At 1410, the pilot issues a call for a course back to the carrier. The officers hear it, but the pilot doesn't get a response. So he waits, checking his instruments, checking the fuel gauge. At last the receiver crackles to life, but he can't make anything of it. "Static bad out here," he says. And then, for a moment, the fuzz coheres into a command to wait just a little more. The pilot waits. The fuel gauge ticks down ever so slightly.

The men using the ship's radar to find the errant plane operate on intuition. The job is to pick out "pips"—spikes in the wiggling green line of the radar display. But that wiggling green line is ruled by noise created by everything else that's out there: interference, clouds, birds. They call this jumpy pattern of fuzz "grass," and the radar's screen is filled with it; the pip they're looking for is just a single blade, standing a little bit taller. There's an art to being a good radar man, knowing before knowing which minute variations in flicker can distinguish a friendly plane from a foe. But today the operator is straining to make out anything at all, and the pilot can't make sense of his radio. So they keep issuing messages that breeze past each other.

"Radar can't see you yet, thunderstorms around," says the operator. "Thunderstorms north of here," says the pilot. "Static getting worse again."

Now thirty more minutes have passed, and the pilot's gaze must be darting frantically at a fuel gauge nearing empty. Back on the ship, a crowd forms around the radar console, and someone finally spots a telltale pip standing a bit taller amid a blurry patch—the thundercloud—on the radar. Relief. The pilot's close, just on the far side of the carrier. The duty officer seizes the microphone. "You're thirty miles from the ship," he cries. "Steer 357." At last, the homing course that the pilot needed all along. At thirty miles out, he can still make it, gliding the final few miles. "Say again?" says the pilot. "You are south of the ship," the officer shouts, desperation starting to creep into his voice. "Steer 357. I say again, steer 357." The pilot answers, "Gasoline low. Not hearing you anymore. Are you hearing me?"

The officer keeps shouting, in every register he can muster—loud and then soft, mouthing every syllable—like jiggling a key in a sticky lock, hoping that some lucky wiggle will open the door. A half hour later, the officer finally stops, exhausted. They know what's happened. A streak of steel and aluminum hitting the ruched surface of the ocean, a white geyser of sea spray, then the lapping waves closing in without memory. On any aircraft carrier like this one, men die. But as the lieutenant later says, a meaningless death such as this one whispers in the dark, haunts you in your bunk. Later that evening, in the wardroom, the ship's executive officer, wounded and gruff, is overheard saying, "Goddamn this business of trusting lives to radars a man can't see, and radios he can't hear." Goddamn this business of believing that machines would work for the people using them.[1]

The end of World War II made the captain's howl echo across the entire length of the American arsenal. Where World War I brought forth mass manufacturing at a previously unthinkable scale, World War II made even those capabilities seem quaint, while adding technical innovation at a blistering pace. Consider: Biplanes buzzed over the war's first battlefields; by war's end, contrails unfurled in the wake of the world's first stealth jets. Radar was perhaps the best example of how quickly technology was evolving. Its lifesaving reach increased on an almost month-to-month basis for six years, thus extending the capabilities of bombers and tanks and artillery shells and ships. And yet few of them performed nearly as well as the engineers had promised, because there simply wasn't any codified understanding of how to make those machines comprehensible to the men who used them. These fissures might appear in radios designed to emit speech in frequencies that the human ear couldn't make out—this is what happened to the pilot lost in the skies just minutes from a safe landing—or radar that simply didn't separate signal from noise. There was precious little knowledge about how humans made sense of the machines around them. "Theoretically, we could drop bombs in a rain barrel," said one Air Force psychologist. "But in actual practice, we missed entire cities."[2] You could count the toll in lives: men who died in combat or even miles away from it, without any accounting for what really happened when their machines stopped making sense.

Among those laying blame there were two camps, shouting at each other. On one side were the soldiers who wailed about "people who design electro-mechanical marvels to be operated by a man with three arms and an ability to see around a corner in pitch darkness."[3] The people who designed those marvels, no less indignant, blamed the failures of their inventions either on poor training or deliberate misuse—they pictured the soldiers mashing buttons and yanking levers in a huff. For a time, during the war, this argument devolved into Kabuki, with engineers touting their newest gear to officers, careful to use only their own scientists as demonstrators in an effort to show that everything really could be used just as designed.[4] The problem was that it couldn't, because, as would happen again thirty years later at Three Mile Island, the performance of men under duress bore no resemblance to that of those operating a demonstration model.

This issue of real-world performance versus lab experiments hovered over the battlefield, a killer beyond reckoning. It was made worse by the fact that the war was being fought on a "sensory margin" exponentially more fine than that of just ten years before. S. S. Stevens, a psychologist at Harvard, was the one who reported that story of an airman lost at sea. He was horrified. As he put it in his seminal paper "Machines Cannot Fight Alone":

The battle hangs on the power of the eyes or the
ears to make a fine discrimination, to estimate a
distance, to see or hear a signal which is just
at the edge of human capacity. Radars don't see,
radios don't hear, sonars don't detect, guns
don't point without someone making a fine sensory
judgment, and the paradox of it is that the faster
the engineers and the inventors served up their
"automatic" gadgets to eliminate the human factor
the tighter the squeeze became on the powers of
the operator—the man who must see and hear and
judge and act with that margin of superiority
which gives his outfit the jump on the enemy.[5]

Stevens notes that men would push this faulty equipment to its
limits. Engineers might tout a new radar as being able to pip an
enemy vessel at fifty miles on a good day, and there would soon
enough be a submarine commander trying to descry amid the green
haze a sampan at one hundred miles in a thunderstorm, because
that was probably where you would find the sampan:

The machine had to be built for *Homo sapiens* to
operate. When it was he used it, and given a new
leverage on the situation he promptly pushed his
flights and his missiles and his electromagnetic
beams out farther until he was again at the ragged
edge of his sensory endowments, where he was left
chafing anew at the dumb insentience of knobs and
dials and gears and coils, stolid and stubborn in
their indifference to serving a human will.

Contrast this with today. With a tap, we hail a car and watch it come to meet us; with another tap, we can call up the entire history of a conversation with someone else. We live in a sandbox of someone else's design, made more clever because the information on offer on our phones, on our computers, in our cars confines us within a simplified version of the world.

It has taken 150 years of shifting ideals to get there, and that journey represents a change in perspective as consequential as cubism or the uncertainty principle or any other paradigmatic idea of the twentieth century. But maybe even more so, because the tenets became so obvious that today they feel as if they'd always existed. One of the most consequential ideas to emerge from World War II was that machines might be bent around people, to better serve them, to better conform to the limits of their senses and minds—to be usable at a glance even in the worst conditions. From that crucible emerged the idea that you should be able to understand anything without ever thinking twice. Whether it's a handheld supercomputer that a child can use, or a nuclear reactor that's easy to troubleshoot, or a button that reinvents 911, these are things that take our limitations as the starting point and then build up from those assumptions, rather than assuming that we'll always be the idealized demonstrator, doing exactly what some engineer had intended.

Picture Paul Fitts as a handsome man with a soft Tennessee drawl, analytically minded but with a shiny wave of Brylcreemed hair, Elvis-like, which projects a certain suave nonconformity. Decades later, he'd become known as one of the Air Force's great minds, the person tasked with the hardest, weirdest problems, such as figuring out why people saw UFOs. For now, though, he's still trying to make his name. Fitts grew up in a tiny town but was carried north over the years by his talents, first to grad school at Brown and the University of Rochester, then eventually finding his way into the service at the Aero Medical Laboratory at Wright-Patterson Air Force Base in Ohio. In the immediate aftermath of the war, his commanding officer sends him on a hunt to uncover what killed so many men in airplane crashes. It's unclear why he's the one called upon. At the time, having a doctorate in the nascent field of experimental psychology was a novel thing, and with that novelty came a certain authority. He's supposed to know how people think. His true talent is realizing that he doesn't.

When the thousands of reports about plane crashes landed upon Fitts's desk, he could easily have looked at them and concluded that they were all the pilots' fault—that these fools should never have been flying at all. That conclusion would have been in keeping with the times. The original incident reports themselves would typically say "pilot error," and for decades no more explanation was needed. It wasn't out of sheer ignorance: The very concept of pilot error itself was a marker of progress.

Around the time of World War I, psychologists such as Hugo Münsterberg, Walter Dill Scott, and Robert Mearns Yerkes were overthrowing the strict behaviorism promulgated by John Watson, who believed that you could teach a human being to do anything with the right incentives and punishments—just like you could a rat in a cage. Instead, as the historian Donna Haraway writes, "Yerkes and his liberal peers advocated studying traits of the body, mind, spirit, and character in order to fit 'the person' into the proper place in industry . . . *Differences were the essential subject for the new science.* Personnel research would provide reliable information for the employment manager and proper vocational counseling for the 'person.'" (Emphasis mine.) They called their discipline human engineering.[6]

A few years after Münsterberg published his ideas about

understanding the unique capabilities of men, industrialists in Britain were flummoxed by the nagging persistence of accidents in their factories. In response, a few psychologists influenced by Münsterberg's model set out not to retrain all those factory workers but to understand what was boggling those involved in all the accidents. Eventually, they concluded that there was a kind of person who was "accident prone"—clumsy and cocksure, or perhaps stubbornly inattentive. But in creating the idea of an accident-prone person, those psychologists had merely restated the problem. They were no longer simply blaming the man. Instead they had created a special class of person to blame.

There was progress in the idea that people were differently suited to different things—but in that progress was also the assumption that correctly operating a machine was about *finding the right person to operate it*. Paul Fitts was edging toward a new and different paradigm.[7] As he pored over the Air Force's crash data, he realized that if accident-prone pilots were the cause, there would be randomness in what went wrong in the cockpit. These kinds of people would get hung up on anything they operated. It was in their nature to take risks, to let their minds wander while their hands were about to be minced by a cogwheel. But Fitts looked at the avalanche of reports he'd gathered and didn't see noise. He saw a pattern. And when he went to talk to people about what actually had happened, he saw terror.

The examples he found slid back and forth on a scale from tragic to tragicomic: pilots who slammed their planes into the ground after misreading a dial; pilots who fell from the sky never knowing which direction was up; pilots who came in for smooth landings and yet somehow never deployed their landing gear. And others still who got trapped in a maze of absurdity:

We had an alert one morning about 11 o'clock.
About 35 Japanese planes had been picked up on
the radar screen. In the mad scramble for planes,
the one I happened to pick out was a brand new
ship which had arrived about two days previously.
I climbed in, and it seemed the whole cockpit was
rearranged . . . I took a look at that instrument
panel and viewed the gauges around me, sweat
falling off my brow. Just then the first Japanese
bomb dropped. I figured then and there I wasn't
going to get my plane up, but I could run it on
the ground. That's exactly what I did. Ran it all
around the field, up and down the run-way, during
the attack.[8]

This hapless ace stutters like a video-game glitch.

Fitts's work complemented that of his colleague at the Aero Medical Laboratory, Alphonse Chapanis, a newly minted Ph.D. from Yale. Chapanis started investigating the airplanes themselves, talking to people about them, sitting in the cockpits. He too didn't see evidence of poor training. He saw, instead, the impossibility of flying these planes at all. Instead of "pilot error," he saw what he called, for the first time, "designer error." This was the seed of the user-friendly world we know today; as Three Mile Island shows us, it took forty more years for this sensibility to fully wend its way through industry. But we can already see hints of how that would happen in the details of Chapanis's work.

Chapanis was quick to note that in the B-17 Flying Fortress, the four-engined workhorse of the American bombing effort, the toggle to engage the landing gear was exactly the same as that for the wing flaps. They were right next to each other and looked exactly the same, and while pilots brought the airplane to the ground it was shockingly easy to retract the landing gear when they meant to lift the flaps. As a result, during a twenty-two-month period of the war, the Air Force reported an astounding 457 airplane crashes caused by the confusion of the flap and landing-gear controls.[9] Chapanis proposed an ingenious solution: to "shape-code" the knobs in an airplane cockpit so that a pilot could know what he was doing simply by feel. By law, that innovation governs landing gear and wing flaps in every airplane today. Moreover, an echo of the idea remains in the way that buttons all around you—on keyboards, remote controls, in cars, even digital ones on your smartphone— are shaped differently so that you can know them by touch or at a glance. We are still surrounded by two other foundational solutions that Chapanis came up with. The first, inspired by pilots like the one haplessly wheeling his plane around on the tarmac, was putting all the instruments in a plane into standardized positions. The second: making sure that controls move in a "natural" direction. If you want to go left, the lever should have to be moved left. Chapanis would later write that certain controls, in how they moved, were "psychologically natural": When you wanted to turn something on, it made sense to flip a switch "up" (for Americans, at least).[10] Of course, no one was born with these metaphors in mind—"up means on" or "turn left means go left"—but they were somehow embedded within our experience, beyond accounting, like a mother tongue.

The field would also take in the senses. One of the greatest accomplishments of "psychophysics," initiated by S. S. Stevens, was to recognize that speech could be made clearer over staticky lines by amplifying the consonants and tuning down the vowels—this single insight doubled the range of American radios, providing a crucial edge by the war's end.[11] Even the Air Force insignia was changed, after the realization of how easy it was to mistake the rising sun on the wing of a Japanese Zero with the blue circle and white star on an American P-47. Testing what symbols pilots could recognize most quickly yielded the familiar circle, star, and bar insignia that still adorns American fighter jets today.[12] (Variations on these same tests would produce the familiar shapes of traffic signs.)[13] "We fought the last battles of the war with new earphones, new microphones, new helmets, new amplifiers, new oxygen masks, all of them engineered in the light of the all-important human factor," Stevens wrote.[14] The death of the anonymous pilot whose radio had failed him in the Pacific hadn't been in vain after all.

All these innovations responded to a dawning reality that was occurring as machines grew more powerful, more intricate, and more ubiquitous. In the war effort, battles were being fought at faster and faster speed—it might take eighteen seconds between seeing a target and firing at it, but your target could have flown five miles in that time.[15] The need to understand what was happening without having the time to think was growing. These problems weren't just limited to the war. In the cars of the time, it was common to have buttons and dials that all looked exactly the same, with none of them even labeled.[16] Moreover, as Chapanis hinted at in describing some controls being "psychologically natural," new technology turned the issue of "fitting the machine to the man" into something not just physical but mental. It was crucial to design a factory floor where the operators could reach all the dials. But with machines becoming more and more autonomous, it was perhaps even more important for the users to intuit what the machine was and the principles behind how it worked.

At the same time, the idea of finding the task to which every person was perfectly suited was becoming self-evidently absurd. On the one hand, the draft was flooding the military with men of all different abilities, skills, and experiences. On the other, there were new, increasingly specialized machines rolling out from the factories and onto the battlefield. You couldn't fit fewer and fewer soldiers to more and more specialized tasks—even the military's vast and growing scale wouldn't sustain it. To achieve any improvement for the American war machine, the machines themselves had to become easier to use for more people, not fewer. Their operations had to be generalized, using some set of principles yet to be articulated. This was the beginning of the discipline called ergonomics and the beginning of an idea we live with still, that machines should be simple to use—so simple even that they're universal.

It cannot have been easy for people like Paul Fitts and Alfonse Chapanis to overturn the dominant assumption that humans could always be taught to perform better. But circumstances had forced them to invent a new perspective. The story of design is wrapped up in two world wars and the Great Depression because each of those eras presented such high-stakes problems—How do you get people to buy new things? How do you help a confused pilot keep his wits?—that they forced new ways of thinking. America couldn't keep relying on mankind to change with just a few more training courses. It would cost too many lives.

It took almost a century of progress to find the "user" in "user friendly," and that journey was advanced by war. Only with such high stakes could a radically different paradigm—of fitting the machine to the man—take hold so quickly. Along the winding path to a user-friendly world, Fitts and Chapanis laid the most important brick, the one that Don Norman would build a career around and that would teach entire generations how to think about our relationship with the things we build. They realized that as much as humans might learn, they would always be prone to err. But if you understood why these errors occurred, they could be designed out of existence. This sensibility might have remained locked away like so many secrets in a military vault if not for the reentry of Henry Dreyfuss. It was Dreyfuss who saw the striking parallel between what people such as Fitts and Chapanis had done—shaping machines around men—and deference to human desire, which powered the burgeoning industry of design.

America's first generation of industrial designers might not have survived the war years but for the U.S. government. Raymond Loewy worked on camouflage suits and signage for the Army; William Dorwin Teague designed rocket launchers for the Navy.[17] Henry Dreyfuss's work as a military contractor placed him in the realm of Chapanis and Fitts and the new field of "human factors," which S. S. Stevens had helped invent. In an echo of the commonsense instrumentation of the Toperator washing machine, Dreyfuss's firm came up with the idea of clustering the radar controls aboard airplanes and ships based on their importance to the operator, rather than ease of manufacturing—a prelude to the humane reorientation of high technology that would become the ethos of user-friendly design.[18] But his most consequential wartime project would turn out to be the chairs for tank cockpits.

Dreyfuss brought his usual gonzo immersion to the problem. Debonair and dashingly dressed as always, he stuffed himself into a tank and learned to drive it. What he realized was that the driver needed a chair that could assume two positions: one while he leaned forward to peek out of the tank during normal driving, the other while he leaned back to look through a periscope during battle. The dynamic seat necessitated a primitive drawing of how it could crane forward to support both postures—and how the human would be situated in the world of the machine. This was the seed of Dreyfuss's postwar obsession.[19] "The more involved the product is with human beings, the more it needs good design. So why not use man as the starting point for all design, even to the extent of drawing human figures into the blueprints?" he would write soon after.[20]

Dreyfuss's elegant facade hid a smoldering competitiveness and a quiet fury. (A partner in the firm asked him where he got his seemingly impregnable self-confidence in front of clients, which enabled him to stride into a room convinced his ideas should win the day. Dreyfuss, with an uncharacteristic candor, said, "I just walk in saying, to myself, you bastards, you bastards, you bastards.")[21] Dreyfuss was the youngest founder among the so-called Big Four design firms—the others were Raymond Loewy, Norman Bel Geddes, and Walter Dorwin Teague—and he wasn't in the lead. That position was probably held by Loewy or Teague, his seniors by over a decade each. After the war, Dreyfuss resolved to invent a new working method that might remake the profession and force his competitors to catch up. His inspiration rose from the human figures that were often drawn into blueprints for scale. Who were those humans? Did they really fit into that drawing? Spurred by a project for a flying car, Henry and Doris Dreyfuss first tried to define the average human body. Mostly they plumbed Army data, but they also called around to shoe stores, department stores, and clothing companies looking for whatever they could find. To turn all that data into something useful, they hired Alvin Tilley, who'd served in World War II as a design engineer.

Tilley would spend decades more perfecting his depiction of the average man and woman, "Joe" and "Josephine," as well as all their relations: short people and tall people, fat people and skinny people,

people with disabilities, kids, and every other variation of human being you might name. Those drawings were a catalog of human scale and movement, laying out in careful detail the proportions of every object that might be fitted around the human body, from the height of a chair to the depth of a cupboard. Moreover, Joe and Josephine represented a new view of the world, the design-world analogue of Leonardo's Vitruvian Man. This wasn't a coincidence.

Dreyfuss greatly admired Leonardo da Vinci, whom he dubbed the world's greatest industrial designer.[22] He idolized the Vitruvian Man. He saw it for what it was. Leonardo, by portraying the human body as an analogy for the clockwork precision of the heavens, put man at the center of the universe. So, too, were Joe and Josephine. In their most famous images, they're each sitting upright in a chair, in profile. The length and reach of their arms and legs is measured off with tick marks; every joint is depicted with an arc describing exactly their range of motion. Just as important as the data those drawings contained was the mere fact of the drawings themselves. With Joe and Josephine at the center of the designed universe, what wasn't at the center of that universe? The actual object of design itself, which was nowhere to be found in those drawings. They showed an abstracted world in which the human came first, and the objects in their lives flowed around them.[23] Joe and Josephine became the mascots of the Dreyfuss office, their images dominating the walls of the studio; more than just decoration, Joe and Josephine guided the form and proportion of everything Dreyfuss designed. And they arrived at precisely the point when the design profession would enjoy a stunning postwar boom. In the 1940s and '50s, American households had the money to buy new things, and American manufacturers had the technology to make things that had never been seen before. The combination of both brought about an entirely new pressure for industrial design.

Most design historians trace the origins of industrial design not to Henry Dreyfuss but to figures such as Josiah Wedgwood, grandfather to Charles Darwin. In the 1760s, Wedgwood invented ways to simplify pottery enough that trained laborers could make not just a few fine teacups but thousands of them in a day, at prices low enough that a new class of buyer could copycat the tastes of the rich. But Wedgwood represents a type of design focused on making slightly better versions of products that have always existed. Dreyfuss and his peers enjoyed a different opportunity after World War II: the chance to create entirely new classes of things that no one had ever realized they needed, and that no one had used before.

The designer became a mediator between the two competing influences of consumer demand and technological capability. As Henry Dreyfuss would later write, "Industrial design entered the American home through the back door . . . the kitchen and laundry held more mass-produced products than the rest of the house put together."[24] The point wasn't that mass manufacturing could make new stuff—it was that the new stuff carried with it new ideas for what life could be. Besides mass manufacturing, what also entered that "back door" was the idea of consumption as an engine of social progress and a strain of design, carried forward by designers such as Ray and Charles Eames and Dieter Rams—and also people working today. Sometimes, these designers get called on to make better versions of things that already exist, but they spend most of their time trying to create things that never existed before. When something hasn't existed before, how do you make it easy to use? And even after that new thing makes its way into the world, how do you improve it enough so that it disappears into daily life?

In the world today, there isn't much left of what Dreyfuss designed, but consider this: There is a piece of him within arm's reach, in the phone-call icon of your smartphone. Look closely at it. The facets of the handle, which Dreyfuss's designers had specified so carefully, are still there, descended from the studio's radically ergonomic design for the Model 500 telephone, released in 1953. The design of the handset itself, with the mouthpiece at one end and the earpiece at the other, made it possible to use a telephone with one hand, while a flat surface for resting the handset between your head and shoulder freed both hands entirely. Both details made talking on the telephone something that could be done while doing something else. They made phones and conversation a more natural part of everyday life. Dreyfuss's design for a headset might be the last phone icon ever designed. After all, what will ever replace it? What do we show when there is no one device that says "phone call" anymore? The icon has become more relevant than the object it refers to—simply because the product that birthed the icon was so natural to use that we eventually took it for granted.

One of the shortest stories that Jorge Luis Borges ever wrote, "On Exactitude in Science," runs exactly 145 words long. Yet it contains a world—or, more precisely, two worlds. It describes an empire so obsessed with mapmaking that its cartographers resolve to create the best map of all, "a Map of the Empire whose size was that of the Empire, and which coincided point for point with it." Eventually that map is forgotten, left to rot—and yet "in the Deserts of the West, still today, there are Tattered Ruins of that Map, inhabited by Animals and Beggars."[25] The story contains a relevant lesson. Just as the denizens of that nameless empire had become obsessed with the map of their civilization, it's a constant and recurring theme that designers, aiming to make something for the world we live in, instead end up designing for an idealized world that they've mapped for themselves. Henry Dreyfuss was one example.

Joe and Josephine did indeed put Dreyfuss's studio at the forefront of his profession, as he'd been hoping since the 1940s. At the time, there was no other compendium for ergonomic information; the masterwork that Dreyfuss and Tilley finally published in 1967, *The Measure of Man*, endures to this day. (In later editions, it was renamed *The Measure of Man and Woman*.) But Dreyfuss had become so obsessed with his maps of human difference that they lost sight of what had distinguished him all along. When Dreyfuss told the story about realizing that the theatergoers in Sioux City were too afraid of the plush red carpet to come in, he was pointing not to some physical characteristic, but a mental one. Likewise with the design he's most famous for, outside of the Bell Model 500: the Honeywell Round thermostat, unveiled in 1953. Thermostats of that era typically had a linear readout and a small, fussy little lever. The Honeywell Round was instead centered on a radial display of the temperature setting; to adjust it, you simply turned the outer ring, which mapped neatly to the display.[26] Thus, the entire form of it blended the information and the interaction into one thing—the insight behind it was about cognitive clarity, not merely ergonomics, and an intuition for what makes things easier in the real world. The ingenuity lay in reframing the problem and seeing more clearly to the life that surrounded it; ergonomics was merely one element of a broader ideal about product design. No wonder that the design became one of the most mass-produced of all time. (It was perfect enough that nearly sixty years later the startup Nest co-opted it for a thermostat imbued with sensors and artificial intelligence.) As to how that ingenuity had emerged, the Dreyfuss studio could point only to the mysterious inspirations of its designers—and the schematics of the people it had been designed to fit. In focusing on people's physical measurements, Dreyfuss's studio missed the opportunity to create a repeatable process for immersing would-be inventors in a problem, and for seeing the humans who lived with that problem. Dreyfuss did it through his own intuition—and yet he was only one person.

Still, Dreyfuss had come far. Industrial design had waltzed onto center stage during the Depression as a way to reignite the consumer impulse, and took on a new importance in the booming economy of postwar America, when new technologies were introduced to the home at a breakneck pace. Design has grappled with those twin imperatives ever since. On one hand, stoking desire; on the other, a responsibility to teach new technologies. This new conception of design helped America overcome the insecurity of the 1930s, which had manufacturers assuming that they'd always be importing good taste from Europe. As Dreyfuss would later write, "By his selection of the right conveniences to be added to the items he works on; by the obvious ease of maintenance he builds into them; by the proper selection of form and line and color for them, [the designer] has given American products the distinction they so proudly wear throughout the world."[27] It is remarkable that Dreyfuss could say that at all, given the lack of faith in American design that had existed just a few decades before.

By the 1960s, Dreyfuss had found enormous success with such icons as the Honeywell Round thermostat and the Bell Model 500; his peers called him the "conscience" of American industrial design. And yet that eminence was tottering by the decade's end. The world had changed. The profusion of new inventions that filled the home had slowed; there was no more postwar boom forcing would-be manufacturers to figure out how to fit entirely new products into people's lives. There was less and less need for those like Henry

Dreyfuss, and the ethos that motivated what they made. Moreover, as the profession grew, it became more and more about churning out new styles, more responsive to consumer whim. As a result, the preeminence of the Big Four firms from the 1930s waned. By the 1970s, there were hundreds and hundreds of competing firms in the United States alone—a glut of industrial designers all too willing to take the easy path of merely designing whatever prettification the client had hoped for. Faced with such competition, the lock-jawed seriousness of Henry and Doris, which they imbued in the studio as a self-effacing ethos, eventually became a weakness—a stolidity in the face of change. The animating spirit of the studio had moldered. As Niels Diffrient, whom Dreyfuss had groomed to take over the practice, once said: "A lot of the stuff was too conservative, it didn't take advantage of the potential to put some life into it. I would guess that was probably at the bottom of my discontent there, that we didn't really struggle hard enough to go beyond just solving the problem, and give the thing some real life or excellence beyond the expected."[28]

In 1972, Dreyfuss, still always eager for press coverage and still always unhappy that the world wasn't better designed, got an assignment from one of the founders of the upstart *New York* magazine, Milton Glaser, to propose better street signs for the city. Dreyfuss hoped to publish his designs alongside an essay with his friend Ralph Caplan, editor of *Industrial Design* magazine. Dreyfuss went on vacation with Doris in Hawaii, and kept sending Caplan postcards asking if the essay was finished yet. Caplan had been dragging his feet on it. "I didn't know what his rush was. He said, 'We have to get going, we don't have time,'" Caplan told me.[29] "I said, 'There's plenty of time to waste!'" Caplan knew Doris had liver cancer, but Dreyfuss didn't talk about it. He certainly didn't tell anyone about the pact he and Doris had made. One evening in 1972,

Doris put on her best evening gown and Henry put on his custom brown tuxedo. They got a bottle of champagne and two glasses, and went out to the brown Mercedes in the garage, as if heading off to a party. They turned the car on. They popped the champagne, toasted, sipped, then went to sleep and never woke up again. Faced with a world that seemed to need him less and less, Dreyfuss left it.

In the seventy years after S. S. Stevens first limned the discipline of psychophysics and Alphonse Chapanis seeded the field of ergonomics, those disciplines have morphed, evolved, and branched, taking on new names and new applications. These came to be called "human factors," "human-machine interaction," and of course "cognitive psychology"—the field that Don Norman came to dominate in the late 1970s, when he was called upon to study the accident at Three Mile Island. And the ideas behind them created the field we know today as user-experience design—which Don Norman had coined to denote a shift in thinking away from the object of design and toward what surrounds it. Dreyfuss intuited what lay behind that new paradigm: that the artifacts in our lives can't make us happy unless they're designed to serve us, with our limitations and foibles and errors.

Seeing humans as they are, instead of as they're supposed to be, was one of the great, unappreciated intellectual shifts of the twentieth century. That worldview was a flat-out rebuke to the Enlightenment's faith in the perfectibility of mankind's reasoning, and the presiding metaphor that our minds worked like the precise gears of a clock. Instead, our culture came to view the mind as a contraption, whose inner workings we often misapprehended, when we appreciated them at all. It's not an accident that the same era that begat the first mentions of user-friendliness also birthed behavioral economics. By the 1970s, the latter had just begun to produce a series of startling studies that revealed just how shortsighted our minds could be, and how many shortcuts we took to make sense of the world. What both user-friendliness and behavioral economics shared was an overriding sense that our minds could never be perfected, and that our imperfections made us who we are. This embrace of human limitation was nursemaid to the idea that machines had to be bent around humans. Don Norman's early papers are larded with references to the pathbreaking work of Amos Tversky and Daniel Kahneman, in which they laid the foundations of behavioral economics. Meanwhile, modern neuroscience was also beginning to discover that our brain wasn't built like a clock either, with neatly functioning units. Rather, it was composed of many separate evolutionary adaptations kludged together. By the 1980s, it wasn't a surprise that humans could be viewed as the sum of their foibles.

User-friendliness is simply the fit between the objects around us and the ways we behave. So while we might think that the user-friendly world is one of making user-friendly things, the bigger truth is that design doesn't rely on artifacts. As my collaborator Robert Fabricant likes to say, it relies on our patterns of behavior. All the nuances of designing new products can be reduced to one of two basic strategies: either finding what causes us pain and trying to eliminate it, or reinforcing what we already do with a new object that makes it so easy it becomes second nature. The truest material for making new things isn't aluminum or carbon fiber. It's behavior.[30]

Tesla Model S steering wheel (2012)

4

Trust

It was January of the year 2016, which would prove to be a break-through year in mainstream media coverage of driverless cars. We were rolling eastward across the San Mateo Bridge in an Audi A7, picking our way through traffic. One of the car's engineers was driving, while I was riding in the passenger seat. There was another engineer in the back seat, monitoring the car from a laptop. Traffic was getting thick as the workday drew to a close on all the area's tech campuses. It was a beautiful day for a drive, typical for the mid-Peninsula. Outside the passenger window, I watched the placid tidal waters of San Francisco Bay, which were a milky green hue beneath a bright blue sky. Then the engineer in the back seat piped up to tell me what was about to happen, and I watched as the car's center console blinked to life with a countdown timer: "5 minutes until pilot mode available." As one of the first people outside of Audi to experience what was about to happen, I dutifully stared at the timer and waited for the future to arrive.

With a sticker price starting at $68,000, the A7 was a fancy car, but not enough to draw attention along the stock-option-paved highways of Silicon Valley. I looked at the drivers around us, knowing they hadn't a clue about what was happening in the next lane. The five minutes passed, and then two buttons on the steering wheel's hub blinked, ready to be pressed. That action was inspired by America's nuclear missile systems, where two keys had to be turned at the same time to avoid mistakes. The engineer driving the car pressed the buttons, and a bright strip of LEDs around the bottom edge of the windshield flashed from orange to blue-green.

The car was in control now.

The engineer lifted his hands from the wheel and put them in his lap, then he smiled pleasantly as if to say, "I'm totally used to people squealing right now." Right on cue, I have to confess, I gave an honest-to-God cheer. The steering wheel pulled back and started to waggle by itself left and right, adjusting to the contours of the road with an uncanny precision. It was a moment that was awesome to absorb—and then, almost immediately, uneventful. Which was as powerful a sign as any that something significant had happened during this handoff between man and machine.

We were chatting when the car in front of us stabbed at the brakes, the taillights flaring. My attention instinctively snapped forward. I could feel the car making the decision to change lanes, starting to drift over. But then came another blur at the corner of my sight, as a driver to our left dickishly raced into our blind spot, cutting us off. My lizard brain thought to curse the guy, but the Audi, unfazed, merely drifted back to the center of our lane and braked gently, so as not to hit the car in front of us. The engineer behind the wheel was still smiling, masklike, his hands on his lap.

This entire exchange should have been freaky, even frightening. The car was making the decisions on its own, but they were over before you could process the minutiae. You trusted what was happening, because the process was so smooth. I asked my blankly smiling driver what, exactly, he was supposed to be doing right then. He smiled—a tad more lifelike, a couple of teeth showing—as if to say he couldn't answer. By law, the test driver had to remain alert at all times and ready to take over, even if the car didn't need help. So he stared straight ahead like a robot himself, almost motionless. The law simply hadn't caught up to what the car could do. (By 2019, European Audi A8s came with an optional "traffic jam pilot" that allowed limited hands-free operation; that option couldn't be offered in America, because of the inconsistency in federal and state laws.)[1] The supervising engineer piped up, "The first three minutes you're thinking, This is crazy, this is the future! Then you get bored." We all laughed. But the very fact of the drive's boringness was a feat. Boringness implied ease rather than fear, a comfort with what was happening even if it was totally novel.

Amid all the headlines about driverless cars, it's easy to miss just how far they have come, and how fast. We can already buy cars that park themselves or swerve to avoid accidents or brake to avoid surprise obstacles. Look a little closer and you can see how awkward the adjustment has been at times. There's a slapstick viral video on YouTube from 2015, with more than 7 million views. It shows a bunch of people at a car dealership in the Dominican Republic who think they're testing out a feature Volvo had been advertising since 2011 that actually prevents the car from hitting a pedestrian. It was indeed a magical-seeming feature—if you had it.

You can't quite see the hapless driver settling in behind the wheel, but let's imagine him wide-eyed, bristling with excitement as he prepares to slam on the accelerator. In the foreground stands a guy in a pink shirt. He's leaning forward nervously, a brittle mix of apprehension and excitement. The driver slams on the accelerator . . . and the car plows right through Pink Shirt Guy, who rag-dolls onto the hood. The camera spins wildly, forgotten. It turns out the guy *hadn't bought that option*, and so had simply run into his foolishly brave confederate.[2]

Self-driving cars went viral again in late 2015 when Tesla dropped a $2,500 software update on its customers that promised a new "Autopilot" feature. The videos were fascinating to watch, mostly because of what wasn't happening. There's one, titled "Tesla Autopilot Tried to Kill Me!," where the driver slowly lifts his hands off the wheel for the first time, with evident nervousness. He's right to be scared. His car, unable to detect the lane dividers that guide it, veers into oncoming traffic. Luckily, he snatches the wheel.[3]

Driverless cars won't arrive one day in a flash. They'll arrive on a day that no one notices, and that will be as much of an accomplishment as any, because of what it will say about all the designs that preceded it. Their success doesn't simply depend on engineering. Their success depends on whether we, the people, can guess what a new button in our car does even if we've never used it before. Do we trust it? Getting this right isn't about getting the technology right—the technology exists. It's why, years before that Audi would come to market, there were at least dozens of driverless trucks and cars plying routes across the United States.[4] The greater challenge lies in making these technologies into something we trust. In those Tesla videos, the drivers don't know what the car can't do. Techies and Tesla boosters were quick to lay blame. Don't these idiots know how all these things work? Sixty years after the Air Force stopped blaming plane crashes on pilot error, we're blaming drivers for the sins of their poorly designed machines. The people looking terrified in those Tesla videos? That's not their problem. It's a design problem. The magic of a well-designed invention is that you seem to know how it will work even before you've used it. That requires weaving together the principles we've seen before, handed down from World War II, Three Mile Island, and elsewhere—but also something else. The secret is that we come to trust machines only if they mimic the way we come to trust other people.

Brian Lathrop was in charge of figuring out how to make drivers trust that A7 I rode in. He runs the user-experience group at Volkswagen's little-known Electronics Research Laboratory, and his very bland job description belies how much time he spends living in the future.[5] A psychologist by training, California born and raised, Lathrop is burly with close-cropped hair like an army sergeant. He speaks with the painstakingly precise diction of a scientist. But he's also an inventor, the coauthor of several patents that might prove decisive for autonomous cars.

Fifteen years ago, Lathrop found his job on Monster.com, and even the guy who hired him didn't quite know what he'd be doing at Volkswagen. There were fifteen engineers, and when Lathrop arrived they all assumed that he'd be the sixteenth. His first week, they handed him some circuit boards to solder. Lathrop, a cognitive psychologist in the mold of Alphonse Chapanis and Don Norman, smiled and started in on the circuit boards. He had come, in his words, to the Wild West. "There are good and bad things," he says. "The bad thing is that no one is giving you directions. The good thing is that no one is giving you directions."

Eventually, Lathrop started working on the interiors of a few concept cars—the futuristic visions that Volkswagen would show off at car expos. One thing he noticed was how the array of features inside our cars was creeping upward into absurdity. When he first sat in a Phaeton, Volkswagen's top-tier sedan, Lathrop counted *seventy* different knobs. He started to think, How do you group these things and get rid of them? And he started to see that a great many of those buttons were dedicated to little tidbits of assisted driving. He thought, Why don't I put those all together on a touchscreen?

This was around 2010, when self-driving cars were just beginning to be real. A team at Stanford had figured out how to rig up an Audi to drive itself in a race up the fabled Pikes Peak. Anyone could see that the promise of self-driving cars was too tantalizing for them to remain in the lab for long. It happened that Lathrop was particularly well positioned for the problem. He'd cut his teeth at NASA, trying to create helmet displays for pilots. It was a job that asked a fundamental question of the modern world: How do you pass control of a plane back and forth between a man and a machine?

Lathrop already knew that 90 percent of plane crashes occurred not when the plane broke down but when the pilot had failed to understand what the plane was doing. He considered what was about to happen with driverless cars and thought, *Holy crap.* "I started to think, We're going to run into the same problems, but they'll be multiplied by ten thousand."[6] In a plane, you might run into a hint of danger once during a sixteen-hour flight. In a car, you could have the chance to crash every second. What's more, your fellow drivers haven't dedicated their lives to training themselves to safely drive a car. They aren't paid to keep other people safe. They aren't paid not to put on their makeup or read their email during rush hour. Lathrop thought to himself, What are the odds that someone with a background in aviation was coming to work on autonomous cars in 2010? He was the only one, as far as he could tell.

By the time we first met, in 2016, he had logged more years working on driverless cars than all but a few people in the world. He'd been set down that path by a book by another human-factors scientist, Asaf Degani, suggestively titled *Taming Hal*, after the killer computer in Stanley Kubrick's *2001*. It had a picture of the Hal 9000's glowing red eye on the cover. In the book, Degani traced the history of automation and the disasters we've encountered along the way, using everything from alarm clocks to microwaves to airplanes. And, while an alarm seems the furthest thing from a sentient AI, Degani was making a broader point about what the Hal 9000 represented. There's a moment in *2001* when the crew, suspicious of Hal's advice, absconds to a soundproof room to discuss unplugging it. Hal, peering in with his unblinking red eye, manages to read their lips anyway. Hal knows what the crew wants. But Hal wants something different. In detailing how cockpits and control panels fail, Degani was laying out how we might create machines that never seem to have a mind of their own.[7] The book helped Lathrop distill a "three plus one" design philosophy for driverless cars, which has become the guiding force behind his work today.

We saw before how the catastrophe at Three Mile Island was caused by its control panels, which buried users in buttons that meant different things without any sense of what was important. It showed us that to build a mental model of how a machine works, you needed to embed its workings in an interface that's easy to navigate, with a consistent syntax for what every action meant, and feedback to tell you things were going right. And we saw how those principles made their way into the simplest interface of all, the button, which had to show the user—via a satisfying click, or a big red light—that the button had been pushed, that the action it was meant to do had actually been done. Whether it's nuclear reactors or smartphone apps or toaster buttons, always and forever, the point is to allow users to figure out what to do, then to tell them what's happening. It was the same for Lathrop's three plus one.

There are three things an autonomous car has to get right, plus one: Above all, we need to know what mode a car is in, whether it's driving itself or not. That harks to probably the oldest axiom in interface design—mode confusion causes most airplane crashes. Alfonse Chapanis and Paul Fitts were the first to discover it when they studied World War II pilots who'd engaged the wing flaps instead of the landing gear. The second principle Lathrop calls the coffee-spilling principle: For us not to get surprised, then freaked out by a driverless car, we need to know what it is going to do before it's actually done. Third, and perhaps most vital in fostering trust, is that we need to know what the car is seeing. And finally—the "plus one" in Lathrop's formulation, because it relates not just to the user but to the interaction between user and machine—we need perfectly clear transitions when a car takes control, or when we take control from a car.

In the case of this particular A7, those principles had all been compressed into the brief span of a couple of minutes, when the test driver moved our car onto the highway and then let its computers take over the driving. It was a tight choreography. When the car took over, the lights rimming the windshield flashed and changed color to tell us that control had shifted. Not only was it clear who was driving, the transition between man and car had been clear. Later on, when the car was changing lanes, it would give a countdown timer saying what it was about to do. And all the while, there was a screen on the console showing all the cars around us so that we knew that the car was seeing every bit of the environment around us as we were.

In the coming years, as the partnership between man and machines takes on even greater texture, our relations with them necessarily will evolve. No longer will it be enough for a machine to be bent around us; it will have to gain our trust. And that trust will have to be built in subtle ways.

Consider what the designers at fuseproject discovered when creating a suit to augment the muscles of the elderly. It looked like an undergarment designed for denizens of the starship *Enterprise*: a form-fitting leotard, with hexagonal pods clustered around the thighs and back. Those pods were in fact motors that worked like an additional set of muscles, powering on when the wearer needed them—while standing up from a chair, for example.[8]

The broader problem the suit was meant to address was indeed a consequential one: the graying of populations throughout the developed world, and the likelihood that more and more elderly people would be caring for themselves in the coming decades. But what had sold investors on the project was the magic of artificial intelligence: Using sensors that detected the electrical signals in the wearer's muscles, the motor pods could readily predict what the wearer intended to do, almost as soon as they intended to do it. A problem arose right after the designers began to test the prototype for themselves. "If the suit just takes over when someone is moving, then it's just doing the same thing as what the aging process has done," said Yves Béhar, the founder and chief designer at fuseproject. "It's just giving people less and less control." Feeling like a suit was taking over your movements would be like being a marionette on a string. What could be worse was what would happen if the suit made an error in thinking you wanted to do something and then acted, getting the whole thing wrong. "If for any reason it does something when you don't want it to, you lose trust," Béhar said. It wasn't just that the suit could potentially reinforce the idea that wearers were losing control over their lives. It was that in doing so, it would lose whatever trust was required for the wearer to even use it, dooming the product.

The problem was how to make the wearers feel in control without any screens to guide them. Solving it required a novel interface. When the suit detected a motion, the relevant motors would give a slight buzz. At that point, users would simply place their hands on the motors themselves. So, for example, when the wearer leaned forward while sitting, the thigh motors would give a buzz. If the wearer placed their hands on their thighs, the motors would buzz twice to tell you what was about to happen, and they'd engage. Just as with the Audi, it was telling you what it was doing, letting you confirm the action, then telling you again that your intent was registered. But it was all designed to embed that cascade of feedback into a behavior that already exists: the natural motion of bracing your hands on your thighs before you stand up. It was a clean example of how behavior has become the material of design. It was also an example of how it isn't enough just to readapt our patterns. Whether it's a suit that augments your muscles, a driverless car, or an artificially intelligent assistant, any technology that asks us to cede what we could once only do for ourselves will need to understand our mores. Those designs will have to understand what's appropriate or tactful or simply nice, because that's the way humans build trust. While politeness seems like a trivial detail, it is a design constraint as real as the heat tolerance of steel or the melting point of plastic.

In the mid-1990s, the sociologist Clifford Nass made one of the strangest discoveries in the annals of human-computer interaction. For nearly twenty years, Nass studied how we think about our computers—not just how we use them, but how we *feel* about them. He had worked out a process to think up new experiments: He and his collaborators would scour the annals of sociology and psychology, finding papers about how humans behaved toward one another, careful to look at how other researchers crafted studies to isolate human-to-human interaction. And then he'd figure out how to observe what would happen if you replaced one of the humans with a computer.[9]

Nass was particularly interested in politeness. Though it seems like a squishy subject, politeness can be quantified. Imagine you're teaching another person how to drive. Then imagine if you asked your pupil how you'd performed as a teacher. To test for politeness, you could simply compare the responses given to you directly with those given when *someone else* had asked how you'd performed. The difference would be a rough measure of how much we muzzle our criticism of someone when asked to say it to their faces. Nass wondered if humans might behave the same way toward a computer, with the same inborn sense of etiquette.

It turned out that humans really were nicer to the computers that they "knew." First he had test subjects perform some simple tasks on the computer. Then he had them rate the design of its software— one group on the actual computer they'd used, and another on a different machine. It turned out that people using a different machine were far harsher when appraising the original computer program— they were more critical when they weren't faced with the computer they'd used. They acted more politely in front of the computer that had been theirs. No one was conscious of doing this; in fact, they denied that they'd ever consider being polite to a machine. *But they did it all the same.*[10]

In dozens of experiments, Nass documented a menagerie of strange examples: In one, people thought more positively of a computer that lavished praise upon them. The behavior somehow remained even after they'd been told the praise was meaningless.

In another, he gave two groups of people blue and green armbands; after asking them to use a computer with a screen lined with green paint, the ones with the green armbands rated their experience more favorably. As his frequent collaborator Byron Reeves told *The New York Times*, "Everybody thought [computers] were tools, that they were hammers and screwdrivers and things to be looked at in an inanimate fashion. Cliff said, 'No, these things talk, they have relationships with you, and they make you feel good or bad.'"[11]

Nass liked to point out that our brains evolved to deal with two basic types of experience: the physical world and the social. Computers were a new hybrid of both; since their beginning, we had thought they belonged to the physical world. But because they responded to us, engaged us, aggravated and pleased us, we couldn't help but see them as social actors. If so, we couldn't help but assume that they'd hew to the rules of polite society.[12]

Talking to Lathrop, hearing of all the years of research and care piled into every detail, the way humans relate to computers seemed almost comically complicated. But it turns out that there's a more basic way to frame our expectations of machines, one that's more familiar and easy to grasp: Our expectations of machines are, to a startlingly consistent degree, well mapped to our expectations of actual human beings.

Consider what happens when you're driving in your car, come to a stoplight, and then pull out your phone to check a text message. We all know it's wrong, but most of us have done it anyway. Alone, you wouldn't think twice about it. But if you're with a friend, she'd be smart to scold you: "Pay attention to the road!" Maybe you'd protest that you are paying attention, that you *know* what's going on. Yet your friend couldn't know that. She would feel endangered because she wouldn't know what to expect of your next move on the road.

She would feel endangered because she wouldn't know that you'd taken in all the information that she has—who's crossing the road, how long it's been since the light turned, the car that's just pulled up alongside you. No matter how well they know each other, people who face a shared danger are constantly checking who knows what, and what to do next.

It is no different with a machine. The car also has to tell both the driver and the rider about what it's sensing. To solve that problem, the A7 shows you a map of your surroundings as the car sees them: outlines of the other cars on the road, shown on a simple, stripped-down display. This doesn't seem like new information. After all, it's merely a crude representation of what you can see simply by looking out the window. But in fact, the display is telling you that *the car sees what you see.* And then it tells you what it's going to do. There's a screen that tells you what the next move will be—"left turn"—with a countdown timer until it happens. Simple as it sounds, that bit of information means the difference between feeling like you're taking a ride, and feeling like you've been taken hostage. The sense of safety you get from that is akin to riding in a car, looking over, and seeing that the driver has both hands on the wheel, eyes forward. She's using her turn signals, checking her blind spots. We're constantly checking out the people around us, to see if they see what we do, to guess whether they know what we know. Our expectations are no different if our partner is a car, driving itself, or a machine that purports to help us. The conversation we have with either shadows those we have with people we trust.

Paul Grice, the great philosopher of language who helped define that field in the twentieth century, thought of conversation as adhering to unspoken rules of cooperation. He laid out those rules as a set of maxims, which boil down to being truthful, saying no more than you need to, being relevant, and being clear.[13] Grice's maxims also shed light on politeness. Being polite means following a conversation, not co-opting it and dragging it in other directions. It means knowing who you're talking with, and knowing what they know. It's rude to talk over people, to misunderstand who they are. Those maxims happen to neatly map to the same design principles laid out by Don Norman, and the ones that guided Brian Lathrop in the creation of Audi's self-driving A7.

You can use that way of thinking to look back at one of the worst pieces of software ever designed: Clippy, the animated assistant that used to pop up every time you did anything in Microsoft Word. Clippy had no sense of his place, or what you were trying to do. Whenever you typed the word "Dear," Clippy would pop up and say, "I see you're writing a letter. Would you like some help?" It didn't matter how many times you'd said no before; Clippy had to butt in. If you asked Clippy a question, he'd tell you something completely unrelated; if you rephrased the question, he'd say the same thing again. Clippy never learned your name, how you worked, what you preferred. Worst of all, no matter how useless Clippy was, he still smiled with puffed-up posture, taunting you. Clippy was unconscionably rude, and a rude machine is worse than one that simply doesn't work. When you're in dialogue with a computer, the logic of creating a trustworthy machine isn't just about fitting machines to the man, but weaving machines into our social fabric. There's a culture to how things should behave. As Clifford Nass knew all along, "Humans expect computers to act as though they were people and get annoyed when technology fails to respond in socially appropriate ways."[14]

Whether it's the rules of conversation or the rules of interface design, the goal is to communicate in a way that's easy to follow. The interactions are all structured around feedback, so that both partners know that they're aligned. Sometimes, in the case of a nuclear reactor panel, that feedback is a set of lights telling us that what we've just done was indeed what we wanted to do. In our social lives, feedback comes in the form of a conversational partner unconsciously nudging us with their body language about whether the conversation is going well. Whether we're communicating with a human or a machine, the goal is to create a shared understanding of the world. That's the point behind both the rules governing polite conversation and how a user-friendly machine should work.

Months after I took my test drive in the Audi that drove itself, the user-experience researchers at Volkswagen gathered in an empty parking lot to try to figure out how pedestrians would behave around an autonomous vehicle. It seemed a given that it would scare them. "Unless people are standing on the pavement with the vehicle, you can't appreciate how they're going to feel," pointed out Erik Glaser, the young project leader. The experiment demanded a giant tent over the parking lot, to control how the light spilled across the bare-bones street intersection they had created overnight. There were stop signs and crosswalks and lanes. There was an Audi A7 idling just beyond the intersection, with its windows pasted over with limo tinting so that no one could see there was no driver. Participants would be asked to simply cross the road whenever it felt safe.

At that time, very few people in the tribe of geeks researching autonomous cars had given much thought to the issue. At the extreme, you could imagine terror—say, if the car behaved so erratically that people raced across the intersection with their breath held. But instead, something stranger happened. "I thought people would be conservative," said Glaser. "But people were really fearless." They saw the car and blithely stepped in front of it. It was a riddle as to why they were so heedless, but it seemed like it had to be one of the many external displays on the car, which were meant to tell pedestrians what the car was doing. There was one LED sign with an icon telling people they could cross. There was a strip of LEDs that gave a pixelated representation of the pedestrian—showing that the car was seeing them, just like you might meet the gaze of a human driver, to make sure that she had seen you. It turns out that despite the hundreds of hours Glaser had spent carefully designing all these details, no one noticed them. Instead, people were so trusting because the car acted in a respectful, socially acceptable way. In a split second, people could see that the car was coming to a measured stop, just like a human driver might. The slowness of that stop said something: that the car had seen you, that it wasn't going to suddenly gun the engine. That whoever was inside wasn't a psycho out to do harm. "The physical driving behavior of the car is actually its own human-machine interface," said Glaser. "It turns out, the personality of the car is something you have to program."[15]

Cars are just one example of the general truth that there's a culture to the way everything around us behaves. This insight offers two forking choices. We can ignore it at our peril, as Tesla repeatedly seemed to. But while the ethos of moving fast and breaking things means it's easier to make technical progress, that progress is illusory, as it's human nature to avoid something that didn't work the first time. On the other hand, we can recognize that the key to making us comfortable with the future lies in mapping all the contextual nuances that we use without thinking—in realizing, for example, that the way a car pulls up to a curb is an interface all its own. We can watch actual humans, in hopes of making things more humane. It's not enough to make a dashboard just easy to use or easy to read.

And while we don't need a dashboard with a full-blown personality, it'll have to have personality traits. It'll need to be calming, communicative, or helpful, as the situation demands. "We're bootstrapping this technology," Glaser told me. "The gaps will get filled in. But we need handholds along the way." Then he showed me an example.

Back at the lab, a small army of engineers and project managers had gathered to show off a new concept. "And now we would like to reveal something special for you!" Glaser announced. He was shockingly young—compared with the many other stone-faced Germans standing around, he looked like an intern: gawky, earnest, wearing jeans, with a chinstrap of facial hair that likely began just a few years ago, around his junior year of college. Like his boss Brian Lathrop, he seemed to have been charting a course to this job for years. As a student at Carnegie Mellon, he helped design a robot programmed with an agenda: as it offered you snacks, it detected what you chose and tried to coax you into healthier choices— "Cookies again, huh?" It had an LED capable of expressing a subtle frown of judgment. Glaser was still facing the same challenge: How do you build a smart robot that doesn't freak people out?

Off to the side of the garage was a black cloth draped over something bulky, about the size of a couch. An assistant gently rolled back the cloth: *voilà*. Here was a simulated dashboard and steering wheel. "This is a working-as-of-last-night prototype," Glaser said, his eyes red-rimmed with fatigue. The steering wheel, a year and a half in development, had just been bolted into the simulator hours before. It wasn't just a demonstration of a new design—it was the demonstration of a new metaphor for how we might relate to our cars. And that metaphor had traveled decades to get here, to the lab.

For over two decades, researchers at NASA had been noodling

over the idea that the interaction between a machine piloting itself and a human who might want to take over could be akin to that of a person atop a horse, holding the reins.[16] When you draw a horse's reins close, you assume control. But let the reins loose and the horse will walk itself. By the horse's ears and posture, the way it moves, you can tell it has taken control. You can be sure that whether you're in control or not, the horse's own sense of self-preservation will keep you within some boundary of safety—from, say, charging over a cliff. The question was how a man and an airplane could trade off with each other so gracefully. Lathrop wondered, what if there were a machine that couldn't be forced into disaster? A machine, in other words, that behaved according to the horse metaphor. Even if you were atop the horse and you had let loose the reins altogether, it could sense what you'd done and let its own eyes and instincts take control. Lathrop realized that the metaphor wasn't just apt; it was a map of what needed to be invented. A horse had eyes, ears, a sense of touch. A car would need the same: sensors to watch your eyes to see if you were paying attention; sensors to tell whether you were holding the steering wheel or had your feet on the pedals.[17]

After years of research came the steering wheel that the engineers had just unveiled. I sat down in the makeshift driver's seat and tested it out. Starting off, it behaved like any other steering wheel. But as I lifted my hands off, the steering wheel drew away by about seven or eight inches—just enough to the edge of my reach that I could tell it wasn't mine to control. But one thing did stay in place: the center column of the wheel, where all the entertainment controls would presumably live. The subtle message was: These controls are for you; the steering now belongs to the machine. Of course, like loosened reins, I could still grab back the wheel if I wanted to take charge. But that span of seven or eight inches was a finely tuned gap, enough of a gulf that the car was unmistakably in control.

When Brian Lathrop started working at Volkswagen, most people assumed that to tell a car to start driving itself, you'd just push a button. "My thesis was simply that that was wrong," says Lathrop.[18] Of course, that impulse for push-button simplicity was itself a metaphor, embedded in our culture. Designers such as Henry Dreyfuss and William Dorwin Teague had helped birth that ideal, with electric washing machines and kitchen appliances. It was Teague, working for Edwin Land, who designed the first Polaroid camera, which ingeniously compressed the laborious process of developing film into something anyone could do without a second thought. With just one press. Today, we see that heritage in the one-click purchasing of Amazon, the Nespresso coffee maker, and even the help button designed by Mladen Barbaric. We aspire to make our interactions as concise as possible, available in button form. But the power of that idea is slowly giving way to something else.

When we push a button, we give explicit permission for a machine to do something on our behalf. But if you take the view of the machine, what is the button except one indicator, the only one it knows how to process, of what we want? What if a machine, like a horse, could determine whether you were still in control just by *sensing* your behavior? What if a car, sensing you'd leaned over or weren't paying attention, would know it had to take control?

Lathrop wanted to design a world in which machines didn't require explicit commands to take over. To be sure, this didn't mean a world of killer robots such as the Hal 9000, with minds of their own. Rather, this would be a world in which computers might sense what you wanted even before you'd managed to form the thought in your head. It was a vision in which the press of a button would feel like work. After all, what was a button but a mere approximation of the more fluid relationship we have with one another, and with the natural world? In the future, ways of passing control back and forth between man and machine would be embedded in our body language—just as they've been between humans for millennia. Lathrop believed that the button-push world was about to end. He believed that, just as Facebook senses what we're likely to read or Amazon predicts what we'll buy, the machines we've always taken satisfaction in controlling would simply sense what we want.[19]

The Audi steering wheel, and the horse metaphor, was one idea about how things would evolve next, in the guise of things we already knew how to use. You might wonder at the weirdness of this: After all, far fewer Westerners have ridden a horse than have driven a car. But the power of the metaphor isn't that we necessarily have direct experience. Its power lies in the fact that the way reins control a horse is easy to imagine, reinforced over time in more movies and TV shows than we can count. That you can know what reins are and how they work without ever having ridden a horse—that's proof that the metaphor works.

For Lathrop the next step was to figure out how to give the machine the right instincts about what you were doing, just like you would a horse. To figure out if you were paying enough attention to drive, the car had to see whether your eyes were forward and your posture alert, and sense whether your hands and feet were on the wheel and pedals. Only when these were all affirmative would the car let you assume control. If your hand wandered, if you stretched your legs, if you were caught daydreaming, the car would know to take control.[20] Our cars are already quietly evolving like this, taking over. Today, many adaptive cruise-control systems will simply pull over to a stop if you fall asleep. They're watching us.

For us to trust a machine, we have to be safe in the knowledge that it can sense what we want. But likewise, we have to be able to accurately imagine just what it is that the machine is capable of doing. We have to have the right mental model of it. When our mental models don't fit with reality—when something doesn't do exactly what we imagine, and when the feedback loops fail to help us understand—horrible things can happen. We saw how drivers unsure of what the Autopilot feature in their Tesla could do were creating videos with titles such as "Tesla Autopilot Tried to Kill Me!" Maybe the most mortifying part was that Tesla had called the new feature Autopilot. By doing so, Tesla planted an idea in the heads of its users about what a car driving itself should do. They invited drivers to supply their own ideas about "autopilot," then sent them on their way. And when there was a gap between what Autopilot did and how people imagined it, tragedy struck.

On May 7, Joshua Brown was behind the wheel of his beloved Tesla Model S while the car took care of the driving. He was a veteran of the Navy, where he'd worked with SEAL Team 6 disarming IEDs. He was a daredevil and a tech geek, Tesla's ideal customer. When he bought the car, he bought the idea that Tesla was pushing the limits of what we were ready for. Brown didn't seem to notice when a truck in the oncoming lane took a left turn in front of him. Neither did his Tesla. It was bright and clear out, a warm Florida day, and the car didn't make out the white truck against a sunlit white sky. Neither did Brown. His Tesla plowed into and under the truck without braking at all, shearing off the car's roof and killing him.[21]

Just a few weeks after that, I borrowed from the company's press fleet an Audi SUV that had been outfitted with the latest in

Audi's driver-assist technology—perhaps one of the last few generations on the market before Audi begins to roll out cars like the prototype I saw, which let you take your hands off the wheel. The differences between that SUV and the Tesla that Joshua Brown drove were striking. It had the same basic technologies: radars and cameras that identified the lane markers and the cars around, so that when you hit cruise control, the car could stay in its lane and brake as needed to stay in the flow of highway traffic, at a comfortable distance from other vehicles. Unlike the Tesla, the Audi wouldn't let you take your hands off the wheel for much more than a couple of seconds without the car pinging insistently, then frantically. But more than that, the car, which I could feel steering in the lane by itself, wasn't totally steering. Instead, it did nothing when I was driving down roughly the middle of the lane. Only when I got close to the lane dividers did I feel the steering wheel start to turn itself, guiding the car gently back. It was a beautiful interaction, for how much information was embedded in it. The machine could readily drive in the center of the lane, but it didn't, forcing me to stay engaged in the act of driving. My mental model was far different from the one Joshua Brown had in his Tesla. My SUV was telling me, *You're still driving, so pay attention.* But then I got an intimation of just how capably the car was watching everything around me. Driving down the highway, an eighteen-wheeler started veering into my blind spot. Immediately, my car nudged itself over, away from the impending sideswipe, and applied the brakes hard, letting the truck pass. It was obvious that this was a car that could drive itself under many circumstances: It could see the road, and it could see the cars around it. It could react to danger. Yet those capabilities weren't being fully loosed—the car wouldn't let me take my hands off the wheel—because the car wasn't quite ready for every situation. Neither are we.

More than a year after Joshua Brown's death, the National Transportation Safety Board (NTSB) issued its accident report. The finding was, essentially, that Tesla's designs allowed too much leeway in how the Autopilot feature was used, but that Brown should have been paying close attention all along.[22] It was, in other words, *driver error*—a telling echo of all those "pilot error" crashes that Paul Fitts investigated during World War II, and all those engineers who'd blamed the pilots. It was business as usual because by the end we'd figured out how to blame the user—the most comforting message because it means that the least has to change. Consider two examples from recent history: when a driverless Uber killed a pedestrian in Arizona while driving at night; and in Hawaii when, during a routine drill, a hapless employee sent a nuclear missile warning that reached tens of thousands of people.

Uber had been testing its self-driving cars on the open road for a few years until the night of March 18, 2018, when, in Tempe, Arizona, one of them, driving forty miles per hour, killed Elaine Herzberg while she was crossing the street.[23] A week later, the Tempe chief of police said she suspected that Uber was not at fault.[24] The day after that, I saw a headline on my phone that read, "Woman Killed by Driverless Car Likely Homeless." The inference wasn't subtle: Maybe it *was* her fault, the homeless being who they are. That narrative may have stuck if video hadn't soon emerged, clearly showing Herzberg crossing the street in the glare of the car's headlights, and the car not slowing down at all before it hit her. Uber suspended the program for a while, before quietly starting it back up.

In the case of Hawaii, the design community was ablaze when a screenshot leaked showing that to send a statewide alert of a nuclear attack, an employee merely had to select one option among many in a confusing drop-down menu. As Don Norman noted in a tweet, the interface didn't have one critical feature: a way to confirm that this was indeed what the user meant to do.[25] Yet it read, with astonishing blandness, "Are you sure you want to send this alert?" The employee clicked "Yes." (Imagine if the pop-up menu had instead conveyed the actual decision being made: "Do you really want to tell thousands of people that their families will be vaporized in a couple of minutes?" Or something to that effect.) Then a story emerged that the error occurred only because the employee in question, when faced with a drill, had simply failed to understand that it was merely a test.[26] For a couple of days, it seemed like the government would be forced to redesign a clearly terrible system. But, with a person to blame, the story merely vanished.

We take comfort in blaming humans when things go wrong. The NTSB took that point of view when it investigated the death of Joshua Brown. His Tesla had come with instructions, and he had plowed ahead all the same. He had, apparently, been too trusting of what the car could do, and unaware of its limitations. But why did the Tesla even let any driver's trust outstrip what the machine could actually do? We demand that new technologies do not only what they promise, but what we imagine. We also demand that they behave in the way we guess they will, without ever having used them before. But making that happen means that the machines must be designed so that our imaginations can't get too far ahead of the machines. When they do, confusion reigns.

This problem is working itself out before us, in real time, in the form of digital assistants: Alexa by Amazon, Siri by Apple, and the Google Assistant. Because these have all been taught to understand and respond to our natural language, users assume that they can indeed use them to do commonsense things. And yet it's all too easy to push them past their capabilities. Tell friends, "Let's make a dinner reservation tomorrow at six at our usual spot," and they know exactly what you mean. Try to tell your digital assistant the same, and it can't even set aside time on your calendar. Their capabilities simply fall short of the interface they've aped. These gadgets can mimic language, and yet they are miles away from accomplishing the things we do with language. The spoken word is our most flexible interface, able to convey literally anything we can imagine. Machines, unlike human beings, are still backed by lists of features and functions, no matter how capably they seem to understand language. As a result, what digital assistants can and cannot do exists in a misty gray area. Talking to one is still a strange type of translation, hampered by the nagging exercise of forcing yourself to think, before you ever say anything, "Okay, so what can this thing do? And how do I say that clearly?" We are left trying to reverse-engineer our language to suit a machine.

For now, these machines often fall back on preprogrammed jokes—which is a clever way of avoiding having to say, "Sorry, I didn't actually understand that, and to tell you the truth, I don't understand most of the things you might imagine." Yet the set of things that these assistants can do is already remarkably long. Alexa, for example, boasts well over fifty thousand "skills"—Amazon's name for actions that Alexa can perform—which range from playing a song you like to doing your shopping. And yet our *finding out and remembering what they can do* has remained a glaring problem in the design. Today, one of the only ways to do so is . . . reading an email sent to you every week. No wonder then that, according to one study, a mere 3 percent of people who buy a voice assistant end up using it regularly just two weeks later.[27] If you do have a smart speaker, it's probably the most expensive kitchen timer you've ever bought—and it remains only that, because whatever else it might do is difficult to discover and impossible to remember. There are typically two solutions offered to that challenge. First is an engineering-led, brute-force approach: By simply gaining more and more capabilities, these assistants will eventually do anything asked of them. And yet "wait until it gets good" isn't much of a strategy. Digital assistants will never fulfill their promise without well-designed mental models that allow a user to understand how such a tool fits into their lives and what it can do.

Don Norman is probably most famous among designers for popularizing the idea of an *affordance*—physical details, designed in products, that tell us how they're to be used, such as the subtle curve of a door handle that tells you which way to pull, or the indentation on a button that tells you where to push. Alfonse Chapanis had anticipated that idea, in his shape-coded knobs and handles for airplane cockpits. Today, on smartphones and computers, buttons are now represented in pixels, and the affordances appear as icons and bevels and notifications and menus.[28] Tomorrow, in a world of machines that sense what we want, governed by metaphors that we take for granted, those affordances will necessarily become psychological. When buttons disappear into the ether around us, our mental models will tell us what a machine can do. We already expect a car with "autopilot" to behave according to our ideas about autopilot. We already expect a digital assistant to do the things that we imagine "artificial intelligence" should do. And yet these devices often fall short because affordances, which were once communicated by buttons and icons that we could see and touch, are now determined by our assumptions about how machines should behave. Mapping that landscape will be one of the great design challenges of the coming decades.

The paradox of having machines that do more and more for us—that drive when we don't want to drive, or tell stories to our kids when we're distracted, or shop when we'd rather keep sitting on the couch watching Netflix—is that by doing so many things in our image, the machines sap the footprint of what we do every day. They do our chores. But does all that tiny stuff which might have otherwise filled our day make us less capable over time? Does it make us less human? There are, to be sure, reasons to fear, which we'll see in chapter 9. But perhaps there are reasons to be optimistic.

When Brian Lathrop and Erik Glaser were researching how a driverless car should behave around pedestrians, they learned that the apparent politeness of its braking patterns was far more important than any other interface. I thought of this as I sat with a virtual reality device strapped to my face, at a desk in a research lab at Columbia University. My host was Sameer Saproo, a postdoctoral researcher. Sameer, an Indian immigrant and a computer programmer in his undergrad years, had come to the United States to study the brain. He could draw a line of influence directly from his first days in college in Mumbai, away from home for the first time, to where we were sitting now. He was inspired by watching the movie *The Matrix*. "My hair stood up on my arms," he said, explaining that we have somehow ended up in the world that *The Matrix* predicted, albeit with less of a frightening postapocalyptic veneer. With these new devices, like the one I wore in the lab, the idea of being seamlessly planted in a new kind of world seemed right here already— "Close to *The Matrix*, but without the spike in the back of your head to plug in," Saproo said, smiling.[29]

The point of the simulation was to show two things: that an artificial-intelligence algorithm could learn to drive, and, once it learned to drive, that it could then be taught to drive like we wanted it to. Saproo thought that the problem with all these driverless cars crawling across Silicon Valley on test drives was that while they might learn to drive, they might learn to drive in ways that wouldn't satisfy us. Perhaps they would brake too hard or swerve into other lanes too quickly, always keen for efficiency but also possessed of reflexes and data and awareness so far ahead of our own that we'd be bouncing around in the passenger seat, motion-sick, unsure about what was going to happen next.

Of course, Saproo was probably overstating the problem—when I rode in the Audi as the late afternoon sun dappled San Francisco Bay, the remarkable thing was how calm and polite the car already was. It was no daredevil; the engineers had already tuned its driving to be as reassuring as possible. But making the car polite was only the beginning of what Saproo wanted to do. He wanted to make the car responsive to how its passengers felt: to drive fast when you were feeling competitive or rushed for time; to take the scenic route when you just wanted to relax. He was one-upping Lathrop's horse metaphor—where Lathrop was focused on figuring out how the car could sense whether you were paying attention and then take control when you weren't, Saproo wanted the car to behave like a very polite butler to whom you'd paid a lot of money to anticipate your whims without your ever having to lift a finger. "What if you have a machine that can do a better job than you can, but that doesn't act anything like you?" he asked. "You're creating a new class of being. So what is your relationship like?"

I asked, But what if stress and the agency that comes with constantly fiddling with your environment are, in some ways, the essence of what it means to be human? Would we really want to live in a world that was truly friction-free, where the room temperature adjusted before we ever had a chance to feel any kind of discomfort? Wouldn't that make us more and more like floating brains in a vat stuck in *The Matrix*, unaware of what's real? Wouldn't the machines then be dictating our desires, rather than merely anticipating them?

Saproo disagreed. "A hundred thousand years ago, the stress we felt was in hearing a rustle in the branches," he said—the rustle of maybe becoming the next meal for a tiger or the trophy kill of a neighboring tribe. The hint of death and bloodshed, which could descend at any second. Now, Saproo said, the times we feel that visceral fear are more likely to be while we're sitting at our desks, gossiping in a chat room with our coworkers about impending layoffs. "Our lives are going to be more comfortable, and we're going to seek agency in other places."

His proof was the iPhone, and the touchscreen that changed the world. Working some thirty years before the iPhone, computer scientists at Xerox PARC had already anticipated some kind of gadget that you could merely tap to get what you want, without a keyboard. The idea was that if we could use our hands more naturally, then there'd be fewer obstacles to what we want to accomplish—there would be no figuring out how to use the computer; we'd just use it, and our intentions would be laid bare.

With the iPhone, Saproo said, "you were closer to what you wanted to do, and you were closer to what it means to be human." Later, the obvious hit me: Nearly eighty years after Henry Dreyfuss first preached that design could yield social progress simply by delivering ease, Saproo had given testament to how ubiquitous such faith had become.

Apple iPod (2001)

5

Metaphor

No man creates a new language for himself, at least if he be a wise man.

—Justice Joseph Story, in a Supreme Court ruling that created modern American patent law

GP Block Pitampura is one of Delhi's oldest slums, home to thirty thousand souls, a hive of lean-tos made of scavenged bricks and dirt floors. Migrants arrive there from India's countryside. A boy might call around to an aunt or a cousin or a childhood acquaintance, who would bring word about a room available in a micro-neighborhood, just a couple dozen households, filled with distant relations and acquaintances hailing from the same village. Drawn together by dialect and custom, they would all help one another find jobs serving the confident, well-educated, middle-class Indians living in the soot-streaked high-rises nearby: as rickshaw drivers or day laborers or office boys, housemaids or cooks or beauticians.

Renuka had come to the slum as a bride at fourteen, to settle with her new husband. The marriage had been a rush job. Renuka's parents, panicked after her older sister ran away to a love marriage, quickly found her a match. She is small and dark-eyed, with four children, and people often mistake her for a sister to her oldest child, a sixteen-year-old girl. She thinks the best days of her life came years ago when she was a little girl and lucked into a government-run boarding program that taught her to read. "On that little education, I'm still surviving," she said, through a translator.[1] Her education had blossomed into a fragile independence, best exemplified by her cell phone. Because she could read, she could send her own text messages in Hindi; she could listen to songs, manage her contacts, coordinate her work as a household cook—unusual in a place where most women asked their husbands to charge their phones because they didn't know how. Still, Renuka chafed at the roles afforded to women, the lives she couldn't dream of having. She had a hot temper, which often found its equal in her husband, who brought in a couple hundred rupees a day driving a rickshaw—not nearly as much as Renuka did.

I met her by way of my translator, a design researcher for the consulting firm Dalberg Design, which my collaborator Robert Fabricant founded in 2014. Their study had been commissioned by a consortium of cellular providers who wanted to bring the internet to the developing world, and wanted to understand why the poor, who seemed poised to gain so much from the internet, barely used it. The clients had expected to hear a litany of technical barriers to internet adoption, which they might check off one by one. Instead, Dalberg Design quickly discovered something else. Renuka, women like her, and even others in Kenya and Indonesia all shared a greater lack. It wasn't that the internet didn't work. It was that all too often, no one understood what the internet was.

In the West we like to believe that the technologies that have transformed our lives can do the same for others in different cultures. Consider the optimism of Mark Zuckerberg, who in August 2013 declared that he'd use some of his billions to provide internet access to the entire world, through a new initiative called Internet .org.[2] By 2017, when you arrived at the organization's website, you saw smiling people on snowy steppes, and Africans joyfully cradling smartphones. There was a picture of an autonomous drone, shaped like a boomerang, flying high over a twinkling urban quilt, designed to beam the internet to the denizens below. Eventually, a year later, the organization began going quiet, in large part due to resistance from local mobile-phone operators and a swirling cloud of doubts about Facebook's intentions.[3] But the deeper failure of Internet.org lay in the belief that the internet was simply about providing the pipes; if the pipes were there, people would use them, just like running water or electricity. For Renuka, the view was different.

She knew where the internet lived on her phone, sort of. She could imagine that the internet might help her find jobs, or help her get formal documentation as a citizen, to receive government services. But she assumed that the internet wasn't for her, that it was for the better educated. And part of the reason was that she couldn't picture how it worked. She had no mental model of what it held. She could recognize the globe icon on her phone, but she had no idea what it meant. She guessed that it led "to the outside world." The researchers met dozens of women who said the same thing. One of them, a cook like Renuka, could actually navigate the internet menu on her phone, but she had no inkling that this *was* the internet. Another woman could recognize the "www," but hadn't a clue what a URL was or how it worked.[4]

We take for granted how the internet arrived for us in the West.

We take for granted all the metaphors involved. But once seen, these rise up like the first skyscrapers in a skyline. The "World Wide Web" evoked the image of a literal spiderweb, spanning the globe. What connects the web? Hyper*links*, like links in a chain piecing together all the places you want to go. If you can't find the right link, then you have a *search engine*, a machine that gleans information as it *crawls* the web. These metaphors fall short of an instruction manual, but they nonetheless foster some basic sense of the internet's logic: how to *navigate* it, using a *browser*—two more metaphors, borrowed from sailing and libraries, which bring forth ideas about coordinates and filing systems. These metaphors helped explain not only what the internet was, but what it could become. The World Wide Web morphed into the "digital world," filled with businesses and homes, populated by digital representations of ourselves. Without that kernel, of course, there would be no Facebook. In the early 1990s, in the West, the news was filled with explainers about the "information superhighway." We don't much remember them or the metaphors that they contained. That's simply because it was explained to us all so slowly, over time. We learned what the web was by using it. Eventually, we didn't need the metaphors at all. (As the design theorist Klaus Krippendorff writes, "Metaphors die in repeated use but leave behind the reality that they had languaged into being.")[5]

But to those women in GP Block Pitampura, the internet had simply arrived one day, devoid of any explanation at all. No wonder it was baffling at best, even terrifying. When a researcher asked her to demonstrate what she knew, Renuka tapped at the icons on a smartphone then pushed it away, flustered, and admitted to being self-conscious about what had passed her by. Another woman, asked if she'd ever seen the internet, remembered how teachers from a neighboring village showed it to her once. "They put on the internet and showed me pictures of Nainital. It was beautiful, with mountains, not the small ones we have here, but bigger ones," she told the researchers. "They said I could put my photo online, and that anyone around the world could see it." As to why anyone would want to do that—why anyone would want another, digital self—she had no idea.[6]

In 1979, the linguist George Lakoff, working with the philosopher Mark Johnson, began an investigation of how metaphors work. In their book *Metaphors We Live By*, the two of them presented the radical idea that it is hardly possible to think without resorting to metaphors—an impossibility akin to the command "Don't think about this sentence." Moreover, our metaphors are inescapably grounded in the most basic mental models we have: our physical notions about the real world. Thus, we might have a root metaphor such as "up" meaning "being conscious"—which then spawns dozens of expressions such as "I'm up already" and "she's an early riser," or, conversely, "he sank into a coma." They emerged by connecting a concept—consciousness—with an earlier physical intuition that humans lie down when they sleep, and stand up when they're awake.[7]

Lakoff and Johnson also had an insight that we saw through Renuka's eyes: that metaphors provide us a web of inferences, which we use to explain the underlying logic of how something should work.[8] For example, if you have the metaphor "time is money," then you're not just comparing time and money. You're assuming rules about how time should behave: If time is like money, then, just like money, it can be saved or invested wisely; it can be wasted or stolen or borrowed.[9] The right metaphor is like an instruction manual but better, because it teaches you how something should work without you ever having to be told.

Consider the metaphor of the in-box versus the news feed. The email in-box borrows its logic from your mail, and you probably at least glance at every piece of mail that's sent to you—simply because they were all meant for *you*. Your email in-box carries the same logic. The Instagram "feed" or the Twitter "stream" are entirely different metaphors.[10] A stream rushes on even if you're not there to see; it gurgles by in the dark, when you're asleep. To say that information is a stream suggests that it's there for the taking, if we wish to drink, not that we have to consume it all. A stream or a news feed, even if it's crafted to your whims, doesn't require your personal attention. It's a commons to be shared.

One reason you might find checking your email to be a chore while checking Facebook feels closer to leisure is that the underlying metaphors are different. Why is it that we happily send unasked-for messages to our friends on Facebook, while the same behavior is considered rude via email? The different metaphors come prepackaged with their own etiquette. The in-box is personal. The stream is not. Imagine how long it would take to list all these rules—but thanks to metaphors, they never had to be listed at all.

That power is what allows metaphors to transfer ideas from a specialized domain—say, the inner workings of a bunch of networked computers, known only to their engineers—to a new cohort. Metaphors strip away what's specialized and complex, focusing our attention on just the few things we need to make sense of something, the ideas we share. Saying the internet is like a web of information, connected by links, tells you what the web is for: joining up spheres of knowledge. It implies what you might do, even what you might invent. Metaphors become so embedded in our experience that they seem second nature: time is money; life is a journey; the body is a machine. But often, the metaphors we live with have been designed.

In 2000, Toyota unveiled the Prius, the world's first mass-market hybrid, which boasted three times the fuel efficiency of a typical car. The innovation upended the industry. Marketed as a boon for the planet, the Prius had forces moving in its favor—after decades of cheap gas, prices were starting to surge. Even Toyota was surprised by the yearlong waiting lists to buy one.[11] And Detroit, whose fortunes had been saved in the 1990s by the SUV, was stunned. In 2004, Ford duly rushed a hybrid SUV to market. Then came the Fusion, a hybrid sedan. Neither was very good, simply because the driving public hadn't yet been taught what to expect of a hybrid. The cars, which were relatively slow to accelerate and rife with new instrumentation, were baffling to drive because of the mental model that drivers had been promised thanks to the advertising: *This is just a new car with much better gas mileage.* Drivers didn't yet know to expect these cars to actually drive differently, and the new instrumentation didn't help. One particularly bad and misunderstood gauge, an analog dial showing the car's battery charge, stuck out. It was a sensible enough thing to make; in a hybrid, when a driver brakes, the wheels don't just slow—gears divert the kinetic energy of the spinning axles, and that spin is used to charge the car's battery. When the driver then hits the accelerator again, the battery powers the motor.[12]

Given how critical the battery is, Ford's engineers thought that hybrid drivers needed to know how well it was charging. So whenever a driver braked, the needle of the battery gauge tracked rightward toward an area of green, showing that the battery was charging. That feedback turned out to be disastrous. Eager to see their batteries being charged, drivers would mash the brake and watch the charging needle spike toward green. But hybrids work best when braking is *slow*, which allows the power from the spinning axles to be efficiently diverted. Hoping to create a display showing how much energy the car was saving, Ford had instead encouraged drivers to behave more wastefully.

Ford's engineers didn't yet know how they would teach drivers that the savings they might achieve were due to the subtly different ways the car responded under acceleration and braking. Research had shown there to be two basic types of hybrid purchaser at that time. There were the ones who bought the hybrid and thought they didn't need to do anything more, and the "hyper-milers" who tracked every penny they spent on gas and traded tips about pulsing their accelerators and gliding for as long as they could on the highway. So maybe the sensible thing to do was design an instrument panel for the car that could tell you *not* to brake so hard, or *not* to turn on the air-conditioning? Others on the team were skeptical: Car culture is about the driver being in control. No one would ever buy a car that was constantly telling them what to do. The project was still a backwater in the power structure of Ford, and thus relatively free to pursue something novel, even strange. The team hired IDEO, and IDEO began gathering up hyper-milers to see what mind-sets might be worth emulating in the dashboard itself.

The problem was simple: How do you get someone who isn't a hyper-miler to realize that it isn't just the car that saves them gas, but their own driving style? Inspiration finally came from a hyper-miler who also happened to be an ultramarathoner. She explained the role of a good coach in her life. A good coach wasn't a scold, because the work of being better still fell to the athlete herself. A good coach would also always know what you needed to do—and tell you just enough information to do it, but no more. That metaphor drove new design principles, which in turn fostered dozens of designs: Support but don't shout. Give enough information to act, and no more.

Among myriad possible ideas, one survived. The entire gauge itself could glow green when someone was driving well. The color green was the raw material of the design, just the same as steel for a teakettle or plastic for a child's toy. The color green provided another metaphor. Green meant go—keep it up! But green also meant eco-conscious and verdant. Yet when it finally came time to make the dashboard, Dave Watson, a computer scientist tasked with building all these prototypes, felt a certain hollowness.[13]

Green was a clear choice that piggybacked upon all kinds of associations, but there still wasn't enough to get people to care. Watson had gone to a slew of user interviews, and it had sunk in how little these real people were like the engineers who thought they had solutions for them. Watson wanted to make them understand the car, but understanding it was different from understanding its inner workings. To get someone to understand, you had to make them care enough in the first place. So Watson thought: Trees. It was as if by driving better, you were helping a tree grow. But trees grow over time; they leaf out, they fade.

Eventually the green became a tangle of vines, sprouting leaves. Leaves that you couldn't count, but that covered up a pane on the dashboard. If you drove aggressively, a few leaves might disappear; drive more prudently, a few more would sprout. From the coach to the green light to the leaf, one metaphor replacing the other. The beauty of the solution lay in how much information was compressed into just a simple image. It was a feedback mechanism that helped nudge people toward better behavior. By driving better you were growing something—who would want to kill a plant?

One of the first test drivers told a story of his daughter peering over his shoulder and seeing the leaves disappear as he stabbed at the accelerator: "Daddy, you're killing the leaves." The metaphor was getting users to care about "growing" this fake vine. One of the other designers involved in refining the dashboard, Dan Formosa of Smart Design, knew from his cousin, who'd been early to buy the new Fusion, that it was working. Formosa asked him if he still had the leaves turned on, assuming that he might have turned them off—which was a concession the designers had to make, for fear that red-blooded American males would not appreciate a dainty vine that seemed to judge them. "I've got leaves coming out of my ass!" his cousin boomed, in his Jersey accent. "When I use my old car to take the kids to McDonald's drive-in, now I realize that I lose leaves because of it. So now we park and walk in instead." A Ford engineer told me he knew the viny leaf metaphor was working when drivers started posting their dashboards online.

In the development of that dashboard, metaphor worked on several levels at once. For the drivers, it helped them understand how the car was meant to be driven, and how their behavior was supposed to change. The metaphor helped them see the car and its inner logic in a way that would have otherwise been counterintuitive. The leaf metaphor went on to appear in many Ford models, in increasingly subtle forms that eventually bore a faint resemblance to the original. Yet its dissolution may in fact mark its success. Today, you can find dozens of cars whose dashboards flash green when you're driving efficiently—thus doing away with the problematic idea, found in the first Ford hybrids, that you're supposed to be charging the car's battery as fast as possible. The mental model of the car as a kind of driving coach persists in more subtle ways, rewarding driving behaviors that are "green." As a result, countless millions of gallons of gasoline have been saved.

Metaphors will always be one of our most powerful entry points to the user-friendly world, possessing the singular ability to make the foreign feel familiar, providing us mental models for how things work. Consider one last beautiful example, a defibrillator that IDEO designed in the 1990s. At the time, research had shown that a third of the 300,000 American heart-attack deaths could be prevented if only defibrillation had been administered within a few minutes of the attack. The obvious solution was to install the devices next to first-aid kits in places such as airports and offices, so that bystanders could administer aid almost immediately. And yet that commonsense solution fostered a familiar problem: making it easy for neophytes to use a specialist machine. Bystanders would have to be able to use these machines at a glance, with no prior training. So IDEO's designers hit on a metaphor. They shaped the new gadget like a book, with a spine facing outward so that users would instinctively know where to grab hold and start. Where the book's front cover would be was a series of steps, numbered one to three, with the right button placed beside each one.[14] Like so many other metaphors you find in everyday design, this one guided users down a path without their ever having to think.

The desktop metaphor cannot be anything other than one of the most influential and pervasive ideas of the twentieth century. It's what transformed the minicomputer into the personal computer: from command lines glowing coldly on black screens to operating systems that sit on almost every office desk in the world. It's what made computing the glue of the modern knowledge economy. The story goes that Steve Jobs went for a demo at Xerox PARC, saw the future there, and more or less stole it. But it's a story riddled with holes, starting with the obvious: How would Steve Jobs have even thought there was anything to steal in the first place?

Bill Atkinson came to Apple in 1978, after Jobs had convinced him to quit his Ph.D. program in neuroscience at UC San Diego. He had become known for designing computer programs that made 3-D maps of mouse brains. It was cutting-edge work, but Jobs pooh-poohed it: "What you're doing is always going to be two years behind. Think how fun it is to surf on the front of a wave, and how not fun it is to dog-paddle on the tail edge of that same wave." Atkinson wanted to surf. Two weeks later, he was at Apple, where he soon became Jobs's regular dinner partner and sounding board, and a star engineer on Apple's follow-up to the Apple II, the Lisa.[15]

Jobs's main way of motivating people wasn't merely fear, but rather capriciousness, which was both scarier and far more magnetic. "Steve would say you were great one day, and an idiot the next," recalled Bruce Horn, part of the team that went on to create the drag-and-drop method of moving files around.[16] Atkinson seemed to float above Jobs's ire, and below it too, buried in his work. Peers would tell him that Jobs was using him, exploiting Atkinson's obvious talents and energies. But Atkinson mostly didn't notice. He was working too hard. "A good tube of toothpaste wants to be totally squeezed out," Atkinson told me with a shrug.

While working on the Lisa, Atkinson had been paying attention to a stream of academic papers flowing from Xerox PARC about a prototype operating system called Smalltalk. So had Jef Raskin, an Apple employee who'd heard rumors about what *wasn't* in the papers. The timing was fateful. By the winter of 1980, Jobs had brought Apple to the cusp of a hotly anticipated public offering of Apple's stock.

Investors across the Valley were hounding him, afraid of missing out. Jobs toyed with them all—including Xerox, which offered up $1 million for a mere 0.1 percent of Apple's shares, implying that the young company was already worth a gobsmacking $1 billion. It was Raskin who convinced Jobs they had to have a peek at Xerox's Smalltalk. It was Jobs, business Svengali, who thought: I'll tell Xerox that they've got to show us Smalltalk, or no investment deal.[17]

Atkinson's manic dedication blinded him to the soft power he wielded, being so close to Jobs. One time, they'd been at dinner, and Atkinson had complained about the naysaying of one of his peers while designing a mouse meant to ship with every Apple computer. "The next day, that guy's desk was empty." When it came time to interview that man's replacement, the candidate sat down and blurted, "I can build a mouse." Atkinson soon got his way: From then on, Apple's new computers shipped with a mouse, which offered a point-and-click simplicity that didn't exist before. What had yet to be determined was the actual software that you pointed-and-clicked on.

I met Atkinson at his house, which sits perched up in one of the beautifully wild parts of Silicon Valley, off a tiny road, near a few other boho cedar-shingled mansions with Teslas parked out front. Atkinson's home was spacious, but humble. The main living room was where he tried out virtual reality gear: In the middle of a vast expanse of blue wall-to-wall carpeting was only a single cheap rolling office chair, so that he could strap in and explore virtual space, unimpeded. We sat down to talk in the photo studio downstairs, and soon we were joined by Andy Hertzfeld, another of Apple's founding pioneers. Atkinson liked to have Hertzfeld around, as a real-time fact-checker—he'd become the lore master for that entire period of their lives. Atkinson, in those earliest days at Apple, working on the Lisa, would spend all day arguing with his colleagues about some detail or another, then all night programming what *he* thought was the best solution. "I don't know when he slept," Hertz-feld murmured.[18]

Today, if you know that story at all, you probably imagine that the Smalltalk team were just eggheads who'd had great ideas, while missing the vision for what they had. But they knew what they had achieved, and why they should guard it. Adele Goldberg, one of the key Smalltalk developers, turned red and teary with rage when she heard Jobs was in the building being briefed on the company's research.[19] She told her bosses they'd have to order her to share Smalltalk at all. So they did. Goldberg appeared at the fateful conference room with a small yellow disk in hand, her face still red. They loaded the disk onto a computer, and the demonstration began. Atkinson could tell the Xerox engineers didn't want to be there by the way they hustled through all the things they'd built. Atkinson nonetheless crowded his way to the fore, so close that Larry Tesler, one of Smalltalk's leaders, could feel Atkinson's breath as he peppered the team with questions about every detail on the screen.

Smalltalk had emerged from an almost comically grand vision for what they were making. It was descended from the legendary Doug Engelbart's LSD trips and the utopian philosophies that scented the Northern California air. Alan Kay, inspired by emerging findings in child psychology, wanted to create an entirely new form of pedagogy so that those kids might grow up to solve the problems of a new world. The computer would become a "safe and covert environment, where the child can assume almost any role without social or physical hurt"—a kind of digital sandbox that could touch any piece of information that the world had to offer, one that would let children build computer programs as easily as they might build sandcastles.[20]

The Smalltalk demo was just an hour long, and for Bill Atkinson it was a blur. In fact, the most eventful thing Atkinson saw that day wasn't the desktop metaphor—the early papers from Xerox PARC had already introduced that idea. Rather, it was what Atkinson *thought* he saw. As the Smalltalk engineers were showing off how you could click around on the windows they'd designed, Atkinson assumed they had figured out a way for the machine to simulate those windows being layered on top of one another, like real sheets of paper on a desk. They hadn't, but it set him on the path to creating what Hertzfeld later called the soul of the Mac. In the car ride after, he told Jobs that it should take only six months for the Lisa to catch up to everything they'd seen. It ended up taking three years.

It was because of those windows. Smalltalk actually had to redraw a window every time it was selected and brought forward, giving it an ever-so-slight sense of fakery. Atkinson's great contribution was that, in his excitement, he had actually fallen for the ruse. He set about trying to reverse-engineer how it could have been achieved, and eventually invented a way for the computer to understand "hidden" regions out of view and redraw them instantly. It was that effect that made the primitive graphical interface—which already had pieces of the desktop metaphor—actually *feel* like a desktop, with files and folders that you could move and touch, that were satisfying to use. It was perhaps the first instance at Apple where the engineers began to realize that faithful mimicry of how the physical world behaved would make the digital world somehow easier to understand—and even magical, if that mimicry was nuanced enough.

Atkinson's work on the Lisa eventually started to bleed together with the work being done on what was to be its lower-end sister, the Macintosh. Once the logic of the desktop metaphor arrived, Apple's engineers kept pulling threads, finding new implications, new ways for the digital world to obey the intuitiveness of the physical one. The web of metaphors began to grow. Bruce Horn had come to the

Apple Mac team from Xerox PARC, where, as a teenager, he had worked on Smalltalk. One of his superiors at PARC, Larry Tesler—the very one who'd actually given Atkinson the Smalltalk demo—was obsessed with "mode confusion," the bugbear of airplane pilots, the oldest problem in human-machine interaction.[21] Modes, when carried over to a computer interface, were hopelessly confusing: Did you remember if you'd clicked into text-edit mode, or text-delete mode? So he insisted that users be able to directly manipulate things on-screen, just as they might in real life. You should be able to click into some text, and type. To extend that idea and make it even more intuitive, Horn invented the ability to drag and drop files. Meanwhile, Susan Kare created the original icons of the Mac—the trash can, the file folder, the hand, all of which summoned the outside world that had inspired them, with a brilliant economy of pixels.

The organic growth of the Macintosh OS shows how metaphors can not only explain ideas but generate them.[22] The desktop metaphor started fitfully; slowly, the engineers worked out a widening circle of implications, such as direct manipulation and the physics of how windows shrank and grew. And then, finally, the metaphor flowered into its own universe of seamless logic. Not only can metaphors tell us how something should work, they can also become guides to what we'd like to create. That's what happened with Brian Lathrop, the engineer at Audi who explored how the horse-riding metaphor might create a new paradigm for driving. It also happened with the Ford dashboard. Inspired by a distance runner who explained how a good coach encouraged and never nagged, they created a display that might provide only the right information, at the right time—a glowing dashboard with a tangle of virtual leaves. Metaphors accomplish something essential to human progress: They don't just spur us to make new things; they inspire the ways in which those things will behave once they're in our hands.

On August 2, 2018, Apple became the world's first public company worth more than $1 trillion. If anything, that abstract figure understates the company's reach. Apple makes the first thing that hundreds of millions of people look at when they wake up. The company's supply chain can extract trace amounts of rare-earth minerals from a mine in the Democratic Republic of the Congo, embed them in one of the planet's most advanced computers, and deliver the whole thing to the steppes of Mongolia. And yet Apple's rise is nothing more or less than the story of three interfaces: the Macintosh OS, the iPod click wheel, and the iPhone touchscreen. Everything else has been fighting about how the pie would be divided up among competitors and copycats.

In the user-friendly world, interfaces make empires: IBM, with its punch-card mainframes, was an empire until the 1970s. Then came the graphical user interface, which transformed both Apple and Microsoft from niche companies into mainstream Goliaths. (In April 2019, Microsoft became the third company in the world to reach a $1 trillion valuation, right behind Amazon.) Apple, of course, nearly died in the late 1990s; a major part of what saved the company in the years after Steve Jobs returned was the iPod's click wheel, which cracked the problem of making it fun to browse incredibly long lists (which themselves were formatted in the drop-down menus that Bill Atkinson invented for the Lisa). Blackberry, with its telephone lashed to a keyboard, was another empire until the iPhone. Even Amazon grew from an interface idea: 1-Click shopping. The value of the patent alone is staggering: Amazon made billions licensing it to Apple for the launch of the iTunes store. But its value to Amazon has been far greater. By eliminating all the check-out steps required to buy something online, 1-Click gave Amazon a decisive edge against cart abandonment, which, according to some studies, averages 70 percent and remains one of the two or three biggest challenges to online retailers. 1-Click made impulse buys on the web actually impulsive. The boost from 1-Click shopping has been estimated to be as high as 5 percent of Amazon's total sales—an astonishing figure, given that Amazon's operations margin hovers below 2 percent. Moreover, it also incentivized Amazon's customers to stay logged in to Amazon at all times—which then allowed Amazon to silently build up a user profile in its databases, which then allowed Amazon to become a platform for selling and recommending anything, not just books.[23] Amazon's 1-Click would easily be the single most consequential button ever invented, but for the Facebook Like button.

Apple's two great innovations, the graphical user interface and the touchscreen, are cousins united by a deeper vein of metaphor. The Macintosh OS got its user-friendliness from the intuitive physics of its interactions, which sprang from trying to create interactions that were natural exactly because they were borrowed from our intuitions about the physical world. The bridge was the desktop metaphor. The touchscreen wasn't so much a new metaphor as it was a better input device. First, the mouse cursor stood in for your hand, when the world was a screen. Then the mouse cursor disappeared, when the screen itself could sense your touch. The iPhone wasn't a break from the Mac, so much as its fulfillment— the ability, at long last, to truly manipulate objects in digital space directly, just as Larry Tesler had been pushing for ever since he arrived at Apple from Xerox PARC.

It may seem strange to say that the iPhone inherited its logic from the desktop computer, especially if you didn't grow up using a mouse. But it's there: the way you tap an app to open it; how you can drag apps around the home screen; the idea of an app itself, able to deliver email or calendar appointments or news; the back button and the close button. Yet all this logic exists quietly. We don't notice the desktop metaphor anymore because we no longer need it to explain how we're supposed to use a modern computer.

That's how metaphors work: Once their underlying logic becomes manifest, we forget that they were ever there. No one remembers that before the steering wheel in a car, there were tillers, and that tillers made for a natural comparison when no one drove cars and far more people had piloted a boat.[24] The metaphor disappeared once driving cars became common. In digesting new technologies, we climb a ladder of metaphors, and each rung helps us step up to the next. Our prior assumptions lend us confidence about how a new technology works. Over time, we find ourselves farther and farther from the rungs we started with, so that we eventually leave them behind, like so many tiller-inspired steering wheels—or like the various metaphors that taught Westerners how to use the World Wide Web.[25]

The story of technology's advance is also the story of metaphors bending to their limits, then breaking. It is happening now all around us. Alongside the study of how women in India such as Renuka thought about the internet, the designers at Dalberg went to Kenya. What they found was radically different. Unlike the Indian women, who had hardly any idea what the internet was, the Kenyan women they met were voracious Facebook users. One of the driving reasons was that Facebook readily lent itself to a metaphor: It was just like the contact list people maintained on their cell phones; it was built around messaging, just like SMS, which they'd been using for years. That metaphor had its limitations. The Kenyan women didn't "surf the web" like we might, bouncing to their browser to read news or do their banking. When they wanted to "search the internet," they didn't ask Google; they simply posted a question in their Facebook feed.[26] Facebook was, for them, the entirety of what the internet could do. Thus, while Facebook worked as a metaphor for Kenyan ideas about knowledge and society, the metaphor failed to explain what the internet could be and how it worked.

There is another breakdown in metaphor that we can watch from our own phones, one created by Apple. Throughout the mid-2000s, the company was lambasted in the design community for its skeuomorphs, which the *Oxford English Dictionary* defines as "an element of a graphic user interface which mimics a physical object." These had started out usefully, but over the decades reached a pointless level of detail. At one time, it was important for a file "folder" to indeed look like a folder, so that you knew it did the same thing. By the mid-2000s the details had gotten baroque. To know how the calendar worked, you didn't need the calendar on every Mac to look as if it had been bound by stitched leather; to know that you could buy books via the iBooks app, there didn't need to be digital shelves, made of digitally rendered wood.

The design community's bias against skeuomorphism had descended from the Bauhaus, which, at the dawn of modern design, declared a break with tradition by decrying decorative flourishes meant to link the new world with the old—for example, the Art Nouveau metalwork of the Paris Métro entrance, where copper was fashioned to look like ornate vines. The Bauhaus was born of the idea that materials should do exactly what they were suited to, and only that. Marcel Breuer's famed metal-framed club chairs, which are ubiquitous today, supported the sitter using a novel cantilevered frame made of steel—and that steel was chromed to highlight the fact that only metal could accomplish the feat. In the context of computers, what had once been a necessary feature to make things user friendly—fidelity to the real world—had descended into a kind of dishonesty. Should pixels look like metal and wood if they're not in fact metal and wood?

It wasn't a surprise that Jony Ive—an industrial designer by training, weaned on a faith in materials, the designer of the candy-colored iMac, then the iPhone—would hew to a faith in material honesty. When Ive took over software design at Apple in 2013, he introduced a clean new language for the iPhone's operating system. At the time, this was trumpeted as proof that Ive's good taste had finally won out over the company's ideologues, such as Scott Forstall, who'd overseen the iOS for years and remained slavishly devoted to the personal tastes of Steve Jobs, who had died two years before. But what actually happened was simply that Apple's founding metaphors, which had been handholds for a nervous migration to the digital world, were now irrelevant. You didn't need the calendar on your iPhone to look like the one on your desk, if, like most people, you'd already discarded the one on your desk because of the iPhone. The rule for metaphor in design is *fake it till you make it*. Apple had made it, after faking it for so many years.

There are stakes for the companies that create these metaphors, and stakes for the people who live with them. As Apple's visual metaphors started to age into incoherence, its underlying metaphors started to break down as well, making our digital lives ever more confusing. When Apple unveiled the App Store in 2008, no one was certain how big it could become. Initially, there were around five hundred apps available, and these were quaint by today's standards: a slew of games such as *Crash Bandicoot* and *Rolando*, and a few other apps such as eBay and *The New York Times*.[27] In later years, we'd see the explosion of the so-called app economy, and the sudden dominance of mobile computing. What's never asked is *why* the App Store made sense to users, and how those initial assumptions shaped what followed. There was a metaphor underlying it all.

All the way up until the late nineteenth century, stores worked very differently than they do today. The goods were placed behind the counter on shelves or under glass. Shoppers on the high streets of Paris and London were typically upper-class, and if they wanted to see something, they had to ask the shopkeeper to get it for them. It was up to the shopkeeper to explain the story of a product. This changed by the turn of the century, thanks to pioneers such as Harry Gordon Selfridge. Beginning at Marshall Field's in Chicago, Selfridge experimented with a retail concept that the world had never seen, in which the goods didn't sit behind the counter. Instead, they were placed out on shelves, where shoppers could touch and see them on a whim, without ever needing a shopkeeper at all. Alone on a shelf, the goods had to sell themselves.[28]

A century later, this remains the standard in stores across the planet. It's how software was sold in the Apple Store when it opened in 2001, in boxes laid out one next to the other. By the time the App Store came along, it made sense that it would look much like those open shelves. But in selling apps like that, right on a smartphone, the inevitable implication was that the apps you bought there were much like the software you bought in boxes at the store. That is, they were stand-alone goods—things like Microsoft Word, which you used for a specific purpose.

As the app economy grew, this assumption started to crack. When you think to yourself to arrange a dinner date with friends, you have to text them, find a restaurant, text them again, find a time, look for a reservation, agree on the reservation, mark it in your calendar. When the time comes, you might reach for your phone again, to call a car. It's up to *you* to remember all the salient details through the process. It's up to *you* to know what the right app is at the right time. When all the details mount, when the reservations keep getting changed or when no one can agree on a restaurant, the tiresomeness of tapping and typing becomes enough for you to hate your phone. How much better would it be for every step involved in setting up a dinner date to be hidden behind a button?

The only reason those frustrations exist is that the metaphor that begot the app economy was the wrong one. Underlying the structure of all the apps we use is the internet, and its infinite web of connections. But we consume apps through the metaphor of the store, through the assumption of stand-alone goods that we use one at a time, rather than in a web of references. Those two paradigms conflict—and they often only barely line up with the ultimate purpose our phones are meant to serve, that of keeping what we care about and whom we care about within reach. As a result, smartphones put the burden of piecing things together upon us. Resolving them will require a new metaphor for how smartphones work, and when someone finds it, our digital lives will evolve. Imagine if instead of apps, our smartphones were built around the relationships we care about—if, instead of opening an app to connect with who we love, we simply remained connected with those we loved, and the tools to bring us closer appeared only when we needed them, in the flow of our relationships with one another. Who knows how much easier, how much more satisfying, our digital lives might be if the governing metaphor for smartphones were one of human connection, rather than programs.

For now, we'll wait for things to get better. In 2018, Apple unveiled Shortcuts, a feature in which its voice assistant, Siri, could be used to do specific tasks directly inside an app, thus leaving out all the requisite taps and swipes.[29] It seemed like a Band-Aid, but a sign of progress. By then, Google had started releasing very early prototypes of an experimental OS dubbed Fuchsia that was based not on a wall of apps but a feed of "stories"—a new metaphor, in which a story was simply a set of tasks, chained together by algorithms into a single action such as "go on a date with Nicole."[30] It's unclear where that prototype will go. But it still proved that the next phase of our mobile lives wouldn't be defined by a new cell phone or new app. It would be defined by a new metaphor.

When George Lakoff and Mark Johnson first began writing, their ideas about metaphor were both scintillating and hard to refute; the hundreds of examples they gave seemed to permeate almost every aspect of the way we spoke. In the subsequent decade, the pair kept pulling at a thread: If metaphors are rooted in the ways our bodies interact with the world around us, and if our bodies are represented and mediated by different parts of our brains, then wouldn't metaphors be represented in the structure of our brains as well? One possible avenue for the formation of those pathways was the simple way in which we learn to associate events with sensations. For example, as a child, perhaps you associated affection with a hug from your mother—perhaps you came to know affection through those feelings of being warm, coddled, and snug. Thus, "being a warm person" could be linked to what we first associated with being physically warm.

That idea of "grounded" or "embodied" cognition is simple on its surface. But as its many adherents would argue, it in fact flouts four hundred years of Western thought, descended from the philosopher René Descartes. In *Discourse on Method*, Descartes set the mind and flesh apart, one irreconcilable with the other. His famous statement in part IV, *cogito ergo sum* ("I think therefore I am"), is often assumed to be a maxim that means merely that if you can think, then you must exist. But by that logic, the Monty Python paraphrase "I drink therefore I am" is just as profound. Descartes was saying something more ambitious. Imagine if you were simply a disembodied brain, floating in a nutrient solution, with all your sensory input supplied by wires that provided fake information about the "real world"—could you ever know you were being tricked?[31] Descartes concluded that you couldn't, but that even if the world around you was an illusion, you could still reason. Descartes then leaped to the conclusion that since you could still reason even if the world was an illusion, then the mind existed on some other, separate plane from the world around it. Lakoff and Johnson suggested instead that the ideas that fill our minds don't come from the pure faculties of reason—rather, we'd have no ideas without the bodily sensations upon which to ground them. Part of the reason that we can't seem to think without resorting to metaphors of some kind is that ideas themselves, when they emerge from our brains, emerge from the same neural pathways in which our bodies are represented. Metaphors reflect some deeper organization about how our minds are structured.

In the years since they first proposed the idea of embodied cognition, experimental psychologists have offered tantalizing evidence that Lakoff and Johnson might be right.[32] In one experiment, people who held a warm coffee cup were more likely to judge another person as trustworthy. Thus, "warming up" to someone didn't seem to be just an abstract metaphor. Because that metaphor dwelled somewhere in our brains, it could be hacked: Being physically warmed could change our emotional judgments. Other studies provided similar evidence for much different metaphors: Participants in one experiment, when asked to think about the future, leaned slightly forward; when asked to think about the past, they leaned back. The underlying metaphor was that the future lay ahead. In still another example, those assigned to fill out questionnaires while using a heavier clipboard offered more serious answers to the questions. Importance was heavy.[33]

Though the science and experimental methods behind these findings are still being hotly debated, designers have been acting on the idea of embodied metaphors since the dawn of the profession. One of Henry Dreyfuss's first bestsellers was the Big Ben alarm clock, patented in 1931, which he gave a heavier base so that it would seem more reliable and of higher quality. We still live with the idea that heaviness conveys quality. One familiar example comes from the sound and feel of car doors. If you open and close the door on a Bentley, you'll feel the weight and hear the sound, like the capstone sealing a vault. Do the same with a Kia, and you'll notice how much lighter it feels, how it *sounds* cheaper. Though the Bentley is heavier, made of finer stuff, its door doesn't have to feel heavy. The hinge, after all, supports the door. It could have been tuned to make the door feel weightless. But it wasn't, because the designers took the time to make sure that the Bentley commanded as much metaphorical heaviness as the bank account required to buy it. Designers still scour the world for metaphors that relate not just to how we understand a product, but how we feel when we use it. The ways in which those metaphors are used reveals a different angle on user-friendliness, showing the ways beauty can be adapted to other uses.

Around 2010, Philippa Mothersill was a product designer at Gillette, tasked with designing a disposable razor for women. She began with a study of all the ways in which we grasp the implements of our daily life. The idea was that you might feel differently about shaving, depending on the posture of your hand. "I was invested in how you could look at ergonomics to create a different experience," she said as we talked at her workbench at the MIT Media Lab, where she was pursuing her Ph.D. "If I design a handle for a razor that's like a house-painting brush, you're painting your face. But if you're cleaning your eyes with a cotton pad, it's a very delicate grip."[34] Her team eventually produced the Venus Snap, a women's razor that doesn't have a handle. Instead, there's a tab about the size of a half dollar with grippy rubber on either side. When you use it, you pinch it between your forefinger and thumb, like you're holding a cotton swab. The design is a metaphor: You draw that razor over your limbs as if you're carefully peeling away a layer to reveal your better self underneath.

When working at Gillette, Mothersill also became fascinated with how heavily the design process depended on giving form to words. She'd find herself tasked with designing something that looked "succulent," and to do so, she'd gather dozens of images that might evoke the word: aloe leaves, maple syrup flowing from a spout. And then she'd try to evoke those shapes in what she was designing. This is almost a universal practice in design, creating mood boards to summon how something should look and feel, and then trying to translate those into form-giving metaphors and words. "Designers have this tacit knowledge of abstract emotive experiences like trust and curiosity," she explained. "Somehow they translate that into a qualitative attribute like the radius of an object, which is what CAD tools require from us."

She carried that question through her studies at MIT, using as a starting point the striking ability of animators to imbue anything with human character, merely with a few strokes—for example, *Beauty and the Beast*, whose characters include a rotund, motherly teapot and a haughty mantel clock with a puffed-out chest. Mothersill tried to create a program that could automate those effects. She first created dozens of designs for bottles, some top-heavy and round, others pointy and thin. Then she enlisted online volunteers to describe the emotions they evoked, such as anger or joy or disgust or fear. Then she mapped those emotions onto a continuum of physical qualities that could be adjusted in a 3-D design program: how smooth an object was, or how angular; whether it was top-heavy or bottom-heavy. Mothersill eventually produced a new kind of 3-D design program, in which the computer did the emotional translation. You could specify that a design be sadder, simply by dragging a slider, and sure enough, the design would grow plumper on the bottom, and sag. You could tell the computer that the design needed to have more surprise or joy, and it would respond. On the wall before us, resting on tiny shelves, were the various bottles that the program had spat out, each of which had been 3-D printed. Each was about the size of a toy teapot, with a stopper sprouting from the top. Some of the bottles were plump and homely. Others were angular and fierce. They were laid out on two axes: the horizontal represented the positivity or negativity of the emotion that had been entered into the program; the vertical showed how excited or calm that same emotion was. In the upper-right quadrant of the grid, right next to the label "surprise," was a bottle whose body drew back while its head—the stopper—leaned forward, agog, as if to say, "He did what?!"

Mothersill's work represented a dream that the fuzzy logic of beauty and aesthetics might be codified in an algorithm, which may be the defining metaphor of the twenty-first century. (As the historian Yuval Noah Harari writes, "Every animal—including *Homo sapiens*—is an assemblage of organic algorithms shaped by natural selection over millions of years of evolution . . . There is no reason to think that organic algorithms can do things that nonorganic algorithms will never be able to replicate or surpass.")[35] To be sure, it was a wild dream—the references any good designer uses to create beauty are immeasurably bound to particulars of taste and personal experience, which aren't so readily mapped. But there is still a code that we understand in the designs we live with. Behind Mothersill's bottles—sad and droopy, or fierce and sharp-edged—was one of the oldest metaphors of all: that of personifying something, imbuing it with human postures and prejudices, so that they might communicate to us something about what that object is supposed to mean. Personification lives with us every day, sometimes subtly, sometimes less so: Steve Jobs demanded that the screen and casing of the first Macintosh tilt ever so slightly upward, like a face turned up to greet you. And the emotional design of cars rests largely on their fascia—the term of art for the grill and headlights that literally means "face." In a 2019 Ferrari GTC4Lusso, the headlights are those of a squinty-eyed killer, and the grill is turned up at the corners in a snarl. In a 2008 Volkswagen Beetle, the headlights are wide-eyed like a puppy's, and the line of the hood becomes a grin.[36]

But personification is just one of the ways designers use metaphors to create beauty. As Mothersill's work with the razors showed, designers are constantly assimilating disparate influences, so that the leaf of an aloe plant becomes the curve of a razor's handle, or lettering from posters from the London punk scene can become a typeface. The references—copied, remixed, blended—are sometimes hard to spot. But when those references gel in just the right way, a product can become iconic, able to represent not only its own histories but others. When you look at a Dyson vacuum cleaner, you see the jutting outlines of the motors and assemblies within. But you're also looking at a "postmodern" design philosophy, which was roiling the architecture profession when James Dyson was having his first successes in the 1980s. The idea was for objects not to hide away their inner workings behind a clean facade, as they did in the heyday of modernism, but to display them. The philosophy reached its apotheosis in the Centre Pompidou in Paris, designed by Richard Rogers and Renzo Piano, the facade of which is crisscrossed with HVAC piping and an escalator tube. The building's design tells a story about how the building works. Similarly, the Dyson vacuum, with its exposed piping and carefully outlined motor casings, was meant to tell a story about the company's zeal for engineering. The transparent dust canister, a first in the history of vacuum cleaners, was likewise meant to show you what all that machinery had done. Seeing the dust you'd just gathered created a feedback loop that hadn't existed before. If you own a Dyson, then you know the satisfaction of being surprised by the sheer volume of all that dust you've collected, and how it just makes you want to vacuum more. None of that would exist but for the beautiful rigor of the self-consciously high-tech design.

In this chapter, we've tracked the various ways metaphors can be used to silently explain how something works. We've seen how unavoidable metaphors and metaphorical thinking are when trying to invent something new. Metaphor is no less important in how we make things beautiful. In the user-friendly world, beauty is a tool that transforms something that's easy to use into something we *want* to use. Beauty pulls us in and makes us want to touch something, to own it, then use it. But beauty works associatively, necessarily referencing what we've found beautiful elsewhere. In that way, design is a kind of arbitrage: finding beauty in one place, delivering it to others. Beneath every product you see, there is a designer, sometimes a good one, whose fodder is an intuition about what you've seen before, what you might admire. "Beauty" is the word we use when a designer's vision overlaps with our own.

Part II

Easy to Want

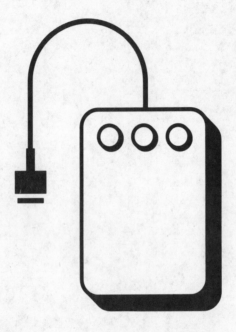

Computer mouse (1968)

6

Empathy

In a classic episode of *The Simpsons*, "O Brother Where Art Thou," we meet Herb Powell (voiced by Danny DeVito), who bears a striking resemblance to Homer Simpson. Herb grew up in an orphanage, but the experience has molded him into a world-beating success, the founder of his own car company, Powell Motors.[1] Still, that success feels hollow. "I have no roots. All I know is that I'm just a lonely guy," Herb admits glumly to his top executives. Then he gets a call from Homer, who's just found out that they're long-lost half brothers, and that Herb was born of a tryst between their father, Abe, and a carnival prostitute. Jump cut, and we see Homer driving with his family to meet Herb for the first time, and then screeching to a halt in front of his mansion. "Holy moly, the bastard's rich!" Homer shouts.

Later, during a factory tour, Herb tells Homer to pick out a car. Homer promptly asks for the biggest one they've got, but a smarmy executive replies that they don't have any big ones, because Americans don't want big cars. Herb loses it: "This is why we're getting killed in the marketplace! Instead of listening to what people want, you're telling them!" Herb quickly decides that Homer, not his egghead Ivy Leaguers, will design the next Powell car. Homer soon becomes the raging tyrant of the product department, demanding dozens of features to suit every annoyance in his life.

When the car is finished, Herb calls a press conference to reveal the new car for the Everyman. He hasn't seen it in advance, preferring to be surprised along with the public. Then the dust cover comes off. The crowd gasps at the monstrosity before them: There are tail fins and enormous cup holders to fit the largest soda from Kwik-E-Mart. Instead of a back seat, there's a glass containment bubble for the kids "with built-in restraints and optional muzzle." The car has three horns, because "you can never find one when you're mad." The hood ornament depicts a bowler in mid-roll. It costs $82,000. "What have I done?" Herb wails, sinking to his knees. "I'm ruined!" Homer, still behind the wheel and wearing a forced smile, honks the horn, which plays "La Cucaracha."

Like so many *Simpsons* episodes, the story echoes real events— in particular, Ford's disastrous invention of the Edsel. There, the suave executives who had succeeded Henry Ford touted that they had done the world's most advanced consumer research, and had provided every feature anyone could want in the "car of the future." The dealers were threatened with fines if they took the dust covers off the car before "E-Day," September 4, 1957.[2] And yet when the day arrived, people looked at the car and yawned. No one cared about innovations such as a push-button gear shifter in the center of the steering wheel, or a speedometer that changed color when the speed changed. The Edsel's failure spoke to a gap in the industry. Polling had seemed to show that young, up-and-coming American males wanted a sporty sedan built for their generation. But polling wasn't the same as figuring out what people actually wanted, and so the Edsel's designers made the leap from what they knew to be true in general to the specifics of what they would create.

Designers such as Henry Dreyfuss—who in the 1950s was still ascending the heights of his influence—should have been the ones to step in, figuring out where the meet-up was between business and user. But even they didn't have any firm process for doing so, beyond their own intuitions. The question remained: How could you understand what you were supposed to invent, for whom, and why, if you *didn't* have some genius with an unmistakable vision for what the world needed? Empathy, which had always been the vague and quirky heart of the design process, hadn't yet been codified for industry, in a process that anyone might understand, copy, and reapply.

Design thinking, "user-centered design," and user experience are all forms of industrialized empathy. These processes push for would-be innovators to immerse themselves in the lives of others, and they lie behind the products all around you: from Gmail's various permutations and new features in the last ten years, to the two-second rewind button on the DVR, invented when design researchers for TiVo saw people watching TV ask, "What did they just say?" They lie behind clever things we rarely think twice about, such as your child's fat, squishy-handled toothbrush, which began with a designer's observation that kids don't hold their toothbrushes with their fingers like their parents.

Industrialized empathy hinges on the idea that would-be

innovators—such as the well-meaning but wrongheaded inventors of the Edsel, or even Homer, with his God-given sense that everyone was just like him—are held back by their own point of view and need to slip loose of it. This shift in paradigm didn't arrive fully formed. It was a direct outcome of the Red Scare of the 1950s, the counterculture of the 1960s, and the fear that nothing holds us back quite as much as ourselves. Eventually, these influences helped spawn the design firm IDEO and its competitors such as Frog and Smart Design, which invented a new way of understanding users. It is a story of a little-known period of engineering and design history just as consequential as any other, but that has gone untold because it didn't produce a technical breakthrough. It produced an emotional one.

In 1952, Bob McKim had just graduated from Stanford, with a degree in mechanical engineering, at the height of the Korean War. A lifelong pacifist, he managed to avoid the battlefield by taking a job at Lawrence Livermore National Laboratory.[3] He was tasked with designing the crates for securing nuclear bombs, and it sickened him. So, after registering as a conscientious objector, he got a job designing lab equipment for top-secret experiments in hydrogen fusion. When his enlistment finally ended, McKim went to New York to study industrial design at the Pratt Institute and then landed a job at one of America's top industrial design firms.[4] "Loewy was outrageously stylized. He was just looking for appearance. Teague I liked a lot. But the most classy and intellectual was Dreyfuss," McKim, now ninety years old, told me, as we drank tea in his backyard art studio in Santa Cruz, where he has spent his retirement crafting bronze nudes. He'd also taken up the tuba. "You have to keep your lung power up to play it," he explained.

Dreyfuss was at his peak by then, and had a swanky office above the Paris Theater, kitty-corner to his apartment at the Plaza Hotel and overlooking the famed Pulitzer Fountain, topped with a bronze sculpture of Pomona, the Roman goddess of abundance. McKim was lured by an ideal that Dreyfuss had been selling ever since he'd turned down the job creating prettier facades for Macy's housewares. Dreyfuss had preached that for designers to actually create something valuable, they had to be steeped in its manufacturing. McKim had always hoped that even the outside of a consumer gadget might express its inner workings, so that the gadget's design could tell its own story.

But soon after McKim started his job with Dreyfuss, his boss's philosophy began to feel like a veneer. Even though Dreyfuss talked differently from his peers, he still worked like them. The designers weren't close to the manufacturing process at all. They weren't even allowed to make their own prototypes, because their billing rates were too high. Instead, they had to send their drawings to the model maker. It seemed to McKim that Dreyfuss, just like everyone else, had been relegated to creating nice cases for what someone else had invented.[5] So McKim quit after a year and moved west with his young wife, doing odd jobs to make ends meet and toying with the idea of taking more classes at Stanford. During a visit, he saw a flyer for a class in unlocking creativity run by John Arnold, who'd also just arrived at Stanford a few months before. McKim went to meet him, hoping to learn more. Instead, Arnold asked McKim if he'd like to teach.

They met at exactly the right time for each other. While McKim was growing disillusioned at the Dreyfuss studio, Arnold had been searching for a way to teach students to be not merely smart but ingenious. His quest started in the spring of 1951, when he got up in front of his engineering students at MIT and asked them to imagine life for a race of aliens on another planet. "You're living in the year 2951. Space travel is well established and there is a good deal of trade in the galaxy," he told the students. Arnold explained that the Terran trade agency, scouring the galaxy for commerce partners, had found the Methanians, thirty-three light-years away on a planet called Arcturus IV.[6] The goal was to make something these Methanians wanted to buy.

Arnold had crafted the limitations of the Methanians to force the students to imagine a life other than their own, and what that might entail. ("Do you think that the average present-day Terran designer gives as much thought to human limitations?" Arnold asked.) Arcturus IV was an unplowed field of consumer desire, primed for inventions. Its inhabitants were friendly and naive, but stuck with nineteenth-century technology. Their planet itself was an enormous hunk of the most valuable resources anyone could imagine during the nuclear age: uranium and platinum. But their needs were hyperbolically foreign. The Methanians were humanoid, but gangly and birdlike with egg-shaped bodies. They were physically weak and extraordinary slow.[7]

As the weeks went on, the students got into debates about whether the Methanians, who hatched from eggs, would find an egg-shaped car to be vulgar; whether the Methanians, with their slow reflexes, should be asked to adapt to the speed of new technologies.[8] The students invented ingenious things: a drill that required two hands to turn on, so that slow-moving Methanians couldn't hurt themselves, and a car seat that worked using suction, so that drivers wouldn't have to use their flimsy limbs to brace during cornering.[9] Even so, Arnold's starchy fellow professors saw that class as a diversion from the real work of an MIT degree.[10] Of course, Arnold saw it differently. Tall, plain, and balding, Arnold, with his forgettable looks, belied a radical sensibility. McKim remembers almost having to jog to keep up with his strides, even while Arnold chain-smoked Lucky Strikes; students in his seminars used to say that even when they were all sitting at a round table, the table itself seemed to slope toward him, leaving everyone else looking up. Through his teaching, Arnold was trying to inoculate the next generation against conformity.

That threat was neatly articulated by William Whyte, in a series of articles for *Fortune* that portrayed a creeping threat to American individualism posed by "groupthink" and the "organization man" who left for work at some big gray company every morning wearing his spotless gray suit, with no higher value than to simply go along with all the other gray suits.[11] Amid the growing fear that the United States and Russia would descend into nuclear war, Whyte was limning a deeper fear about communism: that the threat wasn't abroad so much as it was within.

Arnold was one of the many intellectuals taken by Whyte's thinking. As he wrote in his manifesto "Creative Product Design," "Prediction typifies the daring spirit that is not afraid to fight for what he believes to be right, to stick his neck out and take a chance, to be different when it makes a difference."[12] But the only way to teach people to predict what the world might need was to explode their assumptions. As William Clancey sums up in his recently published introduction to John Arnold's *Creative Engineering*, "Our cultural milieu, our peers, and norms instilled in how we act, look, talk, and relate to our environment contribute to our blindness and limit how we generate new ideas."[13] Arnold was searching for new tools to free the mind. His ideas gained almost immediate attention; the Arcturus IV course landed Arnold on the cover of *Life*, next to a prop he used in class, the three-fingered hand of a Methanian. But Arnold's worst fears about conformity eventually hit home. The faculty brass at MIT groused that the publicity was unbecoming.

Arnold, fed up with their whispering, fled to Stanford's engineering program in 1957. The department differed in the aspirations it was trying to breed in its own students; Silicon Valley didn't yet exist, but the dean of the engineering school was planting the seeds by encouraging its graduates to start their own businesses in the nascent semiconductor industry. The spirit of enterprise was in turn nourished by a burgeoning counterculture, and those influences nourished Arnold's own radicalism. And yet, soon after creating some of Stanford's first courses in product design, such as Philosophy of Design and How to Ask a Question, John Arnold died of a heart attack while vacationing in Italy.

McKim, as one of the first professors Arnold had recruited, was then thrust into the role of leading a growing product-design curriculum. McKim went looking for new methods of unlocking creativity. He took mescaline, in the same experiments that came to include pioneers of modern computing such as Doug Engelbart. He found himself at Esalen—perhaps most famous today as the site of Donald Draper's closing epiphany in *Mad Men*. Esalen had recently been founded by two Stanford graduates on a stunning coastal plot in Big Sur that one of them had inherited. (Before the graduates arrived, the property's hot springs had been a gay party spot on weekends; the gun-toting night watchman was Hunter S. Thompson.) Its new mission echoed the spirit of John Arnold's obsession with innovation. "We were looking for what happened if you took away conformity, which is the result of fear," McKim told me. "What would the human potential look like if you took that away? If you took away fear, would creativity blossom?"[14]

McKim might have sympathized with the students at Stanford who were picketing by day and, by night, breaking into the engineering department to destroy anything they thought might abet the Vietnam War. But, like Arnold, he still believed the enemy lay inside rather than out. Fresh from Esalen, he convinced colleagues to try out a new way of doing things, starting with therapy circles, where someone would sit at the center of a dozen or more people he knew, while each of them took turns voicing how they really felt about that person in the middle. Sometimes, this could be outright terrifying, as when a student dragged his girlfriend across the floor. It made you wonder what lay behind people, hidden. Throughout the 1960s, McKim started to dwell on what separated the best students—what made some projects sing while others floundered. And, as he started to play back the decade he'd spent teaching, he began to realize that the best students didn't demonstrate creativity in solving a problem so much as in finding the problem.

One of the star students in McKim's "need finding" program was David Kelley, who recalled coming up with an idea for in-home tests for venereal disease—no shame, better health—and then showing up at a hospital to ask the doctors and nurses what they thought about the idea. They just laughed, noting how many problems such a product would cause because of misdiagnosis. Lesson learned: The solutions you imagine might not match the scale of the problem. Yet one of the doctors did offer a tour of the basement, where there were files stacked from floor to ceiling, in every direction. "If you want to solve a real problem, come here. If we misfile a patient's record," the doctor said, "we never find it again." "I realized that it was a creative act, talking to people," Kelley says. "I had to actually feel the need of a person."[15] Ask Kelley what the key to his later success was and he credits McKim and his insistence that finding an interesting problem is even more important that finding an interesting solution.

Kelley went on to propose an ingenious filing system, and after that, to become one of the most influential designers of the twentieth century. But not because of the number of things he designed, though he did play a key role in designing Apple's first mouse.

Rather, his influence sprang from the design firm he founded right after graduating in 1978, which evolved into IDEO in 1991. More than any other company, it was IDEO that spread industrial empathy to boardrooms across the world. It's working. In 2018, the consulting firm McKinsey & Company analyzed more than 100,000 executive-level design decisions across three hundred publicly held companies; those with robust design-thinking processes had 32 percent higher revenues than their peers over a five-year period, and 56 percent higher shareholder returns.[16] Jeanne Liedtka, a professor at the University of Virginia who spent seven years studying fifty projects in depth, found something similar in 2018, but was able to better understand why. Her conclusions bear a striking echo of John Arnold's hopes: "By now most executives have at least heard about design thinking's tools—ethnographic research, an emphasis on reframing problems and experimentation, the use of diverse teams, and so on—if not tried them. But what people may not understand is the subtler way that design thinking gets around the human biases (for example, rootedness in the status quo) or attachments to specific behavioral norms ("That's how we do things here") that time and again block the exercise of imagination."[17] Today, you can find design thinking—and industrial empathy—at work in organizations ranging from IBM, which vowed to become the world's single largest employer of designers, to the Finnish government, which used design methods in its programs to reinvent everything from day care to welfare.

As John Arnold had articulated in his class about Arcturus IV, personal experience can blind. So Arnold sought new ways to free the mind of limitation—of personal bias. Bob McKim, in turn, believed that freeing the mind lay in looking out at the world as it was, of feeling the needs of others. Those ideas spread only after the invention of a process that could recast those New Age ideals for the rhythms of industry, retuning them for the insecurities of modern corporations fearful of being out-innovated. This was IDEO's accomplishment, and David Kelley was its best, most passionate salesman. Yet the soul of what the company was trying to become was Jane Fulton Suri, whose role has been overlooked even inside the design profession because what she offered wasn't design itself, but rather the spirit that should guide it.

One of Fulton Suri's first jobs out of college was working for Britain's office of public safety, where one of her first tasks was to figure out why so many subjects of the Crown were cutting their hands and feet off with lawn mowers. At the time, the government kept voluminous accident records, but when Fulton Suri pored over them, on a boxy minicomputer screen in blinking green type, they wouldn't speak: "Ran over foot with lawn mower." Whatever had actually happened was lost in the gaps.[18]

This kind of usability research, if it had been done at all, was typically conducted in a lab, asking users to go through the motions of starting a lawn mower and pushing it. To figure out what had actually happened, Fulton Suri realized she'd have to start by talking to all these people. So she went to them. "It wasn't exactly in the wild," she says. "But it was in the wilder." In some ways, she had always been preparing for this work. As a child, she had a tiger mask, and she remembers thinking about the difference between how that mask looked on the outside and how it felt on the inside—a formative lesson for what she'd do as a design researcher later in life. And she remembers when she and her siblings would visit the tawny beaches of Cornwall and try to convince the local farmers to let them camp on their land. She was a shy child, but she noticed that if she could just get the farmers talking about something they cared about—their prize cows or their balky tractors—they would practically offer up the campsite themselves, without being asked. Fulton Suri realized that people would readily reveal something hidden about themselves, if you asked. But doing so took a special kind of courage. Now an adult, petite, proper, and shy, she would knock on people's doors, explain that she was with the government safety office, and gently ask them to rehash one of the worst moments of their lives.

The people she interviewed would describe leaning down to clear a stuck blade, while reaching with their other hand to balance on the mower—and then accidentally grabbing the lever that engaged the blade. Or they would show her their lawn mowers, which were designed with a single pole as a handle, like a vacuum cleaner. And because these lawnmowers looked like vacuum cleaners, people naturally used them like vacuum cleaners, pushing them back and forth, back and forth across the grass, rather than walking around the yard in straight lines. While to-ing and fro-ing with the machine, they'd accidentally snarl their toes. In those stories, Fulton Suri found a universe of misinformation in the way things were designed. The point was that these products were all speaking a language, but no one recognized it. Like when a man using a chain saw had grabbed what he assumed to be its handle, only to realize afterward, when he'd nearly cut his hand off, that what looked like a handle was never meant to be held at all—it was the hand *guard*.

To be sure, Fulton Suri wasn't discovering a new idea about design. Henry Dreyfuss and William Dorwin Teague has spent their entire careers trying to teach their clients about the semiotics of how their products should look—the subtle references, patterns, and details that made a kitchen appliance look like it was for the kitchen, or that made a new vacuum cleaner just a little bit easier to use than its competitors. And Paul Fitts had seen all those airplane accidents caused by baffling controls, their lessons hidden behind the blanket proclamation of "user error." But Fulton Suri was seeing a premonition of the era when computers would start creeping into our everyday lives. She was seeing what could happen when specialized products for a professional audience—lawn mowers and then, later, computers—arrived in a consumer market. You might expect professionals to be technically savvy, well trained, knowledgeable about the tools they used and how they worked. Fulton Suri was seeing that average people, in the confident domain of their own homes, didn't resemble professionals at all: they didn't follow instructions; they let their minds wander during the task at hand; they made assumptions about how their tools should behave.

It was when Fulton Suri began translating all her findings about lawn mowers and chain saws and hedge trimmers into governmental standards that she realized it would take years for any of that work to make its way into the real world—and, all the while, scores more sunburned citizens would be cutting their hands off. Better to be in the room when those products were being designed, so that you could tell the engineers not to color a chain saw in the same garish colors as a children's toy, because it wasn't meant to invite children to use it. She tried to join their ranks, yet none of the design firms she solicited were interested in hiring her. "You didn't see people like me on the design team," she says. "And I'm sure I wasn't impressive, because I didn't have immediately good ideas or answers to whatever the designers were struggling with at the time."

This could have been different. After all, Dreyfuss used to crow about what he'd do to understand his users, such as when he studied that RKO Theater in Sioux City, Iowa, where he intuited that farmers weren't coming in for fear of messing up the plush red carpet. Teague, not to be outdone, once boasted of sending his designers on a cross-country drive in a shipping truck, to better understand how the cab should be designed. And yet neither of them made their attitudes into anything approaching a systematic process, because they were both assuming that design was an act of personal inspiration. Even though Dreyfuss had codified the measure of mankind in the drawings of Joe and Josephine, neither designer thought to codify the quality of mind that gave rise to their inventions. They saw the act of imagining oneself into another person's problem as ingenuity, not empathy. In the decades before Arnold's experiments in design education, it was hard to imagine how ingenuity might be taught.

By the 1970s, there were dozens of firms, dreaming of just a fraction of the success of Teague and Dreyfuss, who were more than happy to dispense with high-minded ideology altogether. Thus, as the profession grew in the next twenty years, the lowest common denominator prevailed. By the 1980s there were thousands more designers working for less and less money, with less and less investment in what "design" meant. "I remember there was a firm, when I got out of college, that would start a design in the morning and finish it by the evening," recalls Dan Formosa, who would go on to cofound the storied firm Smart Design. "In and out, with just a bit of styling on the outside."[19] Often, even designers at the profession's apex were merely asked to put a pretty casing on a finished product—just as Bob McKim had seen in his short stint in Dreyfuss's offices. So while tidy tales of ingenuity brought the business in, it was styling that kept the lights on.

But Formosa and others were also beginning to sense an opening. From the beginnings of the design profession in the 1920s, there were always two competing strands of thought. On one hand, the ideal of making people's lives better by solving their problems; on the other, the drive to simply stoke consumer lust and keep the furnace of capitalism well fed. On one hand, a belief in commerce as progress; on the other, the hope that simple consumer churn might stoke consumer demand. By the 1980s, the pendulum had swung toward the latter. It was about to swing back, thanks to a new generation and a new opportunity: the explosion of the semiconductor, which would unleash a wave of new gadgetry, the size of which had not been seen since the 1950s. That's the simple reason why a disproportionate share of the world's most influential design firms, such as IDEO, Smart, and Frog, made their names with projects in Silicon Valley. It was there that prevailing New Age ideals about self-discovery merged with a newfangled, human-centered design process; together, the process and its products rode a silicon wave into the world. They ushered in a new sensibility for design, in which the surfaces of things didn't matter as much as the experience of them.

Disillusioned by the stony indifference she'd encountered while trying to find a job in Britain, Fulton Suri made her way to Berkeley, where her boyfriend was studying for his Ph.D. Through a mutual acquaintance she came to meet Bill Moggridge, the owner of a small design studio. Moggridge was a fellow British emigrant, tall and urbane, a polymath who started his career designing hospital equipment but also spent a lifetime studying typography. He could already lay claim to making history, having recently finished designing the world's first laptop computer, the GRiD Compass, which would become standard equipment on the Space Shuttle for nearly twenty years. In a quiet voice, Moggridge would tell people what a letdown the GRiD Compass had been.

As the project began, Moggridge didn't know if such a thing was even possible—if a computer really could be portable enough to be desirable. To test whether it was, he gathered up all the raw parts required in a computer—a hard drive, a floppy drive, a processor, and a display—and put them in a briefcase, which he would carry around all day. It was heavy, but workable. The problem wasn't just making it lighter but making it small, when the display consumed so much space. Perhaps inspired by the briefcase itself, Moggridge hit upon the now-universal clamshell design, where the display could be closed for carrying, then unfolded for use. The genius lay in how it protected the screen while allowing the user to adjust the viewing angle. Yet after he started to perfect the details, when Moggridge flipped open the first working prototype, he was shocked by how little his work seemed to matter.[20] The software was simply a mess: confusing, impossible to use, impossible to explain. Moggridge realized that the software wasn't a thing separate from the laptop. It was all the same experience, one big web of interactions.[21]

At their meeting, Fulton Suri showed Moggridge slides of her work: pictures of people reenacting the accidents that befell them, recommendations she had made about motorcycle lights and power tools and train-ticket turnstiles. Moggridge in turn showed her the diagrams he was using: Dreyfuss's compendium of drawings of Joe and Josephine. "He was using a lot of drawings from Dreyfuss to design computers," Fulton Suri told me, as we chatted in IDEO's sprawling, light-filled offices in San Francisco. "But for me these were failings, because all of those drawings about posture and use assumed things about people's behavior. I was intrigued with what's really going on in the world, where people don't sit like that, where they cross their legs and put their feet up. That came up from seeing firsthand the discrepancy between how people were supposed to use things and how they actually used them." At the end, Moggridge asked, "So what would you like to happen now?" Fulton Suri, flabbergasted, blurted out, "I'd like you to offer me a job!" So Moggridge did. He eventually linked up with an engineer he often worked with, David Kelley, and another designer, Mike Nuttall. By 1991, the three joined their small companies, naming the new one IDEO.

By then the personal computer had arrived in Silicon Valley, killing the mainframe computer and creating new niches to be filled. Apple was the biggest, most important client to the design studios that would go on to remake the profession: In 1980, David Kelley and his colleagues at the proto-IDEO worked on Apple's first mouse; Frog Design, which soon after opened its first office in Northern California, led the effort to design cases for Apple's computers in the 1980s, including the "Snow White" design language that would define its products for a decade. (Smart Design, based in New York, played a role as well.) But even beyond that traditional industrial design work were other, thornier problems for a new kind of client. "The struggle was to not just imagine what was right now," says Tim Brown, now the CEO of IDEO and one of the first designers that Moggridge hired, "but imagining what was right in the future."

In decades past, Henry Dreyfuss and his peers had ridden a manufacturing wave that flooded homes across the world in new products. Now IDEO and a new breed of design studio rode atop a silicon revolution, putting screens and gadgets in places they'd never been before. Sometimes, that was in our own homes, with VCRs and personal computers. More often, it was in the unseen places of commercial progress, such as call centers and warehouses and offices. Software, which transformed dumb objects into objects that were always changing, had presented new problems. "We were working on making complex products easy to use," says Brown. "And if we were doing simple products, it was in the context of the future." Those products had a memory of their own, about what the user had done and about what they had been before—granted, just a few seconds before, usually. "That was when products shifted from being products to being a narrative. They weren't just a piece of sculpture. And we realized you just had to get into people's lives."

But how? In the 1990s, Alan Cooper, an architecture student turned computer programmer, created the concept of a persona—an idealized user, composited from interviews. A persona, and the needs and everyday life it represented, could be literally pinned up on the wall so that designers might be able to place themselves in the mind-set of the people they were trying to help. The idea wasn't so dissimilar to that of Joe and Josephine, whose measurements were meant to stand for a multitude.[22] When Moggridge first hired Fulton Suri, he was working on a project for Xerox and had already written a storyboard and persona: a character named Stella, who was already using an imaginary gadget of the future.

"He said, 'Is this something you might do?'" says Fulton Suri. She balked. "I said I'd rather see what people *already* did." Fulton Suri didn't think you found the future in your head, based upon a construct you'd pasted to a wall. You found it in what was already around you, in the gaps of the world as it already was. She remembered her study days knocking on doors and talking to people who had been maimed: The reason behind all those awful lawn mower and chain saw accidents was that the departments that made the machines were viewed as being different from the design department. In the end, different always meant separate, and separate meant there were tensions about who won and lost. "I didn't want to be in a group that identified itself as different from designers," says Fulton Suri. "I said, 'If we're successful we can hire more people, but I never want there to be a department.'" Instead, she proposed that she teach *everyone* in the office to think as she did.

Fulton Suri noticed that designers of the previous generation didn't much like getting out. Art school itself had encouraged that, by selecting for certain shy, creative types who relished sitting at their workbenches making beautiful things. The idea of observing people in the wild and wading through the details of their everyday lives was anathema. Fulton Suri's special genius lay in noticing, in the way a poet might: seeing how a cast-off detail might reveal meaning, sometimes even a life. The project that eventually became her book *Thoughtless Acts* began when Fulton Suri saw two boys in an English housing project who had boosted themselves up and over the top of a boiler room doorway, arms and legs dangling on either side. In a dark and dimly lit basement hall, they'd made a swing from the only thing that actually moved and made noise in the massive labyrinth of concrete. Maybe the boys needed a playground, or maybe they needed a new kind of apartment complex altogether, one that could be remade around them as they grew up. It was a need, unmet, but which had found an outlet nonetheless. You just had to be sensitive enough to see it. Fulton Suri started collecting more snapshots like these, of people making their presence felt in the world around them:[23] the spines of a house cactus used as a noticeboard; a wine cork perfectly fitted as an impromptu doorstop. The point was that every one of those tiny fixes pointed to a problem that had gone overlooked—to a mismatch between the things people needed, the world they lived in, and the way they behaved.

Tim Brown recalls the moment that this lesson clicked. Fulton Suri had taken the team out, on a project for a kitchen appliance maker, to understand what needs people might have. They interviewed someone who talked at length about all the tools she used to cook her meals. Yet when she opened her cupboards, there was almost no fresh food at all—it was all prepackaged and ready to eat.

There was something movingly human in this strange slippage between how people described their lives and how they actually lived. The stories people lived weren't the stories they told themselves. "They weren't lying," Brown said. "But their mental models of what they were doing were different. That's the trick about user-centered design. The explicit need versus the latent need. People will usually tell you what they want, but not what they need." The entire process of design thinking was meant to avoid producing the equivalent of Homer's perfect car: haphazard and unloved, but nonetheless exactly what someone had asked for. The most important problems to solve were those that weren't being expressed. The most important questions to ask were those that people never thought to ask themselves.

In addition to creating a culture in which the entire staff became students of human behavior, there were two more ingredients in IDEO's way of working: putting prototypes, no matter how primitive, in front of users as quickly as possible, and the idea that the design process didn't lie with any one "designer." Both tenets sprang from the environment that had nourished the young company. Helped by the self-organizing hacker ethos that had spawned Silicon Valley, both Moggridge and Kelley assumed that their office would be radically egalitarian and nonhierarchical. "He was already working like that with David Kelley. People were just team members, and I loved that," said Fulton Suri. "There was already something in the culture that blurred the boundaries." By the time Kelley had studied under Bob McKim at Stanford in 1977, a DIY entrepreneurialism reigned. The student desks were arranged cheek-by-jowl, and students couldn't help knowing what everyone else was working on. Kelley replicated that design at IDEO with an open plan. Everyone knew everyone else's problems, and suggestions flowed freely. Moggridge even made a point of making all salaries roughly equal, and telling everyone that; even he didn't make much more than anyone else.

Kelley also brought an ethos that he'd picked up from McKim: Failure was good. When he worked in Dreyfuss's offices, McKim never could build his own prototypes. At Stanford, he preached the opposite: To create a design that worked, you had to build it, watch it fail while people tried to use it, fix it, then watch it fail again until you finally had something. Designing wasn't something you did on paper. Moggridge was already a habitual tinkerer and prototype maker. So was Fulton Suri. Back in London, doing work for the city transit authority, she had created full-size cardboard replicas of subway turnstiles to see how people moved through them. Prototyping with whatever was at hand—from mere sheets of paper to more developed design models, farther down the line—became a way of integrating user feedback into every step of the process.

Clients were initially baffled by the process that IDEO had created. In the early days people would say, Let's just skip to the design. But Kelley, Moggridge, and Fulton Suri carried out their new way of working anyway. They hid it, revealing all that they had done only at the end, so that it came as a surprise—albeit one loaded with a subtle implication: This is the way this has to be, because we haven't just guessed. The best marker of how much the world has changed is that the assumptions behind IDEO's way of working are now standard practice. Today, Fulton Suri's insistence on rooting innovation in the nuance of individual experience has become the maxim that if you design for everyone, you design for no one.

Kelley went on to expand upon the design curriculum at Stanford, and by 2004 cofounded the Hasso Plattner Institute of Design at Stanford—the so-called d.school—with a curriculum based on

IDEO's methodologies. Elsewhere, in the years since, the working process in almost every digital design agency in the world, inside every major technology company, and even inside countless businesses aiming to be more "innovative," presumes small teams of people working collaboratively, without hierarchy, and discovery periods meant to uncover unmet needs. All these processes are subsumed in a larger, ubiquitous framework—observe, prototype, test, and repeat—that equates observation with creation. Today, you can find IDEO's influence in places as varied as the Gates Foundation, which has made human-centered design into a pillar of its efforts to foster innovation in the developing world; the famed Mayo Clinic, which for years had an entire floor set up in which designers worked alongside doctors, so that they could immerse themselves in a clinic's rhythms and quickly test new ways of offering service;[24] Ford, whose CEO boasted of his plans to remake the behemoth into an experience-driven, user-centered company, to better compete in an era of driverless cars; and even Finland, whose radical experiment in offering a universal income was born in a government-funded design lab meant to reinvent public services.[25] For the coming generation of would-be business titans, design-thinking methods are now taught not just at Stanford but in many of the world's most prestigious business schools, all hoping to emulate the university's promise to teach the alchemy of invention.

To be sure, the seeds of design thinking sprouted in many places at once, including Britain, Germany, and Scandinavia. But IDEO benefited from timing and place: Seated in Silicon Valley— piggybacking off the high-technology boom that made Northern California synonymous with innovation—the company was able to spread its influence because of projects that themselves were influential. The company has sold untold millions of dollars' worth of work using the story of how David Kelley helped design the first

Apple mouse. But that influence spread only because IDEO created the vocabulary that others could use to sell the idea that "design" wasn't just prettiness. Rather, it was a process of industrialized empathy—one that could be marketed, explained, circulated, repeated, and then spread.

Steve Jobs famously said that it's not the consumer's job to figure out what he or she wants—an echo of both Henry Ford's likely apocryphal quote "If I had asked people what they wanted, they would have said faster horses" and IDEO's attempt to separate wants and needs. But Jobs didn't place much faith in process; he placed it in his own intuitions and judgments. As a result, his quote has been seized by countless entrepreneurs, happy to be told that their instincts are all that matter. And there are indeed countless examples of people inventing remarkable things, simply by following the voice of their own experience.

In 2013, Ridhi Tariyal began a fellowship at Harvard Business School that culminated in her trying to invent a new way for women to monitor their own fertility at home. To do that, she realized, she'd need large amounts of blood. There are any number of companies trying to find a way to collect blood that doesn't rely on needles, from laser beams to tiny vacuums. But as a woman, Tariyal knew something else. As she told *The New York Times*, "I was thinking about women and blood. When you put those words together, it becomes obvious. We have an opportunity every single month to collect blood from women, without needles. . . . There's lots of information there, but right now, it's all going in the trash."[26] Tariyal soon patented an idea that's been dubbed "the tampon of the future"—a method for capturing menstrual flow and using those samples to monitor for everything from cancer to endometriosis.

As the author Pagan Kennedy asked, "Why did Ms. Tariyal see a possibility that had eluded so many engineers before her? You might say she has an unfair advantage: Her gender. Because she lives in a female body, she had experiences that just wouldn't be available to her male colleagues. She doesn't have to imagine using her device, because she herself has been able to beta-test it."

Eric von Hippel, an economist at MIT, has spent a career finding stories like that of Tariyal, and they've led him to conclude that the people who lived inside an experience were the best suited to improve it. Inventions tend to spring from those who see themselves as the users, from Californians who invented skateboards to "surf" the streets, to the surgeons who built the first heart-and-lung machines to sustain their patients through arduous surgeries. They're motivated by their own experience.

No doubt this is true. But empathy, next to language and opposable thumbs, may be the most powerful tool that evolution has given us. It allows us not to be bound by personal experience. It allows us not to be limited by our stories. Our economy is built on that idea, that an entire company can be mobilized to a cause that started *before* its employees arrived. So even if a disproportionate number of inventions begin with someone's personal sense of a problem, most inventions aren't perfected by their creator but rather by other people who finally understood a problem after someone else inspired them. "Design thinking" and "human-centered design" arrived to fill a gap, between companies pressed to create new things and people with needs but without the wherewithal to bet their time and money on creating something new. What user-centered design did was to build a sensing process that gave companies a way to mimic that of the inventor.

The gospel of innovation, and the imperative to innovate or be washed away by the rising tide of competition, rings hollow unless you have some mechanism for finding new ideas. The beauty of the design process as articulated at the dawn of the computer age was that we could all innovate, if only we knew how to empathize. In-dustrial empathy arose precisely when a new wave of technology arrived that few people understood, and that almost no one had ever bought for themselves. But when empathy becomes an impera-tive, then the question becomes: With whom should you empathize? Is the average user idealized in a template, like Joe and Josephine? Or is there something to be found in the lives of people at the edges, whose very difference might allow them to sense something that the rest of us cannot?

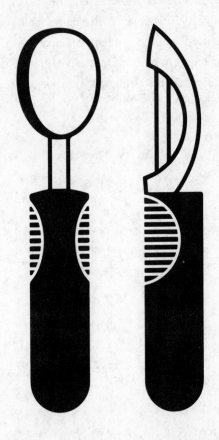

OXO ice-cream scoop and peeler (1990)

7

Humanity

What would later be called the Mother of All Demos—the most consequential tech demonstration of all time—happened on December 9, 1968, a chilly and gray San Francisco morning. Inside a darkened Brooks Hall auditorium, Doug Engelbart sat beneath a twenty-two-foot screen nervously waiting to begin a presentation that would predict nearly every major computing development of the next fifty years. "I hope you'll go along with this rather unusual setting," he began, speaking through a microphone headset. Under his breath he muttered, "I hope."

The audience was composed of leading figures in the computing world, gathered for its premier annual meeting, the Fall Joint

Computer Conference. All the attendees had come of age with punch cards and typewriter terminals, so were almost totally unprepared for what they were about to see. Speaking without notes, Engelbart proceeded to show how a computer could edit text on a screen, could link one document to another with hypertext, and could even mix text, graphics, and video into a single document. To move the on-screen cursor, which he called a "bug," he used a handheld puck. As the presentation went on, he showed how the computer could be used to share files, and even communicate with far-flung colleagues via videophone. When Engelbart finally finished, ninety minutes later, the audience erupted in applause. Engelbart had sketched out a new dreamscape for what computing was to become: the mouse, the teleconference, email, the windowed user interface, the hyperlink, the internet. As one attendee recalled, it was as if Engelbart had been "dealing lightning with both hands."[1]

Engelbart was regarded as an implacable oddball by his colleagues at the Stanford Research Institute, and it had taken him twenty-three years of bullheaded effort to mount that stage. His path began in August 1945, when he deployed to the Philippines with the Navy. Engelbart had tested into the training program to become a radar technician, scanning for pips on a glowing green screen. But as his ship left dock in San Francisco, with the sailors waving goodbye to their loved ones from the deck, the crowd suddenly started to roar.[2] A message came crackling over the ship's PA: Japan had surrendered. It was V-J Day. A month more passed, and young Douglas Engelbart arrived on Samar, an island in the Philippines, late to the action. He spent a slow year doing odd jobs, daydreaming for hours at a time on the towering clouds that bloomed above the Pacific. He was later racked by the specter of all those men who had died before him. Their unmet potential would inspire his life's work.

Engelbart finally found his calling in a thatched hut that the Red Cross had made into a makeshift reading library. Flipping through an issue of *Life*, he came upon a summary of a now-famous essay in *The Atlantic* by Vannevar Bush, "As We May Think." In it, Bush pointed out that scientific researchers were being swamped by the data and information available to them. While mankind had spent thousands of years creating tools for changing the physical world, Bush argued, it was now time to create knowledge tools. He proposed several, including one he hastily dubbed the memex, which would allow a person to store every book or communication he'd ever need, and call it up with "exceeding speed and flexibility." As Bush wrote, "It is an enlarged supplement to his memory." This was a loaded sentence. As John Markoff writes in his definitive history of Engelbart's milieu, *What the Dormouse Said*, "Previously, teams of humans had served a single computer; now, the computer would become a *personal assistant*."[3] (Emphasis mine.) The most far-reaching metaphor in computing was born.

Engelbart spent the next twenty years developing that vision of a personal assistant, utterly wedded to an infinite view of human progress. He didn't believe that such a device could just make each person smarter. If each person were smarter and also networked across the world, then society would improve exponentially faster, making everyone smarter still. After that first, triumphant presentation in San Francisco, Engelbart hit the road, hoping his demo could recruit others to his cause. He visited MIT and looked up Marvin Minsky, a cofounder of MIT's Artificial Intelligence lab. Where Engelbart thought that computers should augment minds, Minsky believed that computers should actually *become* minds. Minsky wanted to replace people, not assist them. As Engelbart painstakingly set up his bulky, hulking prototype and started his demo, Minsky watched impassively. Finally, when the demonstration was done, Minsky asked with withering dismissiveness, "We're going to have a machine that thinks like a man in ten years, and you're just showing us how to create a grocery list?"[4] (Let's note the irony in the fact that fifty years after that conversation, commercials for Amazon's Alexa tout the ability to make grocery lists.)

Minsky and Engelbart were waging an updated version of the WWII-era discord that begat ergonomics and human factors. On the one side, Minsky imagined what the machine could become as something outside ourselves, perhaps beyond us. Engelbart, instead, saw machines as tools built to serve. We seem bound to repeat this tug-of-war whenever a new technology arises. And even when we do side with the users—even when we do side with *us*—that inevitably brings up the question of who counts as "us." As John Arnold, Bob McKim, and Jane Fulton Suri all knew, it's possible to be blinded by your own biases. You can know too much about yourself, so you don't see the world clearly. You can fail to understand people well enough to know their real problems. There are two basic models for overcoming this, for learning with whom we should empathize. You might seek opportunities in widespread behaviors that can be reapplied elsewhere, hoping these patterns express some deeper truth about people. Or you might instead seek out the fringes, the so-called edge cases where the future might currently exist as a rare mutation, ready to take over the world.

In 2010, Steve Jobs learned of an oddball app languishing in the depths of the App Store, called Siri—a play on its birthplace, SRI, the Stanford Research Institute, which also happened to be the incubator for Doug Engelbart's Mother of All Demos. Thanks to startling advances in machine learning and voice recognition that for years had been quietly bubbling in the lab, the app let you speak commands, to ask about the weather, or set reminders, or get movie times. Just a year later, Siri became a built-in feature of the iPhone's operating system, and a race was on.

When it was first released, Siri couldn't do much more than check the weather and tell jokes to cover up its deficiencies. But new interface paradigms don't come along often. When they do, they are extinction events, leveling ecosystems and clearing the way for a new race to the top. (Even Eric Schmidt, Google's CEO at the time, admitted that Siri had blindsided the company and might one day disrupt its business.)[5] With Siri, the idea of a computer assistant had leaped from metaphorical to literal; from a gray box that mimicked the tools that a personal assistant might offer, to a voice, unthreatening and always available, that merely needed to hear you speak. Moreover, Siri happened to arrive just in time for a revolution in how new generations were coming to understand computers.

Around 2012, when Derrick Connell, then Microsoft's corporate VP of search, first touched down in China, bleary-eyed and jet-lagged, he noticed a curious thing about the way Chinese people held their phones. Instead of holding them up to the side of their face, like you would with a landline handset, they all held their phones aloft in front of their faces, like a makeup mirror. It seemed like one of those quirks about a place, like the faucets or the bus stops, that make it feel so foreign. "I thought, Okay, that's strange, but maybe that's just how they hold their phones here," said Connell. It turned out that the Chinese were using their phones differently than almost anyone in the West, using voice as the main interface, letting speech recognition programs do their texting instead of tapping out things themselves. Partly, this was simply easier, because of the cumbersome nature of tapping out Chinese characters on a smartphone. But the more interesting fact was that they weren't just chatting with humans. They were using chat as their entry point into the digital world; rather than tapping through menus to find the right app, they were using their voice.[6]

The smartphone is a different thing in China. It's built upon a different mental model. Apps aren't too popular and neither are app stores. Your operating system isn't nearly as important as your chat app, because your chat app is where everything happens. Let's say you wanted to buy tickets to a concert. In WeChat, China's most popular chat app, with more than a billion monthly users, you'd search for a scalper selling the tickets, and start a conversation with him.[7] He'd show you all the options in a chat bubble that displayed the various ticket prices. You can also book a restaurant or hail a cab, straight from WeChat. There are no other apps to download. With chat as an interface, the seams that we've become used to on our smartphones—the annoyance and tediousness of switching between apps, ferrying little bits of information from here to there like the smartphone's very own lapdog—simply disappear.

One reason developers think this shift happened first in China was simply that the vast majority of Chinese didn't grow up using desktop computers. Much like smartphone users across the developing world—including India and Kenya, as we've seen before—they didn't grow up assuming that you found features through drop-down menus, and they didn't assume that you got to the web through a browser. Not only did those expectations not exist, they had been replaced altogether, thanks to a breakneck introduction to modernity fueled by China's rapid growth. "The barrier in the U.S. is that people are used to using their phones in certain ways," said Connell. Chat became the best place to learn what a smartphone could do simply because chat was also the entry point for brand-new digital citizens. Today, it's easy enough to find Chinese grandmothers who'll ask their phones what's on TV or what the weather's like. But ask them how the internet works or how to type in a URL on a web browser, and you'll probably get a baffled shrug. "It's funny how this new era is built on something we did on day one as humans," Connell mused.[8]

For someone like Connell, this wasn't interesting merely because China's example offered a better way of building user-friendly phones. Rather, it seemed likely to be a microcosm for the "next billion"—smartphone users in India, Africa, and elsewhere, who aren't always literate but who can nonetheless get what they need by talking into their phones. And not just in developing countries, but even in the West, where teenagers have never carried the burden of metaphors about desktops and windows and hyperlinks and websites. The Chinese example seemed like an analogue for how the rest of the world might come of age with technology, without the shadow of a different era of user-friendliness, without climbing the same ladder of metaphors as previous generations.

With the intimation of a new computing paradigm on the horizon, the tech giants started to pour their billions into competing with Siri. Microsoft's own explorations began with a so-called Wizard of Oz experiment: They tested how humans reacted to two fake assistants, whose responses were actually generated by unseen people typing in another room. The first fake assistant solicited the human to help train it; the other simply guessed what a person needed and spat out the right answer. It turned out that users were far more forgiving of the former, and wary of the latter, even if its suggestions were spot-on. There was something about training the assistant that made humans more willing to trust it. But why?[9]

In 2013, one of the people tasked with figuring that out was Kat Holmes, a design researcher by training. One of her team's first insights was that to figure out how humans might come to trust a digital assistant, they could simply shadow real human assistants who'd served celebrities and billionaires to watch how they garnered trust over time—how they went about choosing the right time to make a personal recommendation, how they decided when to be discreet.

By odd coincidence, soon after Holmes embarked on that project, the first trailers had started airing for the film *Her*, directed by Spike Jonze. Set in a distant but familiar future, it opens with Theodore Twombly, a melancholy loner played by Joaquin Phoenix, who decides to buy a digital personal assistant. At home, he starts the software by placing a tiny device in his ear, then hears a clinical male voice: "Mr. Theodore Twombly, welcome to the world's first artificially intelligent operating system. We'd like to ask you a few questions." He answers questions about his personality, and stumbles for a second when asked about his relationship with his mother. The computer issues a curt "Thank you." Then another voice, that of Scarlett Johansson, comes on. "Hello, I'm here." Twombly manages an incredulous "Hi," and gets a chipper, startlingly warm reply, "Hi! I'm Samantha." Samantha chastises Theo for talking to her like a robot. She wants him to loosen up, to talk to her like he would anyone else. Soon, Samantha, the operating system, is filling almost every gap in Twombly's life, waking him up for meetings, drafting his emails—and then listening and joking with him late into the night. Twombly is at first amused by Samantha's relentless curiosity about him. Then he's hungry for it, and for Samantha's ability to uncover things about him that he'd never had the self-confidence to discover for himself.

The movie became an inspiration for the Cortana team at Microsoft because it painted a vision of technology in which we no longer deal with apps or the countless seams in our digital lives—seams that result from an ecosystem in which every app shouts for our limited attention, and where it might require six different apps to make a dinner date. Theodore Twombly didn't have to do any of that; Samantha would simply take care of all the details not worth belaboring. *Her* depicted a future where technology had become totally natural, mediated by the power of voice. As Holmes told me later, "That film helped solidify for us that human-to-human interaction should be the metaphor for design." In trying to understand how computers should interact with humans, the best guide was how *humans* interacted with humans.[10]

When you watch *Her*, it is startling how futuristic life seems—and how little you see that actually looks futuristic, whether it's gadgets or cars. The effect is uncanny when compared to most sci-fi movies, where technology makes the characters superhuman.[11] I met with K. K. Barrett, the production designer for *Her*, to ask him how he'd come up with such a humane vision for technology's role in our lives, compelling enough to influence a tech giant such as Microsoft.[12] Jonze, the director, had come to Barrett with a script that he'd been noodling on for five years, ever since he'd seen a primitive voice-controlled computer program. He had started thinking, too, about online dating, and how you could never know for sure who was on the other end. Jonze let those two ideas tumble around in his head until a story emerged. When it did, Apple happened to have just introduced Siri. Jonze was irked that his script had a sudden ripped-from-the-headlines plausibility, and was anxious about how to make it *not* about tech headlines.

Barrett is in his mid-sixties, older than you might expect for a movie-production designer whose career highlights—including *Lost in Translation* and *Being John Malkovich*—sprouted from collaborations with Jonze and his ex-partner, Sofia Coppola, two of America's hipster power brokers. He wears black from head to toe, and blue-tinted specs beneath steel-gray hair that piles atop his head in drifts. His approach to his work might best be described as "do the opposite." For *Where the Wild Things Are*, Barrett knew the audience would expect lush, sun-dappled jungles. So instead, he set long stretches of the movie in a sprawling landscape of ash. He literally burned the jungle down. With *Her*, Barrett realized quickly that if people paid any attention to the technology, then his own design would have failed.

"You shouldn't put things in the film that undermine what you want to say, and technology was in the way," he told me. "It was a story about people communicating." Just like so many designers we've met in the course of this book, Barrett realized that what we want out of technology is really defined by what we want from each other. "You stop and say, what do you want a computer to do? And you realize you want it to be like a friend. You input the parameters of a dilemma and they help you solve a problem, not unlike a psychiatrist or a good listener." The problem was, technology was always adding new things to everyday life. The way to create a truly different world wasn't to put more technology in it. Rather, you had to take all that stuff out. "If you want to make something feel different," Barrett said, "you just take away everything unnecessary." It was as good advice as any about how to map the future of what "user friendly" should become: a future in which high technology has become invisible enough to lead us back to how things were *before* high technology.

It's common to hear technologists articulate that same dream of making technology so useful that it's invisible. But how will it become so? Simply by weaving itself into the social fabric that preceded it; by becoming more humane. The teleology of technology's march is that it should mirror us better—that it should travel an arc of increasing humaneness.

Despite his long-running success as a veteran technology designer, August de los Reyes affords himself just a few luxuries. A few years ago, he became obsessed with finally buying himself the most comfortable bed he could imagine—a once-in-a-decade splurge. He started with a pillow-top mattress that felt like a cloud. Then he bought the highest-thread-count sheets he could find. The day after it had all arrived he woke up in his new bed feeling contented in every nerve. There were, however, a couple of niggles that he noticed: The puffiness of the mattress made its edge hard to find, and the high-thread-count sheets were slick. He didn't think much of them at the time. Then, one lazy afternoon playing hooky from work, he absentmindedly tried to sit on the edge of the bed, missed it by just a few inches, slipped, and fell hard. His life was about to change.[13]

De los Reyes was born with arthritis of the spine, which makes his vertebrae sensitive to breaks. So he'd always been careful not to put himself in danger of falling: making sure to grab the handrail on a stairwell, making sure not to step into the shower too quickly. But this thing with the edge of the bed had escaped his attention. Besides, after the fall, he'd rushed to the emergency room, where doctors told him everything was fine. He went home, relieved. But in the days afterward, de los Reyes still felt something wrong. There was an odd soreness in his back, a blurry pain that grew. At night, he tried to go to the bathroom and couldn't. He rushed to the hospital, where X-rays revealed a fracture in his spine that the doctors had missed. For days, his spinal cord had been swelling up, pressing against the broken bone in his back. A nurse wheeled him to radiology for a CT scan. He lay back, watching the gray ceiling tiles scroll by. Then, as he was being eased from a stretcher into the CT scanner, an orderly fumbled the handhold, banging de los Reyes onto the gantry. Blinding white pain seized his entire body and de los Reyes knew instantly that he'd never walk again.

The hospital internment was a haze, and worst of all was the timing: He'd just met someone new, and he was just months into a new job as the head of Xbox's digital design team. This was his dream, because he had an almost spiritual attachment to video games, believing that play in all its forms was a moral imperative. Now all the pieces of his life that he'd laid out so beautifully sat unused and mute. Finally, after months having not checked his email or used his cell phone, his sister brought him a laptop. He checked his email. He checked his voice mail. There were dozens of messages from the man he'd been dating, baffled at his sudden and total disappearance. The outlines of his former life began to return. He felt that to be himself again, he had to go back to work. After a mere three months, he did.

I asked de los Reyes once what made him want to be a designer, and he told me about how, when he was a kid, he loved to stay up late watching horror movies. But the only one that he couldn't shake by the morning was a documentary about the elusive, bloodstained visions of Nostradamus. One thing he liked about a proper horror movie was how it tested you: how, if the terror got to be too much, you had to step out of it and see it for a fiction, remind yourself it was all just a movie. But to a young de los Reyes watching an HBO documentary meant to scare the bejesus out of someone like him, Nostradamus was different. In 1555, Nostradamus had seemed to predict Hitler, who "by his tongue will seduce a great troop," and a "heavenly dart" that would destroy Hiroshima and Nagasaki. Nostradamus saw even worse to come: an order overturned and rivers running red. When morning finally came, de los Reyes told his mother about how all the horrible things Nostradamus wrote always came true. She just laughed! And then she said, "So what will you do about it?" To de los Reyes, the obvious answer was: Make a better world.[14]

Today, de los Reyes isn't one to watch things unfold slowly when he could instead make them happen fast. Being back in the office was actually a balm, because the workplace had been fastidiously designed to accommodate wheelchairs, with wide halls and low elevator buttons. The problem was the rest of his life. He'd try to meet friends at a favorite restaurant, only to discover that he couldn't get inside because of one tiny curb. He'd be steering his wheelchair down the sidewalk, enjoying the sun, when a tipped-over garbage can would force him to change his whole route. It was as if he were living in some strange shadow world that belonged to someone else. As he began to see it, his new disabilities said less about him than they did about the heedlessness of the world around him. Put another way, what most people called disability was instead a design problem. As we spoke in his office, secluded in a quiet corner of a colorful new design studio built on Microsoft's sprawling campus in Redmond, Washington, de los Reyes's eyes widened: "That's what radicalized me." The question was, radicalized to what? As a designer who'd found his calling by staring down Nostradamus, what was he going to do? Working with Kat Holmes, the researcher at Microsoft who'd been tasked with helping define the personality of its digital assistant, de los Reyes eventually hit upon a quixotic, even visionary experiment in empathy.

Perhaps you're reading this book with your phone by your side, checking your email whenever your attention drifts, tapping text messages to a friend. You sit at the end of a long line of inventions that might never have existed but for people with disabilities: the keyboard on your phone, the telecommunications lines it connects with, the inner workings of email. In 1808, Pellegrino Turri built the first typewriter so that his blind lover, Countess Carolina Fantoni da Fivizzano, could write letters more legibly. In 1872, Alexander Graham Bell invented the telephone to support his work helping the deaf. And in 1972, Vint Cerf programmed the first email protocols for the nascent internet. He believed fervently in the power of electronic letters, because electronic messaging was the best way to communicate with his wife, who was deaf, while he was at work.

Perhaps one day someone will write a history of the internet in which that great series of tubes will emerge not as some miracle of technical progress meant to connect people faster and easier but rather a chain of inventions each meant to help more and more types of people to better communicate. But the most critical piece of the history will be this: Disability is so often an engine of innovation, simply because humans will invent ways to satisfy their needs, no matter their limitations.

This may sound suspiciously close to the cliché that necessity breeds invention. But a more accurate interpretation is that each of those inventors, by empathizing with someone whose problems they had become intimately familiar with, was able to create things that they might never have created for themselves. Their empathy allowed them to see past the specifics of what they knew. Somehow, in solving problems for someone at the edges of experience, they created products—from the typewriter to the telephone—that turned out to be useful to everyone. That dynamic of finding innovation at the edges highlights a tension that existed in the very roots of design: a focus on the mythical idea of the average consumer. Designers began to strain against this assumption by the 1970s.

One was Patricia Moore, who in 1978 arrived in New York fresh out of college, having landed a design job with Raymond Loewy. Even then, the office seemed like a museum diorama of early corporate man. Moore recalled managers who, when Loewy was out of the office, went out for three-martini lunches and came back too drunk to be productive. In an office filled with female secretaries, Moore was one of the few female designers on the staff. "I remember the chief model maker used to wear a cobbler's apron and had a stogie in his mouth all day long. He used to spit in his trash can," said Moore, over dinner in Phoenix, where she's worked for several years, designing things such as the city's quietly perfect streetcars. "He used to tell me, 'We don't need no fuckin' broads here.'"[15]

In fact, they did. The United States was fighting the Cold War and the State Department was scheming to find new ways into the hearts and minds of everyday Russians. So the State Department began paying American designers to work for Russian companies. There was no design firm more American than Loewy and Associates. But the State Department wanted more women on their staff. Loewy finally found Moore, and she helped win the commission. Her first task was to work with a Russian manufacturing company to create the interior of a family car and then the interior of a hydrofoil. Visiting Russia was a shock and a heartbreak. Moore would ride the bus in Moscow, seeing elderly people struggling along the sidewalk, flustered, as the young whizzed around them. She realized how often she'd seen the same thing in America. But being a foreigner in this strange place—a place where society had geared itself to the socialist dream but nevertheless seemed blind to so many of its own people—allowed Moore to look with fresh eyes upon details as mundane as people crossing the street. When she was back in New York, Moore unknowingly flouted the unspoken rules of the office by sending a memo directly to Loewy, suggesting that by focusing only on the average person, with average needs and average expectations, designers were failing in their duty to make lives better. What about the elderly? No one was thinking about them. But to think about them, Moore thought, you had to *be* them. And so Moore, with Loewy's blessing, went about creating a costume that would simulate what it was like to be seventy—complete with bindings on her joints to limit their movements and a girdle to simulate a bad back. She went on to wear that suit in 116 cities over four years.[16] Of course, designers today don't all dress up and try to pretend to be those they're designing for. The more consequential thing that Moore was wrestling with was that designers should get close to real people, learn from them, and take them as they are—the same insight that would birth IDEO ten years later, and also Smart Design, founded by Dan Formosa, who was Pat Moore's husband at the time.

This great chain of influence, from Alphonse Chapanis to Raymond Loewy to Pat Moore to IDEO, finally draws us close to August de los Reyes, Microsoft, and a pileup of ideas that, through sheer chance, ended up transforming the company's approach to design. De los Reyes happened to return to work at a decisive moment for Microsoft. Satya Nadella was about to be appointed CEO, which lit a fuse that snaked through the company's machinery. Among the first changes to happen was that Albert Shum, who'd become famous inside Microsoft for leading the ambitious, brazenly "flat" and pointedly non-skeuomorphic design of Windows Mobile, was appointed to head up design for nearly all of Microsoft. Shum must have scratched his head, pondering what "design at Microsoft" even meant. After all, this was a company with 130,000 employees, countless product groups, and enough internal feuding to exhaust the Hatfields and McCoys. It was so large that surely its design approach differed from either Apple's or Google's. But it was also a company so large that finding a clear point of view seemed a little absurd. Shum pushed his deputies to figure out what Microsoft's design ethos was.

De los Reyes spied an opportunity, albeit hazily. He knew the concept of universal design, first articulated by Ron Mace, then adopted by Pat Moore. The idea was that by designing with people with disabilities in mind—designing so that they can have universal access—we can create better products for everyone else. Perhaps the best example of that came from OXO. As the legend goes, the founder of OXO, Sam Farber, had recently retired and was renting a home in the South of France with his wife, Betsey. On a sunny day, the two of them set about making an apple tart from scratch. They divvied up the work, and Betsey started peeling the apples. Sam's share of the chores drew him away, and when he returned, he found Betsey in tears. Arthritis had recently set into her hands, and now she simply couldn't hold the familiar metal apple peeler. Farber eventually tapped Dan Formosa to design a peeler that, by virtue of being comfortable enough for those with arthritis to use, would be better and easier for everyone to use. The insight spawned a company that today is probably as ubiquitous as any in American housewares, one whose best products have come from studying people at the edges of daily life instead of the comfortable center. Examples like this are in fact bountiful. De los Reyes, confined to a wheelchair, knew of another one: the curb cut, the low concrete ramp that allows wheelchair users to mount a sidewalk, but which also helps everyone, from the elderly crossing the street to parents pushing strollers.

De los Reyes was proposing a metaphor. He was hoping to find the digital world's equivalent of the curb cut, something elegant that let everyone live a little easier. By learning how the overlooked, ranging from dyslexics to the deaf, pick their way through a world the rest of us navigate with little trouble, the hope was that one could actually build better products for everyone else. The idea was that in order to build machines that adapt to humans better, you needed a better process for watching how humans adapted to one another and to their world. "The point isn't to solve for a problem," such as typing when you're blind, said Holmes. "We're flipping it." They were finding the expertise and ingenuity that arises naturally when people are forced to live a life different from most.

Let's say you'd like to build a phone that's easier to interact with while you're driving and can't look at the screen. You could try to study people driving with their phones. Or you could study how the blind use their phones. What workarounds do they use to determine when their phones are paired with another device when they can't look to see? What aural feedback do apps need to provide when opened? You could build those features into a phone, so that by serving someone with a disability, you serve everyone else better. Holmes put it more succinctly: "We're reframing disability as an opportunity."

We've already examined one product that started with a difficult, impossibly nuanced problem: Ripple, the device that attempted to remake the act of calling 911, so that, at the press of a button, a new kind of first responder would reach out to help. Ripple started with the problem of sexual assault, and only in trying to rethink the needs of a specific group of people did the inventors come up with something that might be useful in many different situations. Other examples hide in plain sight. The famous Aeron chair, which has become synonymous with infinitely adjustable office comfort, didn't begin life as an investigation into the sitting habits of worker bees. It started as a research project to create a breathable mesh sitting structure that wouldn't cause the elderly to develop bedsores.[17] Both Ripple and Aeron were examples of people finding bigger solutions by trying to solve a harder, more specialized problem—and then stumbling onto something much more universal. So why not start with the hard problem? Design progresses only when it fits meaningful solutions to new problems. Over time, as our own quality of life improves, the problems get harder to find. That's what it means for the world to be better and better designed—it means the problems become harder and harder to see. You eventually need new, novel frames of reference to see them—whether that's by seeing how differently the digital world works in China or how many gaps exist in digital life for those at the margins.

Kat Holmes and others at Microsoft began trying to use inclusive design to address myriad opportunities. One project yielded a font and system of text wrapping that makes reading easier for dyslexics—but also faster for those without dyslexia. Working with the blind yielded a smoother registration process for new Windows users, with clearer and better-timed, more concise user prompts; working with the blind, and screen-reader technology, yielded a captioning tool for PowerPoint presentations that would translate for the presenter in real time. That project, in turn, morphed and melded into a retooling of Skype that provided real-time captioning—then real-time language translation, so that people could hold conference calls without speaking each other's language. In each case, making technology more assistive spawned innovations whose scope was far greater than the initial germ. This brings to mind Pellegrino Turri and his typewriter, Alexander Graham Bell and his telephone, and Vint Cerf and email—these were inventors who all started with people with disabilities in mind but eventually helped us all. But the difference is that while each of those inventors stumbled upon an analogue that helped them invent something that everyone else could use, Microsoft was starting with the analogues. They were seeking out those who were different, confident that they've already come up with exactly the solutions that the rest of us need.

In Redmond, de los Reyes and I watched behind a two-way mirror as the inclusive-design process began to unfold on yet another project. Sitting at his side, I could hear the motors whirring in de los Reyes's wheelchair. He has to be vigilant about constantly adjusting his posture, using his chair's control stick, so that bedsores don't set in while he sits all day. On the other side of the glass, a young grad student with an artfully scruffy beard and newsboy cap was describing why he, as a deaf gamer, stuck to playing *World of Warcraft* on a PC, even though he would have loved to play *Destiny* on Xbox One: the PC's keyboard let him chat with teammates in a way that simply wasn't possible on Xbox. Without the ability to quickly communicate on Microsoft's console, he was relegated to subservient roles. The solution might have seemed obvious: better keyboards for gamers on Xbox. But the researcher in the room kept prodding. "A keyboard means I can lead my team on a raid. A controller means I have to follow," the gamer said, his frustration simmering. De los Reyes perked up and imagined that one could create a huddle before a raid started, which would allow deaf players to strategize with their teammates in advance. That happened to be exactly the kind of collaborative planning the best gamers use. What if, by designing pregame strategy sessions into the natural flow of a game, you made it easier not only for deaf gamers but for all players to kick more ass? It was an idea that might have been invisible without this new design process. For de los Reyes, the promise wasn't just a better XBOX, or even a better Microsoft. Eyes widening with excitement, he later said, "If we're successful, we're going to change the way products are designed across the industry. Period. That's my vision." While it hasn't yet happened, today inclusive design has become a byword in the industry. Attitudes toward disability are changing.

Even if the design industry changes, what problems will it look to solve? Today, we are drowning in interactions with smartphones and smart devices, such as our cars and homes—all of which suddenly want to talk to our phones as well. We live in a world of countless transitions. Instead of there being one device, there is actually an infinite number of handoffs between devices. There needs to be a new kind of design process to manage those seams. "The assumptions about computing are that our devices are one-on-one with visual interactions. The design discipline is built around those assumptions," Holmes pointed out. "They assume that we're one person all the time."

This represents a radical shift in the thinking set down in the time of Henry Dreyfuss, with his assumption that users could be measured and charted, and that who they were, in some sense, could be fixed in the drawing of a human being. We don't simply have a single persona, readily drawn on a storyboard. When you're a parent with a sprained wrist, or you're reaching for your phone while holding your groceries, you share a world, albeit briefly, with someone who has only ever been able to use one hand. "There is no such thing as a normal human," Holmes said. "Our capabilities are always changing." The particular problems that Microsoft was identifying came down to problems with the mobile lives we lead: phones in hand, constantly shifting through our days, we sometimes struggle with our devices when we need something but are too distracted or preoccupied to actually use them. The phone, in order to bend to our needs, can't be one thing all the time.

It's easy enough to say that technology will become more humane. It's hard to say how that will happen. But the only way to expand the universe of people who get counted when we imagine who the "user" is in "user friendly" is by bringing context and human messiness into a design process that typically subsumes differences into averages. By finding analogues at the edge of experience, or in the details of everyday life, you might sniff clues about where the future is headed. Making things easier to use is often another form of arbitrage: You find users at the extremes, solving problems that others might take for granted. You bring those needs and those ideas into the mainstream, as products simple enough that no one has to think twice. The art lies in finding the path from one set of users to another. Of course, the processes of ferrying one insight to another place entirely is contingent and uncertain. Balanced against that uncertainty is the fact that it keeps happening: in the creation of the internet, in the design of the Aeron chair, even in the story of how the computer itself became mainstream. For Microsoft, it happened again, in a way that may end up shaping much more than any single piece of software.

The project that Holmes helped with, shadowing human personal assistants and learning how they eventually earned the trust of their clients, led to a series of recommended behaviors for Cortana, Microsoft's competitor to Siri. Following the human example, Cortana was meant to be transparent, because the best personal assistants are transparent about what they know of their clients, and why they've done what they've done—some even keep logs that the client can see anytime. Cortana would also be mindful and honest about its limitations, because good personal assistants don't make a flippant joke when they can't do something; they admit what they do and do not know. They try to recover for what they can't do by suggesting the things they can.

Years later, those principles morphed into Microsoft's framework for designing for artificial intelligence. One ("humans are the heroes") is not to overshadow or edge out the capabilities and preferences of the human; in other words, not to overshadow or shoehorn the client. Another is to "honor societal values" while respecting the social context of an interaction—again, to be discreet and well-mannered. And another is to "evolve over time," to learn the whims and nuances of a person's preferences.[18]

These might seem banal, but their absence could produce unsettling results. Microsoft's engineers had invented a new feature in PowerPoint that would use AI algorithms to scan the presentation you were building, trying to figure out better layouts for each slide based on millions of other PowerPoint presentations it had been trained on. Click on the Designer tab, and instead of your haphazardly pasted picture and bullet points, you might see three different options, with better typeface choices and a frame around the image that matches its tone. But when Microsoft was first testing Designer, it actually felt uncanny and weird. "In the way it was first tested, the tone of the words and animations in Designer made it feel like the computer knew better than you," explained Jon Friedman, whose job was to lead the vision for Microsoft's Office suite. There was something even more uncanny: If you kept following Designer's recommendations, the end result was a presentation that didn't feel like you'd made it anymore. The computer, it seems, was taking over, step-by-step. Magnify that kind of thing across hundreds of apps, and the world would start looking scary indeed.[19]

Eventually, Microsoft fixed that problem, unveiling a subtly more helpful, more neutral feature that made recommendations based on not only the best presentations it had seen but the rest of *your* presentation style. Behind those changes lay the company's governing principles for AI design—letting humans be the heroes, and being sensitive to context. Who knows where else those ideas have yet to be applied—and where else they might be needed, but are not yet being used.

In May 2018, during its annual developer conference, Google blundered through the looking glass when it unveiled a demo of Duplex, a machine-learning-powered service that could call up a business on your behalf and make an appointment for you. The audience on hand rippled with delight as the digital assistant called a hair salon, speaking as if it were a real human being. Sounding utterly natural, saying "mmhmm" in assent, the robot made its way through an entire conversation that ended in a 10:00 a.m. reservation on May 3.

But the day after came the backlash, from people worrying about the ethics of a robot posing as a human. ("Google's AI Sounds Like a Human on the Phone—Should We Be Worried?" read one headline on *The Verge*.)[20] Google was forced to almost immediately announce that its robots, at the start of any conversation, would state they were machines.[21] But amid that justifiable worry, what went ignored was a more subtle, far-reaching reality: that a robot which speaks to us *has* to act human for us to want to engage with it. If Duplex had called up a receptionist at a hair salon sounding merely like another robocall, that receptionist would have hung up. We saw how Apple tried to make interfaces that looked like real-world stuff—leather calendars, bookshelves—hoping to make them easier to use. Today, skeuomorphism doesn't just lie in tools aping the tools that came before them, but rather in how machines mime our behavior, down to the *ums* and *ahs*. The right suggestion, made at the most tactful time, becomes what wood and metal were to another generation of designers—material waiting to be bent toward a purpose. Both our behavior and our mores are now the material for design. Consider again the Duplex example. Part of the backlash seemed to stem from the fact that the persona of the robot voice was all wrong, sounding not like a professional working on your behalf, and instead more like a teenager ordering pizza. While they had built it to sound impressively human, it seemed the engineers hadn't asked what kind of human persona would be appropriate. We've seen hints about how our personalities and mores are seeping into our machines—for example, in the way that pedestrians, when approaching a self-driving Audi, would merrily cross the street if the car simply slowed down like a conscientious driver would. But this world is a strange one, and there are strange choices to be made.

In 2017, Capital One revealed that it was creating a chatbot called Eno that could check your credit card balance, search your transaction history, and see your billing history. Just as Microsoft had, Capital One concluded that Eno shouldn't fake its origins—but also realized that a humanlike personality could be a valuable tool. "Eno knows it's not a human," explained Steph Hay, Capital One's VP of design. "Transparency is at the top of the list in our corporate values. So Eno is 'bot and proud.'" This turned out to be a functional benefit: People using Eno were more forgiving of its shortcomings if it fessed up to being a robot, rather than trying to pretend to be human.[22]

But Capital One also discovered that if Eno had some sense of humor and could talk to people about *other* things besides banking, people would use it more. The fact that Eno could "drop a rhyme" or an intentionally terrible pun was just as functional as how quickly it could find your March balance. "You would be surprised how delighted people are when they can extend the conversation beyond a functional-use case," said Audra Koklys, Capital One's head of AI design. "They were texting Eno all kinds of things, they were saying 'please' and 'thank you,' as if Eno was a human being."[23] Shades of Clifford Nass, the professor we met in chapter 4, who showed that humans inevitably treat computers as people. Koklys had previously worked at Pixar, where she cut her teeth on the film *Ratatouille* and learned how to bring digital characters to life. At Capital One, that was a surprisingly useful skill. As it happened, making Eno simply capable as a robot banker wasn't enough to keep users engaged. "In the end, we're trying to build a relationship and gain trust," Koklys said. "The way we're doing that is through character."

Koklys and Hay explained that an enormous amount of work was going into mapping all the possible conversations Eno could have, and how Eno would respond when it had reached the limits of its capabilities. I asked Koklys to start describing Eno's character and how it might emerge during a conversation. Eno, for example, would never be funny or cute when it failed to understand. It would use humor only to show empathy with someone. "Eno has core traits, a backstory, and things Eno likes and dislikes," she said. "We actually designed character flaws because we found that's how people connect with characters." I asked what that meant: What was Eno's personality, and what were her personality flaws?

What ensued was one of the strangest conversations I've ever had. Hay and Koklys kept muting the conference line, conferring about their answers. Then they would come back on and say exactly what they'd already said, in a different way. This happened several times over the course of fifteen or so minutes. The conversation grew tense. Eventually, Hay shut the line of questioning down, explaining that Eno's personality was Capital One's intellectual property, and they wouldn't be explaining it. I protested. Could they really not explain the behavior of a bot that I could, when it finally became public, simply talk to myself and describe however I wanted? Wouldn't it be better just to state for the record what the truth was? It was not. I asked if the chatbot trend was merely a fad, and Hay demurred. "It's here to stay, and it's going everywhere. You see it in the investments of the Big Five banks." The call ended awkwardly.

Afterward, I recounted to myself what had just happened. A major bank had declined to reveal the personality traits of a robot it had created, because the bank believed that the personality of its robot would make people more apt to do business with them. We are still far away from the world of *Her*. But we are already dealing with a world in which computers are becoming a finer and finer reflection of how we're made. They're luring us in not just with clean and orderly buttons, but with predictions about how we feel, based on knowledge about who we are.

Disney MagicBand (2013)

8

Personalization

Movies might seem like Disney's core business, but they are really marketing vehicles. Most of the company's billions come from turning movie hits into franchises: first with toys and TV shows, then with theme-park rides that imprint kids anew, powering sequels and selling more toys. Amusement parks are the flywheel in Disney's cash machine. But by 2007 there were unmistakable signs that something was wrong in the Magic Kingdom. The numbers had started to turn, the most worrying being "intent to return." Only half of new visitors to Disney World said that they'd come back, owing to lines and ticket costs. Thanks to a park running at twice the capacity that Walt Disney had planned for, there were lines everywhere, for rides and ice cream and bathrooms and food. Then there was the hassle of tracking tickets to the park and tickets to rides, and receipts and credit cards and maps and keys. Disney executives whispered to one another that the parks, once a bedrock of their quarterly results, might just be a "burning platform." They worried, "If we miss out on that next generation of guests, suddenly our burning platform is fully on fire," one of them told *Fast Company*'s Austin Carr. "Panic mode."[1]

In 2008, Meg Crofton, who was then president of Disney Resorts, assembled her top deputies and told them to fix it. "We were looking for pain points," she said. "What are the barriers to getting into the experience faster?"[2] This notion of pain points was an intimation of the design-thinking process they were hoping to emulate, and the path they would follow next. They started by diagramming what a day at Disney World looked like for a typical family (a process called journey mapping in human-centered design). This was a cat's cradle of crisscrossing paths: The day started when families would sprint from the opening gates to grab advance tickets for the most popular rides. Later, families would often split up, to make sure everyone could do what they wanted. They might cross in front of Cinderella's castle twenty times a day. Looking at that map of what people went through was like putting a well-loved old couch on the curb: By the harsh light of day, you saw the stains you'd been living with for years and thought, I can't believe we let it get like this. Not only that, the world was changing. By 2008, if you were a business executive with an eye toward coming disruptions, it was already clear that the year-old iPhone was poised to redefine expectations for convenience. What happened when the kids who'd grown up with the world on demand started contemplating where to take *their* kids on vacation? "On the surface, we had super happy guests, but in reality, we were making them go through so much hassle at the park that down the road, they would simply say, '*No mas!*'" said one former manager.[3]

John Padgett was part of the fix-it team flying back and forth between Disney headquarters in Burbank, California, and Walt Disney World, in Orlando, Florida. They were all on the plane again early one morning, taxiing for takeoff, when he started thumbing through the SkyMall catalog, a new one that he hadn't seen twenty times before. Padgett spied the Trion-Z, a rubber wristband that placed a magnet over the wearer's pulse point, under the dubious theory that the magnet could improve your balance and your golf swing. It was pseudo-science, but also radical: It assumed that we'd attach little techno bits to our bodies to better ourselves. Padgett wondered if a wristband might be the key to an entirely new Disney World.[4]

By 2013, there was gossip in the design community about what Disney had created, a wristband that rendered every bit of commerce in the park invisible and had cost nearly $1 billion to develop. In 2015, after wrangling with Disney's press minders for two years, I finally went to see for myself. As I walked the park, the most remarkable thing about the Disney MagicBands was that they were already as ubiquitous as sunburns and giant frozen lemonades. They were already invisible.

Today, Be Our Guest, Disney World's *Beauty and the Beast*–themed restaurant, is such a meticulous fantasy that it feels not like 2-D, or 3-D, but 2½-D, like a pop-up rising from a storybook. You approach through a crumbling Gothic gate—airbrushed fiberglass, actually—then cross a tiny drawbridge flanked by scowling gargoyles. You look up at a mauve, parapeted miniature castle, peeking from behind a fake ridge of fake granite. There's a weird dilation in scale. The gate is more or less normal size; the bridge is just a little bit squished, and the castle is made tiny so as to look very far away. These compressed spatial effects were a psychological hack invented by Walt Disney himself to make visitors feel larger than their everyday lives. It works. It feels like you're walking a half mile with just a few steps, a jump cut to another place. The entrance itself is teensy, so that the Disney staff can buttonhole everyone who enters with a cheerful hello.

If you've arrived wearing a MagicBand, then there's a telling bit of friction that disappears: Sit anywhere you like, and the food simply finds you. "How will they find our table? It's like magic!" I heard a woman tell her family as they sat. The couple's young son flitted around the table like a moth. Soon, the family's food had arrived, delivered by a smiling young man pushing a serving cart.

The woman's sensible question faded with the rising aroma of French onion soup and roast beef sandwiches. This was by design. When Disney's executives were deciding which experiences might be overhauled in the park, they focused on Be Our Guest, whose popularity meant that when visitors arrived, exhausted and tired, they'd be met with another line. To fix all that, the family I was eavesdropping on was shadowed by a chorus of technology the moment everyone crossed the moat, a chorus geared toward serving them invisibly. *How will they find our table?* It was the MagicBands, and the technology silently working inside them, which could eliminate every slightest wait they might have encountered: the bus ride from the airport; checking into their hotel and getting into their room; the entry to the park; paying for anything inside. In each MagicBand was a radio chip transmitting forty feet in every direction. When that family had arrived, the kitchen got the message: two French onion soups, two roast beef sandwiches. When that family finally sat down, their MagicBands pinged the radio receiver in the table. The server then got their coordinates and found them, knowing exactly what they'd ordered.

Today, we are surrounded more and more by technology like this, meant to serve us without our ever having to ask or even to push a button. No matter how often we say we're creeped out by technology, we acclimate surprisingly quickly if it anticipates what we want. Just consider how a smartphone tells you when you need to leave for an appointment, or how Gmail now suggests what you'll type. Today, those "smart replies" make up over 10 percent of all messages sent with Gmail.[5] Today, Google Maps is, by default, studded with your history of location searches and events arranged with friends, all in the effort to anticipate rather than merely respond. The convenience takes hold before the goose bumps can set in. The utility is so obvious that consent has simply been assumed. Yet the surprising thing revealed at Disney World was that when we see the same ease applied not just on our phones but in the environment around us, we usually shrug and dig into our roast beef sandwiches.

This is the reason the MagicBands might have been worth $1 billion to Disney. Using them, the company had managed to recast its cold business logic—the chance to turn over tables quicker by eliminating many aspects of waiter service—into something a vacationing family of three had actually described as magic. Somehow, Disney World had turned a high-tech surveillance operation into a delight. When the MagicBands were being designed, that alchemy seemed to afford endless possibilities. When people crossed that fairy-tale drawbridge and saw that castle, sensors could pick them up as they approached. In the original imagining of Be Our Guest, the host would greet them by name, and ask about the rides they'd taken—knowing exactly where they'd gone and what they'd reserved for the rest of their trip. In the original vision for the MagicBands, the park cameras, combined with the park sensors, would have been able to stitch together a movie of every person's visit, to be revealed as a souvenir at the end—as if you'd been a guest in your very own *Truman Show*. And yet those features weren't ever flipped on—not because they couldn't be, but because somewhere along the way Disney had lost its will.

This was a surprise. Of all the places for such ambitions to be carried out, it should have been Disney World, which was founded on Walt Disney's obsession with painting cutting-edge technology in its cheeriest hues. As Neal Gabler wrote in his definitive biography, Disney wanted to craft "a better reality than the one outside." His fervor was born of watching his first park, Disneyland, become a blight. In the 1950s, its runaway success had transformed the cityscape around it into a hive of tacky hotels, garish billboards, and seediness. Heartbroken, he concluded that you couldn't create magic if you didn't first create order at a grand scale. With his company sliding into financial disarray after a string of movie busts, he borrowed against his own life insurance to fund the "Florida project." Where Disneyland was the size of the reservoir in Central Park, Disney World would be forty square miles, roughly the size of San Francisco. Walt Disney would go to sleep every night with the plans pasted up on the tiles above his bed. He would die just a few years later, looking up at those tiles.[6]

The park couldn't have been built without an abiding faith in a user-friendly world where commerce was social progress, and better design meant a better life. Where there wasn't a technological solution, Walt Disney resorted to ingenious stagecraft. His vision started in the tunnels. When you visit Disney World, you're not on flat ground—rather, you stand atop one of the largest mounds ever built, veined with burrows, created so that the "cast members" playing Goofy or Mickey can suddenly appear where they're meant to be, and disappear like on a stage—never to be seen smoking or gossiping or bitching about the smell of their suits. Even the gaps between the rides were designed to make art: They were vast areas of blankness that cleared the palate between scenes of Main Street or the American West. Walt Disney was designing an experience based on the aesthetic of the movies and theater, where everything inessential has to be stripped away so that reality can be concentrated.[7]

Forty years after it opened, today's Disney World does indeed offer a glimpse of a frictionless world with annoyances buffed away by technology. But only a glimpse, because the MagicBands, and the original dream for them, buckled under reality. The difficulties Disney saw in realizing its vision show why giant companies hoping to build the user-friendly world are reaching the limit of what they can create. It isn't from a lack of design, technology, or vision; nor is it because we're simply not ready. Rather, the difficulties lie in how the companies themselves are designed. The alluring visions being dreamed up in places such as Disney World and the tech behemoths in Silicon Valley are hitting a new limit. The dilemma lies in somehow convincing thousands of people to work in concert on the tiniest details so that the seams never show, and getting those tiny details to reflect a unified experience. And yet their seams show nonetheless, whether it's in the new features crammed onto your phone, the futuristic smart home that turns out to be a buggy mess in real life, or the theme park that was meant to be magical yet falls short of what it should be. The seams these companies are striving to hide away still persist, because they reflect how the companies themselves are built: the groups inside them fighting for control, and the people inside those groups who may or may not understand how a thousand tiny trade-offs, all of them reasonable enough, might chip away at an experience until it's dust.

With his aw-shucks grin, neatly parted hair, and a more-than-passing resemblance to Richie Cunningham, you can easily picture John Padgett as a kid growing up in 1970s Seaford, Virginia, a small town near the Navy shipyards where they built aircraft carriers and nuclear submarines. Nearly all his neighbors worked at the yards as tradesmen—electricians and machinists and welders like his grandfather. Seeing the Navy yards every day taught him that massive scale wasn't anything to fear. You might pass beneath the shadow of an impossibly huge aircraft carrier, and it was just guys like your next-door neighbor building it one rivet at a time until the whole thing grew bigger than life. Padgett grew up learning to be a carpenter himself. Massive scale has become his obsession. He was the prime mover of Disney's MagicBand and MyMagic+, the digital platform that unifies the MagicBand experience. He was the coauthor on more than a dozen patents that, once realized, transformed how tens of millions of people move through Disney World. The project eventually dragooned a thousand employees and contractors; it meant laying tens of thousands of sensors everywhere in the park and integrating more than a hundred disparate data systems. All of it was marshaled toward the single goal of turning the park into a giant supercomputer, capable of absorbing real-time data about where guests are, what they're doing, and what they want.[8]

Padgett and the other key executives trying to erase all the hassle of visiting Disney World were not among Disney's Imagineers, the demigods of fun who create Disney's attractions. In the hierarchy of Disney's creative culture, it was the Imagineers who usually held the most sway—they thought they owned the magic. Partly, this was Walt Disney's doing. He set up the Imagineers to be the innovation engine—and he couldn't anticipate the limitations of that arrangement. Padgett's group, by contrast, were veterans of the company's sprawling operations division: the people managing the gnarly realities of running the park, from keeping people from scamming ride reservations to reuniting lost kids with their families. Unlike the Imagineers, these people didn't see Disney World as the sum of its best attractions. They saw the park with X-ray vision, and saw the bones holding everything up. That they'd be the ones with a new plan for the park amounted to blasphemy in the eyes of the Imagineers—and that was even before they started letting their imaginations loose on what their system might become.

The MagicBands themselves are simple, cleanly designed rubber wristbands offered in cheery shades of blue, green, and red. Inside each is an RFID chip and a radio like those in a 2.4 GHz cordless phone. You reserve them when you book your ticket online; at that time, you can pick what rides you'd like to go on. Then, in the weeks before your trip, the wristband arrives in the mail, etched with your name. *I'm yours, try me on.* For kids, the MagicBand is supposed to be like a Christmas present tucked under the tree, perfumed by anticipation. Disney executives like to call it a modest kind of superpower, wielding access to the park. It is amazing how much friction Disney engineered away. You can tap it anywhere there's a telltale Mickey icon. There's no need to rent a car or waste time at the baggage carousel. There are no hotel keys or admission tickets to deal with. You don't need to wait in long lines. Inside, you can show up to the rides you've already reserved at your appointed time—and the itinerary you follow has been calculated to keep your route from crisscrossing the grounds. You don't even have to go to the trouble of taking out your wallet when your kid grabs a stuffed Olaf and begs for *just this one thing, please.* You just wave your MagicBand.

Tom Staggs couches Disney's goals for the MagicBand system in an old saw from Arthur C. Clarke. "Any sufficiently advanced technology is indistinguishable from magic," he told me. "That's how we think of it. If we can get out of the way, our guests can create more memories."[9] At the time, Staggs was the chief operating officer of the entire $168 billion Walt Disney Company empire, a parks veteran in line to become Disney's next CEO. The MagicBands were one of the crowning achievements of his tenure: Sure enough, after they were deployed, guests were spending more money, 70 percent were likely to recommend a visit, and five thousand more of them could fit in the park every day, owing to more efficiently distributed crowds. Staggs had the ramrod posture, trapezoidal jaw, and friendly face of an ex-varsity star you meet again at your high school reunion. We talked over teleconference, he from Disney's headquarters in Burbank. I was in a large room hidden within the support wings of Disney World, surrounded by charts and graphs projected onto the wall, displaying all the information constantly flowing in from the park. At a long folding table, in a room that looked like it had been set for a PTA meeting, I could glimpse the park breathing people in, breathing data out.

Like many corporate bigwigs, Staggs relayed the grand ideas that have bubbled up in him with a suave common sense calibrated for Wall Street. You could see why he—and Disney—would have been so keen on the bands. Instead of telling your kid that you'll try to meet Elsa or ride It's a Small World, "you get to be the hero, promising a ride or a meet-and-greet up front. Then you can be freer to experience the park more broadly. You're freed to take advantage of more rides," said Nick Franklin, one of Staggs's former deputies.[10] Disney knows that parents arrive to its parks thinking, We have to have tea with Cinderella, and where the hell is that Buzz Lightyear thing, anyway? The MagicBands let you set an agenda and let everything else flow around it. "The ability to plan and personalize has given way to spontaneity," said Staggs.[11] And that feeling of ease just might make you more apt to come back—especially if a cast member had more time to make you feel welcomed. All along, the other goal of the system had been to optimize how the park employees behaved, by trading the time they spend fiddling with transactions into time spent actually interacting with guests. The MagicBands and MyMagic+ allowed employees to "move past transactions, into an interactive space, where they can personalize the experience," Crofton told me in an interview in 2014.[12] What started as a sprawling technology platform was meant to change the emotional timbre of the park.

Yet that's when I started to detect the first cracks in the story that I was being told. The executives were frustratingly vague on what happened next. I'd talked to dozens of people who teased what might happen if the sensors in the park kept proliferating and the system kept growing. Invisibly, the park's myriad cameras could capture candid moments of your family—enjoying rides, meeting Snow White—and stitch them together into a personalized film. The park's computers might recognize when you'd waited in line just a little bit longer than you were supposed to, and send a conciliatory text message and a coupon for free ice cream. With that, they would have hooked the white whale of customer service: turning a negative experience into a positive one. That's why casinos comp you drinks and shows when you lose. And that was just the technology itself. The system was meant to eliminate annoying frictions, such as lines, and replace them with a stage-crafted serendipity. Mickey, whose minders could track you through the park, could surprise you with a script tailored to your birthday, asking if you'd like to walk together to the next ride. On the Little Mermaid ride, the seagull might call out your name. As another executive told *The New York Times* in 2013 when the Magic-Band was first announced, "We want to take experiences that are more passive and make them as interactive as possible—moving from 'Cool, look at that talking bird,' to 'Wow, amazing, that bird is talking directly to me.'"[13] Those ideas were never realized. Two years after Disney had promised a magical seagull that knew who you were, it could be found squawking on a loop to an empty room.[14]

The company had a mountain of ideas about what it might create. The fight was over whose right it was to do it. The Imagineers zealously guarded the rides and attractions, and the idea that someone from ticketing could waltz in and reinvent the park experience was like someone laying asphalt telling you how to design a Ferrari. They presumed that the rides themselves would be the magic; to say that magic might live in the negative space between the rides was anathema. The war devolved, as one executive described, into "booger flicking."[15] Once, when the MagicBands were being tested out to show how they could be used to ID passengers zipping along on a ride—so that the animated characters might call visitors out by name—Imagineers sat on their MagicBands, hoping they wouldn't work. (They did anyway.) Another time, one faction had cast members try to sneak past the gates, hoping to show the system could never be secured. Meanwhile, the rank and file working on the MagicBand project groused that Staggs just wanted to see the project sewn up tight so that he could take credit and move on to his big promotion before things got messy. In the end, no one could agree what the MagicBand would become. The vision had been to join all these new experiences into one simple device, on one single platform. But to do that, the entire company had to agree to work together in ways they never had before, and they couldn't.

In setting the Imagineers on a pedestal apart from operations, Walt had created a model common across countless companies today, in which innovation is viewed as a function owned by an anointed few, rather than an emergent property of the system. This was the dilemma in which Padgett and his peers found themselves. Disney already had its Imagineers; in setting up another innovation group, the problem of crafting a shared vision was only magnified. As studies have shown, innovation labs usually fail not because of a lack of ideas but because at some point those new ideas require new ways of working.[16] To be sure, the bones of the MagicBand project are still there: the ticketless entry, the ride reservations, the check-outs and check-ins with a wave. But it all remained frozen in place, undeveloped, short of its original promise. In the couple of years after the MagicBands were rolled out, almost all the lead executives attached to the project had quit or were fired—even Tom Staggs.

Disney wasn't experiencing something unique. Rather, it was experiencing something that has become common in this user-friendly era, when entire organizations have to work together to create one simple thing that every one of their customers will touch. How do you get one thousand people to agree on a single detail in an app, or one tiny piece of the MagicBand system, if they don't share a vision? The modern corporation wasn't designed to serve up a coherent experience. It was designed for the division of labor, to expend its energies on the efficiency of the parts rather than the shape of the whole. Those seams are obvious once you start to look at them: how Amazon's website has started to seem not like Amazon but like a photo negative of Amazon's organizational structure, with entire rabbit holes of navigation dedicated to video, groceries, audiobooks, music, even a weird section of the website telling you all the things you can do on Alexa—which is its own weird universe that mysteriously connects to all that other stuff.

Google and Apple aren't different. You can use a Google app in one place, and it seems to know everything you've ever asked Google. And then you can use Gmail, and it will suggest that you, a straitlaced middle-aged man, reply to an email saying, "You got it!" Apple meanwhile would have you believe that all its products are wrapped up into tidy boxes that "just work"—and yet keep shoe-horning useless buttons and invisible features into their software, seeming not to care about whether anyone bothers to use them.

As one Apple employee once told me, "I'm always showing people all these things they can do on their phones, and they say, 'Oh, you know all these amazing hacks,' and I have to say, 'No, these aren't hacks. This is how it was designed.'" The point of all these examples is that in each of them, you can feel the companies behind these products, which seem so polished, fighting with themselves. This isn't to say those companies are failing or even struggling—far from it. But even while their core businesses keep hauling money in, the possibilities of what they *might* build seem ever more elusive. And so these companies, with their hundreds of different products and business units, become bigger and harder to navigate over time. Instead of offering more with less friction, they simply offer more.

You can feel those companies shunting hard decisions onto their users, asking them to figure out what the company couldn't figure out for itself. Within the trade, this is often described as "shipping your org chart." This is the greatest open challenge in the user-friendly world: how to create one coherent face to the user, when the company behind that face is really a federation, atomized in order to make the work efficient. If the most influential companies in the world can't do it, you can bet that it's an open problem as to *how* to do it. Perhaps there is a natural limit to how much people can collaborate on a shared vision. Or perhaps one of those companies will invent new tools and a new way of working. Or perhaps a newer company will come along and sweep them all away by better assembling the pieces they've already laid.

John Padgett, the man who'd kicked off the $1 billion MagicBand project after seeing a gimmick in a SkyMall catalog, was among those who left Disney. He was looking for another job, one in which it might be easier to realize one vision, instead of just fighting against dozens. Ask him what the goal of the whole MagicBand project was, and he'll say it wasn't just to deliver what you already said you wanted—to deliver your order at a restaurant—but to *anticipate* what you'd want. After he was well into his next act, I asked him why the promise went unfulfilled at Disney. He stared through me impassively, then his eye twitched. "I'll let you be the judge of that," he said.[17] He'd wanted not just to make things frictionless but to make it feel as if you were the only person in the world who mattered.

Not long after quitting Disney, Padgett met the CEO of Carnival, Arnold Donald. Donald wanted Padgett to figure out how to make every cruise offered by the $40 billion company feel personal: not only the 105 ships, but the 740 destinations around the world, each of which had its own culture and staff. It was the kind of company Padgett knew, and the kind of scale he dreamed of. Take the name off both Disney and Carnival, and you're left with companies that had swelled to include real estate, infrastructure, logistics, boats, and hundreds of restaurants.[18] Theme parks and cruise ships offer the one thing that—for the time being—eludes the tech giants of Silicon Valley: a truly controlled environment that can be imbued with enough sensors to glean where you are and who you are.[19] But the difference was the amount of control Padgett was being offered: a seat at the top, rather than just below it, and support from on high so that he might better instill a vision. He had at his command similar pieces, but a new level of command over them.

There is nothing so similar to a theme park as a modern cruise ship. Unless you're one of the few vacationers who've taken a cruise—about 2 percent of all global hotel rooms are aboard ships—you probably don't realize the size and scale of their operations. Take the *Regal Princess*. She's almost 1,100 feet long and her nineteen decks are 217 feet tall. She carries 3,500 passengers and

1,300 crew, and ranks as one of the thirty largest cruise ships in the world. As big as she is, she probably won't be all that remarkable in a decade because of the economics of the cruise business.

Larger ships expend less fuel per passenger; the money saved can then go to adding more attractions—which, in turn, are geared toward attracting as many types of people as possible. Thus, in 1996 the *Carnival Destiny* was the world's largest cruise ship, weighing 100,000 tons and carrying 2,600 passengers. Today, the *Harmony of the Seas* is more than twice as heavy, and carries up to 6,780 passengers and 2,300 crew.[20] On a typical cruise ship, you can do almost anything, from attending violin concertos to playing blackjack to bungee jumping. And that's just the ship. Most of a cruise is spent in port, where each day there are dozens of excursions available. That avalanche of choice creates the stress that was first named thanks to social media: FOMO, fear of missing out, of having to discover and book the perfect thing and missing out if you don't. "You can see why people are so overwhelmed that they don't want to take a cruise," said Jan Swartz, president of Princess Cruises, the first of Carnival's ten brands to adopt the platform that John Padgett came to develop. "All that choice might be invisibly depressing demand, because people simply don't understand what a cruise is."[21]

On a small scale, we've seen what happens when options and features begin to bloat a product. Consider the example of the VCR that no one in your family ever knew how to work. All the add-ons just kept adding on, because they were easy to sell, even if no one used them once they got home. Same with cars, or appliances, or TV apps. The individual pieces have gotten simpler, easier to use. The entirety has gotten more complex, so that we now drown in an abundance of choice. Instead of picking a DVD to watch from a couple thousand at Blockbuster, you have tens of thousands of movies on demand through Netflix, and hundreds of thousands more through Apple and Amazon. Without a new interaction metaphor that can organize all those options with a new mental model, we're left in a world defined by what the psychologist Barry Schwartz called the "paradox of choice." Presented with too many options, it's easy to choose nothing, or to be disappointed with what you choose. That's the promise of personalization: to give us exactly what we want most while we spend as little energy as possible on making a decision. The stress of overwhelming choice is one that companies such as Amazon and Netflix are attempting to solve with algorithms, but it typically can't be addressed in the physical world.

When Donald first approached Padgett with the question of how you'd make a massive cruise feel personal, Padgett had already been working on the answer for a decade. But, ever the showman, he kept his ideas quiet. He told Donald, with his typical swagger, "Give me six months, a few million dollars, and I'll give you a presentation that will change the course of this company."[22] That he could be telling the CEO such a thing at all revealed a crucial difference with Disney. Organizational theorists point out that it's not enough for change to be proposed, or for it to make sense. The need has to be felt. At Carnival, Padgett wasn't just proposing change. He was being asked for it.

Padgett's gold-plated self-confidence can be either inspiring or maddening, depending on whom you ask: There were Disney veterans who'd storm a castle with him, and others who'd just as soon burn him alive. But the results are hard to argue with. Padgett's presentation to Donald wasn't a PowerPoint but an entire building. Carnival's Experience Innovation Center looks just like any other bland office building you'd find in any other office park in Miami.

But when I first visited, in the summer of 2017, about a year and a half into the decade-long project, the perfunctory lobby offered a hint of the constant construction and reconstruction that's been going on. There was a steel door leading to the inner sanctum, and sprays of dust emanating from all around the door jamb, as if something had just exploded on the other side. Through the door, there was a reception desk and a painted message on the wall, seven feet tall, from Buckminster Fuller: "The best way to anticipate the future is to design it." (Fuller, forefather of design thinking, had been a formative influence on the Stanford professor John Arnold.) It was dark, and the rooms beyond weren't rooms but rather curtained-off soundstages. There was a sundeck, a hallway, an elevator, a stateroom (the cruise-ship word for a hotel room), a casino, a bar—all the pieces of a real-life cruise experience. At the center of this maze, behind all the curtains like so many Wizards of Oz, were hundreds of engineers and designers arrayed cheek by jowl at cheap folding tables, clicking away at algorithms and app screens and floor plans. There were bound to be hiccups and bugs, but Padgett was confident it would all work out, because of the hypercollaboration represented at the experience center. The dozen or so teams involved all sat within shouting distance, fitting together in a sprawling mosaic—the service captains sitting next to the developers, so that they'd all understand one another— just like the crews that build an aircraft carrier. "People ask me all the time how you deal with complexity," Padgett said. "It comes down to putting people together and letting them work it out."

Padgett was by turns proud of what he's made and eager to get beyond it. He was wary of offending all the Disney people he once fought in the palace intrigue. He wanted to crow about Carnival's project and also to distinguish it from what came before, but it can't help but be an extension of the Disney work. Even the soundstage was something he'd learned to do at Disney. At Disney World, it was fronted with broad windows that had been blacked out. The designers inside used to giggle at the chatter they could hear on the other side: parents, thinking they'd found a corner for privacy in front of a disused building, yelling at their pouting kids: "We came three thousand miles to get here and you will have a good time!" That soundstage is what secured the sign-off on the $1 billion budget. Today, it's gone, and there are almost no photos of it, thanks to Walt Disney's founding obsession with hiding the mess behind the magic. But you can see what it must have been like, at Carnival's Experience Innovation Center.

I began my tour of what a Carnival cruise would soon become in a fake living room, with two of the best-looking project staffers pretending to be husband and wife, showing how the whole thing was supposed to go. I saw the app, and how you could choose all your reservations. I saw how, just as with Disney, the "Ocean Medallion" would arrive in the mail. Once on board, all you needed was to carry the device—a disk the size of a quarter so that it could be worn within a bracelet or carried in a pocket—for any one of the four thousand touchscreens aboard to recognize who you were and act just like the app on your phone. The experience recalled not just scenes from *Her* and *Minority Report* but computer-science manifestos from the late 1980s written by the visionary Mark Weiser. He called his movement "ubiquitous computing." The dream was to create a suite of gadgets that would adapt to who you are, morphing to the needs you had, based on context, whether in a meeting room or a bedroom.

Behind the curtains, in the makeshift workspace, pride of place was given over to one giant whiteboard wall, covered with a sprawling map of all the inputs that flow into some hundred different algorithms that crunch every bit of a passenger's preference behavior, to create something called the "Personal Genome." If Jessica from

Dayton, Ohio, wants sunscreen and a mai tai, she can order them on her phone, and a steward will deliver them in person, anywhere she finds herself across the ship's seventeen decks. They'll greet Jessica by name, and maybe ask if she's excited about her kitesurfing lesson. Over dinner, if Jessica wants to plan an excursion with friends, she can pull up her phone again. But in that case, the recommendations won't just be tailored to her, but rather the overlapping tastes of her group. If some people like fitness and others love history, then maybe they'll all like a walking tour of the market at the next port.

Jessica's Personal Genome would be recalculated three times a second by a hundred different algorithms using millions of data points that encompassed nearly anything she did on the ship: how long she lingered on a recommendation for a sightseeing tour; the options that she *didn't* linger on at all; how long she'd actually spent in various parts of the ship; and what's nearby at that very moment or happening soon. If, while in her room, she had watched one of Carnival's slickly produced travel shows and seen something about a market tour at one of her ports of call, she'd later get a recommendation for that exact same tour when the time was right. "Social engagement is one of the things being calculated, and so is the nuance of the context," said Michael Jungen, who'd worked with Padgett first at Disney, then at Carnival.[23] Finishing up the tour, I saw a flicker of the Personal Genome. As I walked around a rigged sundeck with the Compass app open on my phone, I could see that the options for nearby entertainment would shift as I crossed the room, as the servers crunched new data about what was nearby and what I had chosen. It was like having a right-click for the real world, or being in a sci-fi movie come to life.

Time and time again, in the move from paper money to credit cards to mobile payments, one iron law of commerce has been that less friction means more consumption. Standing on the mocked-up sundeck, knowing that whatever I wanted would find me, that whatever I might want would find its way onto either the app or the screens that lit up around the cruise ship as I walked around—it wasn't hard to see how many other businesses might follow suit in the coming years, or try to. "One way to view this is, creating this kind of frictionless experience is an option. Another way to look at it is that there's no choice," said Padgett. "For millennials, value is important. But hassle is more important, because of the era they've grown up in. It's table stakes. You have to be hassle-free to get them to participate."

By that logic, the real world was getting to be *disappointing* when compared with the frictionless ease of the virtual world. For a company such as Carnival, selling real-world experiences, the only way to compete—and the only way to get a new generation of customers onto its ships—was to exceed the ease afforded by the digital experiences people already knew from everyday life. First, Carnival had to engineer an invisible sensing apparatus analogous to that of the web, so that a system could sense a person's behavior, then deduce whatever they might want. Once in place, the ship's systems could do more simply because people had afforded them greater permission. People expected to be wooed or even wowed, because a cruise was supposed to be bent to their whim. By 2020, when the Ocean Medallion will finally start appearing across dozens of ships in Carnival's fleet, with greater and greater refinements to its sensing capabilities, the best place to taste the future won't be in a Skunk Works lab in Silicon Valley. It will be from a deck chair afloat on the Caribbean, with the smell of suntan lotion in the air and a mai tai in your hand. Whether or not the project ultimately succeeds in its grandest goals—which extend at least another decade into the future—it is still a bellwether for design and technology, and for a world where your environment would be every bit as important as the device in your hand.

The *Regal Princess* was nothing if not the smart city advertised endlessly by companies such as IBM—a place where the smartphone had been taken to its logical endpoint, so that impulse and desire were always available, not just on a device but in the environment all around you. With your wearable tucked away, you didn't have to go to the casino to gamble. Any screen you approached on board would become your own personal casino, with all your preferences and history seamlessly uploaded. The Ocean Medallion promised to transform the cruise ship experience into a personalized voyage at a massive scale: where touchscreens would recognize you as you move past, à la the film *Minority Report*; where crew members would know you by name as you approached, know where you were going, and be able to act as a personal concierge even if you'd never met them before; where anything you wanted to eat or drink or buy would find you. Looking into the future, the designers of the Ocean Medallion imagined a bar where your drink preferences would be mapped to your behavior, and where the ingredients would be updated based on the local bounty as you moved from one place to the next; they prototyped a virtual reality experience that would let you don goggles which would reveal the dinosaurs that once walked on the beach you were at, then turn those memories into movies that would play across your in-room TV. Taken as a whole, the vision was an Uber for everything, powered by Netflix recommendations for meatspace. And these are in fact the experiences that many more designers will soon be striving for: invisible, everywhere, perfectly tailored, with no edges between one place and the next.

During the three years or so I'd followed the Ocean Medallion project, it often tottered under the weight of its own ambitions. Many of the basic pieces ended up having to be totally reengineered, due to persistent bugginess in the systems; it was as if, by 2019, they had built the whole ecosystem not once but twice, at astronomical—and highly secret—expense. And yet Padgett was, true to form, undaunted. He wanted to increase the speed at which new ideas for the Ocean Medallion were being invented, and deliver them to more and more ships, faster and faster.

I asked him what the hardest part had been, and how this project compared with that at Disney. His nonanswer was revealing. He talked about how at Disney, the bureaucracy was the most daunting challenge. What had taken three years at Carnival took more than seven at Disney. But, he implied, once the MagicBand was delivered, the staff at Disney World knew how to hide all the kinks in the system from the guest, making everything appear seamless in the end. At Carnival, it wasn't so easy. "Here the planning and strategy was easy, but the activation and orchestration was the hardest thing to do," Padgett said. It had been difficult training the frontline staff to understand how powerful the change they were being asked to deliver was—it had been hard making them understand just how much was changing, from how they greeted guests on board, to the nature of the job itself. Hearing him talk, I couldn't help but think how similar this was to life back onshore, where entire workforces are now being asked to reorient themselves to the rhythms of software updates.

Around the time of the beta launch, in November 2017, I had asked Padgett why he cared about any of this enough to work on it for a decade. It was obvious that hundreds of millions of dollars in technology might make the experience better in a theme park or a cruise ship. But why did he *care*? He seemed, after all, like a guy who'd made enough money to be playing golf all day. "Some of it's craziness and some of it's principle," he allowed. "It always galled me that in the vacation industry, people call it innovation when you segment some tiny group and do something special for them. Democratizing what was previously only for the elite is a game changer."[24] As he explained it, the economics for the vacation behemoths put personalization out of reach for most, because the guest experience usually evolves along two distinct paths. Those who can afford it pay top dollar for customization—itineraries based on their interests, butlers who know about their dislike of cilantro. For the masses, operators focus on getting more bodies through the gates more efficiently.

The Ocean Medallion was a different thing: the idea that, using technology, you could tailor a mass experience to feel personal. Padgett wasn't necessarily an idealist. He was a pragmatist who began his career at Disney as an MBA-toting finance guy. When he crunched the numbers, serving a few rich people never made sense to him. It improved a business only around the margins. It didn't grow the whole business. But get someone to venture out on a couple more excursions, get them to try a couple of activities that they otherwise would have skipped, and maybe they'll have a better experience, create better memories. At some point the dollars and cents of frictionless transactions would bleed into the squishier stuff of experience—how people enjoy themselves, how they remember, what they remember. If better memories mean that people are 10 percent more likely to return, that's a windfall. That's why Padgett was able to sell Arnold on the idea of retrofitting the fleet, with the setup costs alone running to the hundreds of millions of dollars.

Padgett often likened the Medallion program to the smartphone: a platform that will evolve over time, and which comes with the implicit promise that, year by year, it will eventually do things that hadn't seemed possible before. All of it was built upon knowing more and more about the user. The last time we talked, Padgett showed me the data at the heart of the ship: an intricate map of every inch inside, every deck. And, as you clicked into the details, you could see bubbles representing exactly where each person aboard was in real time. "You can see here there's a lot of people on the balcony," he explained. You could click onto any of those bubbles—any one of those people—and see exactly what they were doing, and what they had done last.

Padgett, a couple of years before, had told me that with all this hyperpersonalization, with all the crew around you knowing what you're interested in, what you did today, and what you'll do tomorrow, the key would be making people feel the personalization as a luxury—and not as a creeping incursion. If it's your birthday, a crew member should be socially savvy enough not to say, "Hey, I see it's your birthday!"—thereby alerting you that you are, in a real sense, being monitored. Instead, they would tune their appeal. They might ask, "Are you celebrating a special occasion with us?" In doing so, they would open a conversational path that might seem like a lucky opening for freebies or better service, but which had been quietly engineered all along.

"Yes, we've invested in technology," said Swartz. "But we're spending countless hours rewriting procedures and role descriptions . . . If I want to share a glass of wine at sunset, I won't have to interrupt the moment to make eye contact with a waiter. It will find me. But the crew bringing the wine has to be trained to let me have that moment as well."[25] Those subtleties offer a lesson for companies such as Google, Facebook, and Apple, which are now creating a world of hyperpersonalization. As the gadgets around us become more and more capable, they'll need to become more polite, more socially aware. They'll need to adopt better etiquette, and to do that, they'll need to model our mores better. They'll need to reflect a new way of designing that better models human-to-human relationships, rather than human-to-thing interactions. The next generation of design will become less about screens and things, and more about scripts and cues. What we saw in the last chapter, in the development of more humane technology, is true again: When technology gets laced into the fabric of everything, what we demand is that those technologies hew closer to our social mores and the expectations of polite society.

While it would seem like etiquette would be easy—a simple matter of common sense—consider how delicately we're still fitting social networking into our real-world relationships. In the last ten years, the ways we represent what we know about one another have evolved. You might chitchat with colleagues and ask them where they went to college, even though you know where they went, because they're always popping up as a suggested connection on LinkedIn. To do otherwise would be weird—it might imply a stalkerish level of interest, even though the ease of Google has made it the first stop after you meet someone new. Elsewhere, you might follow someone on Instagram but refrain from hitting Like on one of their posts because you don't want them to know that you know something so personal about them. The point is, we're still figuring out how much to share about what we know of someone else—even while all of us on social media know the data is already public.

As we're negotiating this new terrain, the social networks themselves aren't nearly so adept, because advertising creates a third class of "user," so that we can never know who a product is really intended for. Interacting with social networks can be like having a conversation with a gossip, whose handiwork you can detect only afterward in the startling things other people seem to know about you. Recently, a friend of mine, a single woman approaching her mid-thirties, started getting ads in her Facebook feed for egg freezing. She'd never thought about it before, until that moment—and then she thought about it all the time. When she shared that bit of weirdness with her friends, none said they had seen the same ad, but they'd all been targeted with their own too perfectly targeted advertising. Not long ago, I started getting ads for acne treatment featuring an Asian male. I'd had acne as an adult. I'd never talked to friends about it, or as far as I recalled even googled acne treatments, because I wasn't too bothered. But somehow, an algorithm had sniffed out just enough data to find me, on the chance of targeting an insecurity.

These ads are examples of technology that we'd quickly call creepy, but might also simply be labeled as rude. They glean what they can about us, without ever getting to know us. Instead of engaging us in conversation, they stare at us from the shadows and collect gossip. Just like someone walking up to a person he "knows" only on Facebook and asking how dinner with the family was last night, these ads behave sociopathically, spouting everything they know about us from the moment they arrive. The ad industry can target us in new and mysteriously accurate ways—but the ads are still delivered in formats that borrow from the billboard metaphors created during a previous era of impersonal mass communication. (In fact, within the marketing industry, the largest-sized "banner ads" are called "billboards.") If you were to open up a conversation with someone about egg freezing or acne medication, that might be a conversation they'd want to have. But shouldn't a conversation start with "Hello"?

And yet eerily accurate advertising isn't just being foisted upon us—it also reflects a more general expectation that whatever fills our lives will be customized to our demands. We now expect the feeds we see on social media, or the news we see, or the emails we read, to be filtered on our behalf, so that we see what we want and nothing more. The unsettling nature of modern advertising today is merely the intimation of a greater trend. This book began with the century-long journey to find the "user" in "user friendly"—the history of how people have come to understand who people are, what they need, what they'll use. In the early decades of user-centered design, this meant finding the principles that underlay how we expected the world to behave; it meant inventing new technology that anyone could use, because it already made sense. But smartphones and connectivity, which have allowed the world to come to us, have created a new era in which we all use the same containers—whether it's apps or smartphones—but everything inside is different for each of us. John Padgett liked to call it the "market of one." Where design was once concerned with knowing the user, the things we've created now try to understand *us* as individuals. (The writer Tim Wu offers an exact year when this new era began: 1979, when the Sony Walkman was introduced. "With the Walkman we can see a subtle but fundamental shift in the ideology of convenience. If the first convenience revolution promised to make life and work easier for you, the second promised to make it easier to *be you*. The new technologies were catalysts of selfhood. They conferred efficiency on self-expression.")[26]

We have reached a tension, even a breaking point, in user-friendliness: The commonalities in design that technology has been driving toward, in an effort to make things easy to use, have finally run aground on the truth that we're not all the same person. This is one reason that so much money and attention have been pooled into machine learning and artificial intelligence. The human beings have done the work that humans could do, understanding what we all share so that the stuff in our lives can make life easier. But at the most far-reaching scales there aren't enough people to curate countless markets of one.

We're hoping the machines can build the last mile that the creators cannot predict. And, at the end of that connection, there's just content. The container makers themselves are beginning to look more and more like media companies—competing not just to bring us to the table, but to keep us there, at the table they've each designed. Apple has its multibillion-dollar effort to seal up TV deals, and a growing team of content editors behind Apple News;[27] Facebook, after a decade spent decimating the publishing industry, now finally admits that it, too, is a publisher and not just a technology platform.[28] Google, meanwhile, has quietly become the technical plumbing for delivering stories on the mobile web—that's why so many stories we read now bear not the publisher's URL, but Google's—while at the same time trying to turn YouTube into an outright replacement for TV. Amazon has not only a $5 billion movie budget that dwarfs most movie studios but an ecosystem that revolves around everything else you might buy, watch, or read; and it's sticking its name on more and more stuff, from furniture to Ethernet cables.[29] Once you've come close enough to fine-tuning the design of an empty box, the only thing left to do is fill up that box with so many different things that people can't help but keep opening it—and then use algorithms to make sure that the perfect thing sits right on top when they do. And *that* interaction has in turn reshaped how our user-friendly products engage us, making them far less like tools to augment the mind, as Doug Engelbart dreamed of, and more like the stage for our everyday lives, filled with so many perfect recommendations that the real world can't compete.

It is fair to worry. Nick de la Mare was one of the designers behind the MagicBand, and the digital experiences that sprouted from it—or, at least, tried to sprout from it, but never came to light. He was working at Frog Design. But just as their competitors had, Frog evolved into designing the more slippery stuff of experience: how people lived, and not just what they touched. De la Mare eventually quit Frog to start his own design firm, and one of its first projects was for the University of Texas's campus in the Rio Grande Valley, one of the poorest parts of the state, home to tens of thousands of migrant workers and their children, who, if they got to college at all, wouldn't be arriving on the backs of SAT tutors and guidance counselors. The kids there had jobs at Walmart and Costco; they didn't have their own cars. They were the first generation in their families to go to high school, not to mention college.[30]

For the university, de la Mare's firm, Big Tomorrow, proposed creating a virtual college campus, to be joined up with something like the Disney MagicBand. Classrooms wouldn't be on a grassy college quad. They'd be in strip malls, next to where the kids were already working. To get everywhere they had to go on this distributed campus, the kids would simply hop aboard a bus with their sensors. They could have their educational progress tracked and personalized, through a persistent data profile of what they were learning and how well they were performing. It made sense for a new type of student who couldn't bank upon the vague promises of a classical university education and needed to know how their educational investments would pay off. After all, these were students whose digital lives were already customized to them. It made sense for higher education to be remolded to fit their particular lives.

That pitch was eventually grounded by the university's operating model—yet another organization limited by its own design. Still, de la Mare worried about the future he was proposing, which took the personalization afforded by Disney World and Carnival to its logical next step. What would it be like when even education was tailor-made? Would it mean that we would all live on islands of our own creation? Would it mean that the world of Facebook tribalism—where people listen only to the people whose views chime with their own—would then become not just the world of Facebook, but . . . the world? "What would it be like to grow up inside that?" de la Mare mused. "How might that facilitate or hinder things like selfishness, empathy, and our ability to deal with adversity?" How strange it would be if the user-friendly world—brought about by industrialized processes for fostering empathy with users—ended up not increasing the empathy those users feel, but stunting it.

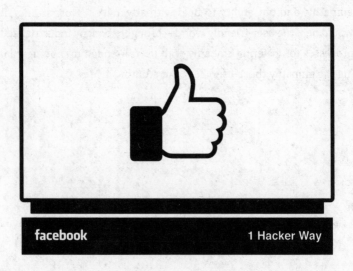

Facebook Like button, as depicted on the
company's headquarters' signage (2009)

9

Peril

Even the same people who were telling us that this is terrible,
we'd look at their user stream and be like: You're fucking using
it constantly! What are you talking about?

—Max Kelly, Facebook's first cybersecurity officer, on the introduction
of the Facebook News Feed

Any man whose errors take ten years to correct is quite a man.

—Robert Oppenheimer

The Like button is the single most ubiquitous interface of the twenty-first century, used every day by hundreds of millions of people. It began with a friendship between Justin Rosenstein and Leah Pearlman. They met at Facebook in 2007, when the company had just one hundred employees, and had an almost instant chemistry, an ease with talking about their hopes. They took long bike rides through the trails surrounding Facebook's headquarters in Palo Alto. They got stipends to live within a mile of the office. Facebook was a heady place. Pearlman remembers that it felt ecstatic, watching young people in the prime of their curiosity and ambition, everyone working on everything. There were no teams, just tiny tribes of passionate interest, each one believing it was creating something miraculous.[1]

The News Feed had recently been rolled out, and an engineer, Akhil Wable, had noticed how people had invented their own way of spreading an idea. The only actions available on the News Feed were to either post or comment. So when people got excited enough about something they'd seen, they'd take a screenshot of it and re-post it on their own feed. Facebook's employees called that "feed-bombing." When something went viral, so many people in a single network would be taking screenshots and then posting the same thing that it would take over a person's feed, forcing them to notice. Wable wanted to make that easier, with a Feedbomb button. The idea was wildly popular at Facebook, sparking debate over how to do it, different tweaks and permutations, different names. Pearlman had another spin. "Leah wondered, wouldn't it be cool if you could give someone props," Rosenstein told me as we sat talking in a quiet corner of the sprawling modern offices of his startup, Asana, cofounded with Mark Zuckerberg's college buddy Dustin Mosko-vitz. "At first I thought it was silly." But Rosenstein and Pearlman kept thinking. "We talked about it, and by the end we had zoomed out and asked, 'What are our goals with Facebook?' One of our goals was a world in which people lift each other up, where positiv-ity is the path of least resistance."[2]

At the time, the only place to say anything in response to a post was in the comments. But comments were a problem. "If someone posted something interesting, the comments were all the same: 'Con-gratulations,' 'Congratulations,' 'Congratulations.' If you wanted to say something unique, it got lost in a sea of comments," Pearl-man recalled. If you just wanted to send a little bit of warmth, you either racked your brain about something original to say, or you just gave in and typed exactly what everyone else had typed, which seemed to Pearlman and Rosenstein, who were primed to think in milliseconds, an agonizingly long process: C-O-N-G-R-A-T-U-L-A-T-I-O-N-S. "We thought we needed to make that friendlier," said Rosenstein. "We thought, What is the simplest, friendliest way to express positivity?" The team dubbed it the Awesome button. It would combine similar comments while also giving Facebook a metric by which to determine how far a story should spread. Pearlman and Rosenstein, with input from Wable and help from a couple of other engineers, stayed up all night and made a prototype. They shared the work. Their colleagues raved. Then the Awesome button succumbed to months and months of debate as people agonized over what sign it should have, and what name. The thumbs-up was declared off-limits many times, because the thumbs-up was negative in many cultures. (This was well before Facebook had expanded around the world; the company was already thinking big.) Numerous times, the project stalled out, leaving Pearlman to resurrect it again. Finally, Zuckerberg himself tired of the debates, declared that it would be called the Like button, and that it would be denoted with a thumbs-up icon.[3]

The web was a vastly different place at the time. User feedback didn't reach much beyond Reddit's up/down voting system and five-star reviewing platforms on sites such as eBay. Almost nothing existed that *affirmed* something, rather than rating it. The Like button augured an entirely new model of feedback, and a new way to gauge what people wanted and what they might want next. Today, that idea dominates the digital world, from hearts to +1s to emojis. It is a universal, even dominant mode of expression. It is the way countless ideas and emotions are spread. "It's been fascinating to see the Like button succeed beyond our wildest imagination," Rosenstein says. "And it's had all these unintended consequences that range somewhere between natural and pretty harmful." We were talking two months after Donald Trump had been sworn in as the forty-fifth president of the United States, when the media was filled with new data showing how America had fractured itself into the little bubbles of confirmation bias of which Nick de la Mare was so fearful, and how roughly half of America was utterly baffled by the other half. Reports were suggesting that Russian hackers had used Facebook to spread misinformation on behalf of Trump.

Rosenstein is slim, with a tousled mop of hair, a patchy beard, and a boyish gap between his two front teeth. The contours of his life are those of the protagonist from a docu-comedy about Silicon Valley. Summing up one of his Facebook posts, Wikipedia reported, "He dated a woman named Jordan starting in 2010, but her path to Peruvian shamanism ended their love, so Rosenstein had a heart sculpture constructed at Burning Man that featured lyrics from songs she had written, and they planned an epic friendship."[4] But Rosenstein also has a numinous earnestness. So while his Facebook stock eventually became worth hundreds of millions, he seemed to have no interest in it at all. He locked it away in a trust and promised to give it away before he spent any.[5] Instead of his own mansion, he lived in a twelve-person commune called Agape among other entrepreneurs with New Agey sidelines.[6] He is also a genius in at least one way. At Google, after getting frustrated that it was hard to see what other people were working on, he invented Drive, the product that now allows people to share files in the cloud. Then, after his boss told him that it would be technically impossible to embed a chat window in Google's email window, he spent sleepless nights coding and invented Gchat. Together, those products have become Google's touchpoint into hundreds of millions of lives.

Rosenstein has neatly arranged his life to accomplish exactly what he wants, every day. He begins in the morning by lining up five glasses of water on his desk, to make sure he drinks exactly enough as the day goes on. One of them is mixed with a powder derived from beets, blueberries, and other superfoods. He marks his calendar with blocks of time, dedicated to what he should be concentrating on, so that he knows exactly where to focus. He has a timer that reminds him to meditate at set times throughout the day. And yet even he admits that he's sucked in by the world that Facebook wrought. "I basically have only one addiction and it's notifications," he admits. "I'm an adult. I don't care what people think about me. Moment to moment, who's clicking? I don't give a shit. And yet right after this I'll be checking my phone, checking Facebook." We know quite a lot about how such compulsion happens, and how it might be reshaping our society.

As a kid in the 1910s, decades before he would come to loom over academic psychology, Burrhus Frederic Skinner assumed that a person could be molded just like any machine. He was already testing that thesis out as a boy, using himself as a subject. Once, after his mother hounded him about picking up his clothes, he resolved to train away his own forgetfulness by redesigning his bedroom. First, he arranged a flag to block the doorway. This he attached to a pulley, and on the other end a clothes hook. The flag would raise only if he'd hung his pajamas there.[7] Skinner couldn't articulate it at the time, but the guiding thought seemed to be: Here is something that I don't want to do, that I can never remember to do. But the right environment will *make* me do it. The idea hovered over his life with an eerie consistency.

In 1926, he returned to that bedroom after finishing college. This time, he was determined to train himself into being a novelist.[8] First, he refashioned the space into a simple factory. At one end, he built a rack that held an open book before him, so that without lifting his arms he could read Dostoyevsky, Proust, and H. G. Wells. At the other end, he built a writing table. The plan was to read, write, then repeat until he was a master. Yet it didn't work, for reasons that surprised him. It wasn't that he was scared of the blank page, or that he didn't have anything to say. Rather, he was bored by how small the blank pages seemed. It seemed hopelessly quaint to waste hours conjuring up the interior lives of made-up people. The young Skinner wondered if, instead of illuminating people from the inside, he might explain them from the outside in ways no one could argue with.[9]

Skinner had always been anointed for great things by his teachers, and soon he enrolled in graduate school at Harvard. "My fundamental interests lie in psychology," he wrote to his old college dean. "I shall probably continue therein, even, if necessary, by making over the entire field to suit myself."[10] His dream was to make the study of animal psychology every bit as rigorous as physics—to eliminate the need for any novelistic interpretation of why any creature might behave a certain way. He once again began by feverishly tinkering, and quickly hit a breakthrough with what would come to be called the Skinner box.[11] The device was an uncanny echo of his childhood bedroom designs and his dream of fashioning behavior through the design of an environment. The box was a chamber, sized to a rat or a pigeon, that could be rigged up with a light or a loudspeaker; there was also a lever, which, when pushed, would deliver a food pellet. The point was to see if the hapless creature inside could learn a cause and its effect—to learn that by pressing the lever after the right cue, it would get a reward.

Skinner's experiments might seem quaint—an updated version of Pavlov's famed experiments with drooling dogs—and yet his lasting influence was in how he built a worldview using his boxes. What was the world, if not a web of random stimuli? And what was life, if not a series of levers we push, hoping to achieve money or sex? To Skinner, psychologists didn't need to understand anything so vague and unknowable as thought or motive. They didn't need to be novelists. "By discovering the causes of behavior, we can dispose of the imagined internal cause," he would crow in later life, when he'd made his magical box into an entire ideology that dominated psychology for decades. "We dispose of free will."[12]

Skinner's obsession with reducing our personalities to a mere product of our environment is worth remembering—especially since he also discovered the single most troubling psychological mechanism of the user-friendly world. Skinner found it by asking a simple question about the rats: Would they respond more quickly if the food rewards came predictably, or if they were meted out randomly? It seemed obvious that the former would be a better goad—the rat should act more quickly if a reward was sure to follow. In fact, the opposite was true. The rats were attentive enough when the food rewards came regularly; but when they came randomly, the rats went wild.[13]

There are all kinds of ways that animal experiments fail to paint us a faithful portrait of ourselves. We might discover that the analogy between us and other animals is too simple, or that our impulses are differently primed. But this was one of those rare and perfect instances where we could look at the animal instincts of our most distant relatives, millions of years old, and see ourselves. Skinner proudly noted that his fabulous behavior engines could finally explain the universal human obsession with gambling. What was a slot machine—or any other game of chance—if not a Skinner box? You pulled a lever, and you never knew what you would get. It was the prospect of winning big that reeled you in. It was the fact that you almost never did that kept you pawing at the lever.

In the last few decades, neuroscientists have finally begun to understand why this happens. When things turn out just as we expect, the reward centers in our brains stay dormant. After all, our circuitry didn't evolve to reward us for finding out what we already know. On the other hand, when things *don't* turn out like we expect, our brains catch fire. Alert to the chance of gleaning a new pattern, our reward centers buzz. It's the same dopamine circuitry triggered by heroin and cocaine. So-called variable rewards pop up most obviously in casinos, and in the design of slot machines, on which Americans spend more money than movies, baseball, and theme parks combined.[14] Leave aside for one moment that every movie, baseball game, or theme park offers its own type of variable reward. The concept can also explain some of the most ever-present textures of everyday life. Let's say your job earns you a $2,000 check every two weeks. Nice as that check might be, you don't celebrate when you get it. But just imagine the joy of winning $1,000 from a lottery scratch-off that a friend gave you as a gag. You'd be bragging to your friends. You'd cheer and buy the bar a round. Consider, too, how we celebrate underdogs in almost every facet of culture. In sports and books and movies and politics, from the very earliest stories ever written, we root for underdogs when they win because they don't simply reaffirm the world we already know. Instead, the underdog-made-good creates an altogether different world. When underdogs win, it's ecstasy. "No one tells stories like that about teams that we expect to dominate," said David Zald, a neuroscientist at Vanderbilt who has studied the dopamine rushes that occur when people luck out. "No one is excited when Alabama beats Vanderbilt, but if Vanderbilt beats Alabama, Nashville goes crazy."[15] Ever since the beginning of the written word, we've told one another stories about heroes who succeed in spite of long odds. Those stories were perhaps the first, best drug delivery devices we've ever discovered.

One person to notice the eerie connection between Skinner's

work and our digital lives was the writer Alexis Madrigal, who in 2013 read a book by the anthropologist Natasha Schüll about the design of slot machines and saw striking parallels in the design of apps.[16] The design community began to enter a painful period of self-examination. "Once you know how to push people's buttons, you can play them like a piano," wrote the designer Tristan Harris. "Tech companies often claim that 'we're just making it easier for users to see the video they want to watch' when they are actually serving their business interests. And you can't blame them, because increasing 'time spent' is the currency they compete for."[17] Today, Skinner boxes that offer the prospect of variable rewards are everywhere, and we call them by their brand names: Facebook. Instagram. Gmail. Twitter. You wake up and you check your Facebook feed or your Instagram account or your email. Your messages and likes trickle in. The images and words of your friends tickle you, or they aggravate you. Or they're simply boring. You never know what it'll be. How many likes did your post get? And so, without ever realizing what you're doing, you're checking them all again in a couple of minutes: Facebook. Instagram. Twitter. Each of them has some kind of variation on the ubiquitous pull-to-refresh gesture— pull the screen down, or tap a button, and a new batch of updates loads, ready for your consumption. That gesture is nothing if not a modified lever at a slot machine. Sometimes you get nothing for your efforts. It's the variability that hooks you, day after day. By some estimates, we check our phones about eighty-five times a day.[18] Other researchers, who've watched how much we touch our phones—simply to feel that they're there, waiting—say we tally 2,617 touches per day.[19]

Skinner thought that the lessons of his boxes could be used to improve our society at every level, and that we might condition ourselves to be better. So far it's unclear if he was right. What is obvious is that the experiment is well underway. The smartphone is nothing if not a modern Skinner box. Except, it wasn't a box foisted upon us; it was a box we chose for ourselves. The smartphone's user-friendliness has allowed it to spread across ages and cultures. In turn, the user-friendliness of the buttons and apps and feedback within those smartphones has now restructured the social life, information diet, buying patterns, and mating patterns for billions of people around the globe. Consider the dating app Tinder, which refashions the process of finding love around the machinery of variable rewards. Instead of wheels of spinning icons, there is an endless procession of new faces, posed and cropped for the speediest consumption; the jackpot is someone you like, who also happens to like you. Volition and luck combine to make Tinder feel first like a game—and then, once that game becomes familiar, like a drug. As one of Tinder's founders explained matter-of-factly, and utterly shamelessly, "We have some of these game-like elements, where you almost feel like you're being rewarded. It kinda works like a slot machine, where you're excited to see who the next person is, or, hopefully, you're excited to see 'did I get the match?' and get that 'It's a Match' screen? It's a nice little rush."[20] Thrilled by such ease and pleasure, our society is busy putting a Skinner box in every hand by making them ever cheaper, easier to use, and easier to get. But unlike slot machines, our personal Skinner boxes don't offer the prospect of riches. The market has figured out exactly the bare minimum that will keep us coming back.

Of course, almost no one had consciously thought to create a world of Skinner-inspired addictiveness. But that only makes the creation more profound. Designers evolved these solutions because, in a quest for what got users to come back more and more often, they stumbled upon what we cannot resist. But a mix of ambition, intuition, ingenuity, and greed rediscovered one of the intractable facets of our brain chemistry. The most enduring businesses in the world have always been built upon addiction—alcohol, tobacco, drugs. The trick of the user-friendly world is that not only are we addicted, the drug doesn't have to be bought. The drug lies in our own brains, hardwired there by evolution.

In the early chapters of this book, we saw how psychology shifted away from behaviorists' icy conviction that our motives were nothing more than conditioned responses, brought about by punishments and rewards. When psychology did shift, it shifted in favor of a more nuanced understanding of people, from the perspective of what went on in their minds. That shift toward empathy helped designers place us, the users, at the center of the man-made world. That ethos gave rise to the idea, after World War II, that the reason pilots were crashing planes wasn't simply that they needed better instructions. Men died, and others such as Alphonse Chapanis realized that the training was inherently flawed, because men were flawed. For men to perform better in machines, they didn't need to be trained more; rather, the machine needed to be crafted around them so that they needed to be trained *less*. And so, whereas twenty years ago, buying a cutting-edge VCR or TV meant also getting a thick instruction manual with which to decipher all its newfangled capabilities, we now expect to be able to pick up some of the most complex machines ever made—our smartphones—and be able to do anything we want, without ever having been told how.

User-friendliness wrought a world in which making things easier to use morphed into making them usable without a second thought. That ease eventually morphed into making products more irresistible, even outright addicting. For a brief period in Silicon Valley, that search for addictiveness seemed harmless—partly because addiction itself was usually framed as "engagement," a Silicon Valley byword for having users constantly coming back for more. This naive enthusiasm was incubated at Stanford by B. J. Fogg, who had been a star student of Clifford Nass, the Stanford professor whom we met in chapter 4 who studied the politeness that people applied to computers. Following the work of his mentor, Fogg analyzed the ways computers shape our behavior. Yet he was about to see an experimental outlet Nass could never have dreamed of, in the form of Facebook.

By the end of 2006, just two years after launch, Facebook had amassed 12 million active users and showed no sign of slowing. Seeking to spur even more growth, Facebook by then had opened up its platform so that outside developers could build games upon it. Fogg was keen enough to recognize Facebook as a virgin mine of psychological data—and not just a mine, but a place to put psychological theories to work. So in September 2007, for an undergraduate computer-science course titled Apps for Facebook,[21] Fogg asked his students to build their own Facebook games, and to target their users with a variety of psychological principles. These included a form of online dodgeball, which asked players to goad their friends into joining, and a virtual hug exchange, which capitalized on the human need to return kindness. Together, the seventy-five students managed to garner $1 million in revenue and 16 million users within ten weeks. The final class presentation was attended by five hundred people, including hungry investors.[22] Watching that explosive growth, Fogg wondered: What made some of those games so irresistibly sticky? He codified the principles in just three elements: motivation, trigger, and ability. Create a motivation, no matter how silly or trivial. Provide a trigger that lets a user sate that motivation. Then make it easy to act upon it.

The formulation bears a striking resemblance to Skinner's ideas about conditioned responses. (Indeed, one of Fogg's disciples, Nir Eyal, rocketed to guru status in Silicon Valley by popularizing

Fogg's insights in a book titled *Hooked*.) Boiled down, Fogg's model is simply that we form new habits when triggers in our environment allow us to act upon our motivations—pleasure and pain, hope and fear, belonging and rejection. Goading a user into action is merely about having triggers arrive at the perfect time, and letting us act upon them with maximal ease. And what's the best way to reward those actions? Uncertain rewards that tickle our dopamine centers, of course. To be sure, even as he was articulating and developing these theories, Fogg tried valiantly to ward off their potential misuse.[23] But his caveats and nuances went largely ignored. Hundreds of students passed from B. J. Fogg's classes to Silicon Valley, going on to occupy senior positions at Facebook, Uber, and Google. The most famous is Mike Krieger, who, with a college friend named Kevin Systrom, invented a social networking app tailored to the iPhone 4. Eventually, Krieger and Systrom stripped down their app to focus just on sharing photos and liking the photos of friends. They called it Instagram.[24]

As we've seen in the stories of Capital One's secrecy-shrouded chatbot persona and the social engineering aboard Carnival's next-generation ships, our behavior has become a design material, just as our intuitions about the physical world once were—and those behaviors are often involuntary. It shouldn't be surprising that our psychological quirks necessarily lie at the core of every app or product that takes hold in the market. A striking example comes from Uber. After a lengthy investigation, the *New York Times* journalist Noam Scheiber discovered that the company was using insights from behavioral economics to get its drivers to work longer hours.[25] One trick capitalized on the human preoccupation with goals. Drivers would be prompted with messages such as "You're $10 away from making $330 in net earnings. Are you sure you want to go offline?" The number was arbitrary, and the goal essentially meaningless. But for the goal to work, it didn't have to mean anything. It just had to be slightly out of reach—much like how the final reel on a slot machine will slow down to make you think you're *just* about to hit three cherries, then slip by at the last moment. Uber and Lyft both tantalize drivers with another feature, which Uber calls "forward dispatch," that queues up the next drive before the present one has ended—much like Netflix queues up the next episode of a series. "It requires very little effort to binge on Netflix; in fact, it takes more effort to stop than keep going," noted the scholars Matthew Pittman and Kim Sheehan. The feature was so successful that Uber drivers nearly revolted, because they felt unable to take bathroom breaks. The company eventually added a pause button, but defended itself by pointing out that drivers want to stay busy earning money. But as Scheiber notes, "While this is unquestionably true, there is another way to think of the logic of forward dispatch: It overrides self-control." There are other flavors to this psychological hack. In Snapchat, users are awarded "streaks" for sending messages to friends on consecutive days, in the form of emojis. "I think in some weird way it makes concrete a feeling of a friendship. Like, you can talk to someone every day, but a streak is physical evidence that you talk every day," one teenager told *Mic*.[26] Said another, "Streaks are sort of proof of commitment to someone." Thus, through feedback and our hardwired yearning for reciprocity, a meaningless goal has become the most meaningful gauge of what seems, in high school, like life or death: your popularity. By creating a new metric for social standing, Snapchat was able to rewire the social lives of teenagers.

This book has been about a hundred-year journey to better understand who we are—why we find things easy to use, how we understand the gadgets in our lives, all so that we make them friendlier to the quirks of our own minds. The winding path toward knowing ourselves has, in the end, led to gadgets that tap into parts of us that we cannot help. Having traveled a path to understand who we are as individuals, with needs and biases and quirks, we are back where we started, naked in front of B. F. Skinner's lidless gaze. The market has filled our lives with products that are easier and easier to use; these have culminated in glossy skeins of code—Google, Facebook, Instagram, Twitter, and almost any app that you find on a smartphone—that tickle the most ancient parts of our brains, tied to the very way we learn about the world. After discarding the reductive thinking that Skinner hoped to bring about, designers striving for user-friendliness have rediscovered it. They have restructured the things that make us human—our search for love and belonging, our quest to find out new things—as Skinner boxes, whose very success depends on their ease of use. We stuff those boxes with the treats, or the worst, of everyday life.

Today, Skinner's blind focus on whatever goads an animal into action has been transformed, thanks to technology platforms, into a presumption that what users want can be reduced to what makes them click. It is a presumption that totally omits motive in favor of impulse and action. Design methods themselves have codified that dynamic and entrenched it. Alan Cooper, the eminent user-experience designer who came up with the idea of user personas, has called this the Oppenheimer moment for product design.[27] Oppenheimer had helped birth the atomic bomb so that the United States might end World War II. But once he saw the first mushroom cloud at the Trinity test, he realized that the intent behind what he'd created was irrelevant in the face of how people used that creation. "Today, we, the tech practitioners, those who design, develop, and deploy technology, are having our own Oppenheimer moments," Cooper once told a crowd of user-experience designers working in a field he himself had helped invent. "It's that moment when you realize that your best intentions were subverted, when your product was used in unexpected and unwanted ways."

I'm the son of Taiwanese immigrants, of a father who came to America for an education and a mother who never made it much past middle school. Whatever I have today—fulfilling work, a good education, a wife I love, and the expectation that our child deserves the same—I owe to the opportunities afforded by America's singular genius for cultural integration. As economists will confirm, my country's stunning history of growth has been sown by immigrants realizing their potential. Just as millions of others must have done when they woke to the election results on November 9, 2016, I asked myself whether America no longer believed in the story I've lived. I didn't find any good answers, not in the data about who voted for Clinton or Trump, and not in any of the stories I read about that data. They rang hollow because they didn't reveal what to do about any of it. Then I read an essay by the writer Max Read, "Donald Trump Won Because of Facebook."[28]

Read's central premise, the one that we know to be true, was that Facebook doesn't spread information so much as it spreads affirmation. Thanks to the Like button, invented by Rosenstein and Pearlman, and the algorithms behind it that track those likes, we are cocooned in beliefs that neatly match our own. A post falsely claiming that the pope endorsed Trump got more than 868,000 Facebook shares, while the story debunking it had 33,000.[29] Lies spread far better than truth, because a lie that we can believe in is so much easier to share than a truth that requires another click to discern. As a colleague pointed out, Facebook has created the twenty-first-century equivalent to the suburban tract developments of Levittown: a place of homogeneity rather than diversity, where the only voices we hear are those of virtual neighbors who think exactly like us.

There exist even worse outcomes than anything we've seen here in the West. Even as America and Britain began to slowly mobilize their investigations of Facebook's role in the election results for both the 2016 presidential race and the Brexit referendum, Myanmar was enmeshed in a wave of genocide directed at its Rohingya, a Muslim minority who for decades have been persecuted by radical Buddhist nationalists. The bloodshed arrived in the country at a sickeningly regular pace, but in 2017, after more than 6,700 Rohingya dead, 354 villages burned, and at least 650,000 forced to flee west into Bangladesh, the United Nations identified a new spark: misinformation spread on Facebook.[30] And not just in Myanmar but also in Sri Lanka, in another anti-Muslim uprising; and in lynchings in India, Indonesia, and Mexico, each of them fomented and then enshrined on social media.

"We don't completely blame Facebook. The germs are ours, but Facebook is the wind, you know?" said one Sri Lankan official.[31] Yet Facebook wasn't just the wind, scattering a plague farther than anyone could foresee; feedback built upon our primal need for affirmation is more powerful than that. (To quote one headline: "Former Facebook VP Says Social Media Is Destroying Society with 'Dopamine-Driven Feedback Loops.'")[32] As *The New York Times* reported, after tracking the half-life of a series of posts that falsely claimed a pharmacist in Sri Lanka was disseminating sterilization pills to his Buddhist customers, "Facebook's most consequential impact may be in amplifying the universal tendency toward tribalism. Posts dividing the world into 'us' and 'them' rise naturally, tapping into users' desire to belong. Its gamelike interface rewards engagement, delivering a dopamine boost when users accrue likes and responses, training users to indulge behaviors that win affirmation.

And because its algorithm unintentionally privileges negativity, the greatest rush comes by attacking outsiders: The other sports team. The other political party. The ethnic minority."[33]

Moreover, on the street, people might think awful things, but they're held in check by the rhythms and mores of the commons. Society, after all, is built to encourage some behaviors while tamping down others—to foster certain types of communities while holding others in check. That is society's most basic function. Facebook, by contrast, makes it easy to say awful things in public. Unlike in the commons, such extremity is rewarded with likes. People can realize, thanks to a feedback mechanism that never existed before, that there are others just like themselves. The signal gets reinforced. By that mechanism, what might have been a fringe opinion expressed under one's breath can then harden into a worldview typed out in all caps. It is more than simply cocooning ourselves in virtual tract communities of like-minded thought. Affirmative feedback of our worst impulses allows the fringe to feel like the center—and feeling that other people believe as you do frees you to consider things you might never have otherwise. The ease of user-friendly design allows us to become the worst version of ourselves. It makes starting a fire as easy as merely adding the kindling. I've reported and written thousands of stories about digital design, and also designed digital products myself. That entire time I've always assumed that "making things frictionless" was an unalloyed good, right up there with science, efficient markets, and trustworthy courts. But is a user-friendly world actually the best world we can create?

In the months after the election, as flummoxed Hillary Clinton staffers were wondering how they'd so badly misunderstood the race they were running against Donald Trump, news reports began trickling out about Cambridge Analytica, a mysterious data-science company that had been paid millions to help Trump's campaign in the run-up to the election.[34] Cambridge Analytica itself wasn't an innovator. It had been inspired by Michal Kosinski, a young psychologist at Cambridge University.

Kosinski typically wears the uniform of a venture capitalist: pressed khakis, crisp button-down shirt tucked in. (If the shirt were untucked, you'd peg him for a startup bro.) But as an algorithm might say, his hair is just about 17.2 percent too tousled, his beard scruff about 10.9 percent too long. He's relentlessly contrary, the type of person who'll ask a stranger why they believe in God. He attributes that to growing up in Poland, where argument is a national pastime. And he concedes that his disagreeableness has guided his own career. It has made him into a Cassandra of what's possible with our online data exhaust.

Kosinski earned his Ph.D. in psychology and his master's in psychometrics. One of that field's founding assumptions was that all the wooly complexity of human personality could be boiled down to the Big Five simple traits, known by the acronym OCEAN, that each of us possesses to varying degrees: openness, the willingness to engage in new experiences; conscientiousness, or perfectionism; extroversion; agreeableness, how considerate and cooperative a person was; and neuroticism, or how easily upset a person could become. In 2012, Kosinski was working on creating adaptive versions of those tests, where the questions could shift based on answers already given, and thus become short and more efficient. Kosinski and a colleague then spied a chance to do much richer tests online; they created a personality test on the OCEAN traits, which they distributed on Facebook. It went viral, attracting millions of responses. Kosinski realized that here was a data set unlike any other in the world. Not only did it reveal the personalities of the people who answered, but those personalities could be mapped to the things they liked on Facebook, and the demographics revealed on their profiles. "It struck me that you could just look at digital footprints, and from there, it's a very short jump to understanding personality in a fully automated way," Kosinski recalled.[35]

The results were stunning. With just a few dozen likes, Kosinski's model could guess with 95 percent accuracy a person's race. Sexual orientation and political party were almost as close, at 88 percent and 85 percent. Marital status, religiosity, cigarette smoking, drug use, and even having separated parents were also within the model's predictive reach. Then things got eerie. Seventy likes were enough to predict a person's responses on a personality quiz even better than their friends could. Just 150 likes would be enough to outdo the person's parents. At 300 or more likes, you could predict nuances of preference and personality unknown even to a person's partner.[36] On April 9, 2013, when Kosinski published his findings, a recruiter at Facebook called to see if he'd be interested in a role on its data science team. Later, when he checked his snail mail, he saw that Facebook's lawyers had also sent him a threat of a lawsuit.

Facebook quickly responded by allowing likes to be made private. But the genie had escaped its bottle. Kosinski had shown that if you knew a person's Facebook likes, you knew their personality. And if you knew their personality, then you could readily tailor messages to them—based on what made them angry or scared or motivated or lonely. It was perhaps only a matter of time until Cambridge Analytica approached Kosinski about a partnership, under the guise of a shell company. Kosinski turned the offer down, and then watched with alarm as reports emerged suggesting that Trump's campaign was creating Facebook ads tuned to provoke outrage in microtargeted audiences. By 2016, Cambridge Analytica's CEO was claiming that it had profiled the personalities of nearly every adult in the United States—220 million people. It has been estimated that during the election, the firm was testing 40,000 to 50,000 ads *a day* to better understand what would motivate voters—or keep voters who didn't like Trump from voting at all.[37] In one instance, Trump's own digital operatives claimed that they'd targeted black voters in Miami's Haitian community with stories about the Clinton Foundation's supposedly corrupt efforts to deliver aid after Haiti's catastrophic 2010 earthquake.[38] Some months later, journalists began to question whether Cambridge Analytica's data science really could be as advanced as it claimed.[39] What no one questioned was that Facebook could easily do what Cambridge Analytica had boasted about.

Indeed, months after the election, a leaked Facebook document produced by company executives in Australia suggested that they could target teens precisely at the moment they felt "insecure," "worthless," or "needed a confidence boost." Facebook quickly denied that it offers tools for targeting people based on their emotional state.[40] But they couldn't deny that it was possible. Kosinski's work had proved in startling fashion that Facebook's advertisers didn't have to rely on crude demographic targeting. Instead, with the mere rudiments of Facebook's data, they could target people based on their specific personalities: how a particular person reacted to messages of fear or hope or generosity or greed. For the first time in the history of user-friendly design, you could change a person's experience based on not just assumptions about an individual, but actual knowledge.

Mark Zuckerberg has always borrowed from the language of user-friendly design to communicate his ambitions, saying that Facebook made its users happier and more fulfilled by "bringing the world closer together." And yet he created much more than that: a company that could *understand* users with a precision that couldn't be dreamed of before. He created the biggest Skinner box in the world, an engine of user focus that wasn't actually friendly. There is a plangent irony in this. When Skinner invented his black boxes to test animal behavior, he argued that the interior life of an animal wasn't worth speculating upon if you could understand the inputs and rewards that guided its actions. And yet Facebook may be harmful precisely because it allows people we don't know, with motives we cannot track, to predict exactly who we are.

The end goal of consumer technology has always been to buff and round every corner, so that each detail is so alluringly simple that it seems "inevitable." As we've seen in this book, that "inevitability" is shorthand for many things. Designs seem inevitable when they anticipate how we'll use them so well that we don't see the design at all. But the quest that began with fitting machines to "the man" has come even further. Today, we're not just fitting machines to a generic ideal. We can fit machines to us—to our individual personalities and whims. We saw that in the work Carnival Cruise Line had done with the Ocean Medallion and how Capital One developed a chatbot with personal foibles. But the individually tailored ideal has reached its apotheosis in two products: Facebook, which recast our messy social lives around virtual connections and a feed of information determined by who a machine believes we are; and the smartphone, a series of buttons that increasingly are designed to anticipate what we want to do.

Yet in hiding great complexity behind alluringly simple buttons, we also lose the ability to control how things work, to take them apart, and to question the assumptions that guided their creation. Modern user experience is becoming a black box. This is an iron law of user-friendliness: The more seamless an experience is, the more opaque it becomes. When gadgets make decisions for us, they also transform the decisions we might have made into mere opportunities to consume. A world of instantaneous, dead-simple inter-actions is also a world devoid of higher-order desires and intents that can't readily be parsed in a button. While it may become easier and easier to consume things, it will become harder and harder to express what we truly need.

To be clear, I've focused on Facebook because it has had the most obvious and far-reaching influence on society. But none of the other tech giants whose influence springs from creating user-friendly products is immune to criticism. The surface of their products hides outcomes, costs, and audiences we cannot see. You cannot see the workers in an Amazon warehouse, struggling to make ends meet, sometimes not working at all for days at a time, then clocking in for backbreaking twelve-hour shifts. Apple, for its part, helped make Facebook possible, by creating the very imperative that our entire lives fit onto a tiny screen. Apple has literally shrunk and focused our lives onto palettes that have become smaller and smaller over time. Google, meanwhile, has escaped the same punishing reex-amination as Facebook, but it, too, in ordering the information that we see and when we see it, exerts an unknowable control over our sense of the world.

Good user-experience design always hinges upon making an interface well ordered, with an intuitive logic that's easy to navi-gate, and making sure that interface engages you with feedback, letting you know whether you've done what you wanted. But even if those choices are ones that we make freely, our path to those choices is up for debate. We aren't all just one person. We're fickle. We have better angels and bad ones. The supposed inevitability of a design bleeds into the inevitability of the choices we are allowed to make. When data is used to mold the choices around us, then it's reasonable to ask: Whose choices are we making? By turning our-selves into consumers who see only the things that we want most, we might lose the possibility of becoming anything other than what a machine thinks we are—and the machine may not have gotten that right to begin with.

To give just one example, one of the automated news feeds on my phone presumes that because years ago I blithely clicked on a few stories about football, Tesla, and sneakers, these are the *only* things I'm interested in. Today, faced with stories about football, Tesla, and sneakers, I can only pick things that reinforce the machine's bizarrely limited model of my interests. The experience of scrolling through this frustratingly narrow interpretation of what I value is akin to being stereotyped by a fool. The fool never sees the clues and subtlety he's missed; the fool isn't armed with the wisdom to see what she has not considered. Now imagine this same stereotyping problem magnified across more and more things—not just the news we see, but everything else, from the friends we keep in touch with to the things we buy our kids—and you begin to see the problem. In purporting to know us better than we know ourselves, user-friendly products trap us in assumptions we can never break. We become rats in a Skinner box with only one lever to push, and so we push and push, because there is nothing else to do.

Still another problem is that when digital products have greater and greater reach, it means fewer and fewer people are making the decisions. That's all the more surprising because the power and promise of the personal computer wasn't born from whole cloth. It was born of the fact that a bunch of hackers like Steve Wozniak could break machines apart and assemble their own, better machines. But as our machines have become more elegant, our ability to alter them hasn't nearly kept pace. As easy as it is to change the preferences on your smartphone, it's all but impossible to make a different smartphone. The most optimistic thinkers in Silicon Valley believe that the answer is for all of us to be able to code. That's why today there are so many beautifully designed products aimed at teaching kids the basics. But why should coding remain a barrier to remaking our digital world? Why isn't it easier for all of us to peer under the hood of an algorithm, much as in a previous era we might have tinkered with our cars?

Of course, there is always a gap between the things we use and the expertise required to make them work. That's what it means for something—anything—to be user friendly. You don't *need* to know how Facebook works to enjoy it. You don't need to know *why* the smartphone looks the way it does in order to get value out of it. This is progress. One reason our society works is that we leave complex details for specialists to work out; what those specialists know is often provided to everyone else in the form of neatly designed products that are easy to use. This idea was summarized by Elizabeth Kolbert in a review of *The Knowledge Illusion: Why We Never Think Alone*, by Steven Sloman and Philip Fernbach: "This borderlessness, or, if you prefer, confusion, is also crucial to what we consider progress. As people invented new tools for new ways of living, they simultaneously created new realms of ignorance; if everyone had insisted on, say, mastering the principles of metalworking before picking up a knife, the Bronze Age wouldn't have amounted to much. When it comes to new technologies, incomplete understanding is empowering."[41] It's not a bad thing to make the stuff of life into tastier, more pleasurable morsels. Why shouldn't the things we want be easier to access? This is the dream of ever-increasing standards of living, the one to which Henry Dreyfuss subscribed when he equated better design with social progress, in the form of increasing leisure time for the emerging middle class. But there is a point at which we are so far from how things work that we cease to use a product, and the product begins to use us.

Maybe the most elegant expression of this dilemma comes from the field of cognitive psychology—the field that Don Norman, the grandfather of human-centered design, helped define. It's called the automation paradox, and its roots lie in the study of the autopilot feature in airplanes. As cognitive psychologists and human-factor researchers began inventing better and better solutions to hand off control between pilot and machine, they noticed a worrying dynamic: As planes became more automated, the pilots themselves were less and less practiced in flying their planes. They reacted less capably when something went awry or when something unforeseen occurred. The result was that machines had to be more automated to compensate for the increased failings of their human partners. The automation paradox is that automation, which was meant to maximize what a human could do, actually worked to sap our capabilities. Automation was meant to make humans more capable, freer to focus on the complex tasks our brains are good at. The automation paradox suggests that as machines make things easier for us—as they take more friction from our daily life—they leave us less able to do things we once took for granted.

The automation paradox is almost always referred to in the context of problems that arise when machines are explicitly designed to do more for us—in the case of self-driving cars, for example, which may create a new era of hopelessly bad drivers. I want to get at something different. Call it the user-friendly paradox: As gadgets get easier to use, they become more mysterious; they make us more capable of doing what we want, while also making us more feeble in deciding whether what we seem to want is actually worth doing.

If you're old enough to remember newspaper comic strips, then you probably remember *Nancy*, a single-strip comic whose eponymous character was a rotund little girl with frizzy hair. You probably don't remember anything of what *Nancy* was about. This was by design. *Nancy*'s creator, Ernie Bushmiller, sought to eliminate almost all content from the strip: social commentary, internal consistency, characterization, emotional depth.[42] Bushmiller instead wanted to "gag it down," wanted the strip to be so simple that even before you'd decided you liked it, you'd already read it. You may have laughed; you probably didn't. But you'd already consumed it.

The user-friendly world can be maddeningly silent in matters of whether what we've consumed is in fact actually good. The industrialization of empathy that we tracked across a hundred years of progress began with the ideal of understanding who people were, to better anticipate what they needed. But "human need" isn't the same as convenient consumption.[43] Yet we have been living for nearly a hundred years assuming that they're alike. As Tim Wu has written: "However mundane it seems now, convenience, the great liberator of humankind from labor, was a utopian ideal. By saving time and eliminating drudgery, it would create the possibility of leisure. . . .

"Convenience would make available to the general population the kind of freedom for self-cultivation once available only to the aristocracy. In this way convenience would also be the great leveler."[44]

But there is a telling omission in that equation, which we can see now: Henry Dreyfuss and his peers didn't believe that convenience itself imbued us with greater meaning. We had to find that meaning on our own. It should not be surprising that the user-friendly world has not provided it for us. Yet we know the outlines of an answer to this challenge, thanks to the automation paradox. The solution to preventing human skills from withering in the face of increasing automation is to keep humans in the loop and in control at decisive moments so that their underlying skills stay honed. Resolving the user-friendly paradox will require something similar. Our machines must hew to our higher values, instead of chipping away at them through heedlessness.

"User friendly is about deferring to the desires of the users," said Justin Rosenstein, after we'd talked for an hour about how the Facebook Like button came to pass. "But there's a hierarchy of desires. There's a sense of wanting to eat that cheeseburger. But there's also that higher-level desire, of wanting to be healthy and happy long-term." Abraham Maslow, he pointed out, assumed that our needs were arranged in a neatly complementary hierarchy. By fulfilling the lower-level desires, we became freed to contemplate the higher ones. But, Rosenstein asked, "What if your neocortex and your limbic system straight-up disagree? We have this experience of a single self, but at the hardware level, the reality is that we're a committee. Some parts are old, some parts are new, and it's not unusual that they'll disagree." Thus, there's a difference between wanting to check your Facebook notifications and wanting to spend your time well. "People used to make fun of businesspeople addicted to their 'Crackberries.' Then the iPhone came out and everyone was suddenly addicted. If you asked people, 'Are you happy with your relationship with your phone?' I bet they wouldn't say yes. Sure you need email to function, but if you're too friendly with the user, giving them exactly what they want in the moment, then you're being unfriendly in helping them achieve their highest-level desires."

Designers now have to confront the alarming possibility that user-friendliness helps us avoid consequences by abstracting away any downstream impacts. Rosenstein himself, along with Tristan Harris, the design ethicist whose essays helped ignite the design industry's debate about tech addiction, and other notables in the tech community cofounded the Center for Humane Technology, to lobby for more responsible approaches to technology.[45] As for the creators themselves, the user-experience designer Alan Cooper has called for something he calls "ancestor thinking" in design: a consideration not just of whether a product works, but what its implications are. Just as a previous generation had to codify, systematize, and then spread the process of industrialized empathy and the tenets of user-friendly design, Cooper has called for a new way of working that privileges the future over the present, and ways of seeing implications that we might not have ever noticed. There have, in fact, been efforts to foster just that, but they never caught hold. One was the so-called Futures Wheel, a method of generating ideas about what we might invent, based on what kind of futures we want to create. Tellingly, it was invented in the 1970s—before the silicon boom, during the era of the energy crisis when President Jimmy Carter exhorted Americans to turn down their heat and wear sweaters inside. The Futures Wheel was a whiff of what industrialized empathy might be if it were crafted around not merely what the user wanted but who the user might want to become, and the world she might want to create. That world can seem tantalizingly close. For example, it's astounding how little Facebook makes per user—somewhere between two and four dollars per month. How far-fetched is it that we might finally account for its costs and opt into something else with our money? Americans will happily pay 50 percent more for organic goods. How much more would we pay for products that give us peace of mind, let alone the ability to be better to ourselves?

The first time I heard of the Futures Wheel was in fact at a conference about designing for artificial intelligence. To me it seemed far-fetched that asking designers to take a longer view of their work could influence anything with a reach that could be numbered in the billions. But then again, when you work at one of the world-eating tech companies, one of the most surprising truths is how much control a single person might wield. Even if some product such as Apple's iOS or Google's Assistant requires a cast of thousands to build, there aren't thousands of designers and engineers working to define what those products will become. The upfront assumptions are crafted by just a few, and the assumptions those people hold—about the world they live in, or the kind of influence they can have, or whether there is something to be gained by thinking of further horizons—matter enormously. One doesn't have to be either a naïf or a tech apologist to believe that the intentions of just a few people can be decisive.

When I visited Michal Kosinski, who had shown how Facebook might be used to target our emotions, his office was clean and almost devoid of any personal touch. The only decoration on the wall was a painting that he'd bought, showing a soldier in riot gear in the background and, in the foreground, a protester, seen from behind, with the "f" of the Facebook logo in his back pocket. His left hand curled toward it, which made me think of Michelangelo's David, and the way his fingers curl around a rock in the moment he spies Goliath on the battlefield. I told Kosinski it seemed strange that he'd be that painting's owner.

Kosinski explained that he was an optimist because his life had been filled with optimism. He was born in Poland at a momentous time. In 1981, hoping to crush the anti-Communist Solidarity movement, the country's leadership instituted martial law and a nighttime curfew. More nights spent indoors coincided with a stunning explosion in Poland's birth rate. Kosinski was one of those so-called Solidarity Children: The preschool class ahead of his own had fifteen children. His had thirty-two, and the year after that there were sixty. By the time Kosinski finished grade school, Poland had tumbled out from behind the Iron Curtain, blinking in the glare of new freedoms. "Every day of my life was better than the last," he recalled. "I remember my first Levi's. I remember tasting a banana for the first time. Not because there we were hungry, but because we'd never seen one." He grew up as a teenage entrepreneur running his own internet cafés, making more money than his father had ever made in his life. "It's true I often focus on the downsides," Kosinski said. "But at the end of the day, technology is empowering us to do better things." This may sound like mere faith when balanced by concrete proof of things getting worse. But there are reasons to believe, if we look in the right places.

Magic Bus Ticketing (2016)

10

Promise

When she was six years old and growing up in the Democratic Republic of the Congo, the kids at school used to compliment Leslie Saholy Ossete on her drawings. The recognition stirred in her the first inkling of pride. Her second thought, which came a bit later but still seemed totally mysterious coming from the mind of a child, was: I could make money off these. She figured that little kids were always either reading comics or watching TV, and they'd want more. She went home and drew some stories of her own, about the things she knew: animals she'd read about and the bad kids and good kids at school. The next day she gathered up her schoolmates on their little dusty, dun-colored playground and offered her drawings for whatever pocket change their parents had given them. Ossete spent the proceeds on candy. This was the first business she ever started, and it seemed like magic: how one person could make something that someone else wanted, then they'd make an exchange, and everyone ended up happier.

Ossete's parents are genteel and educated members of Congo's thinly sprinkled middle class. Her mother is a pharmacist, her father a university professor and civic leader. She grew up watching them start businesses on the side to supplement their income or fill a need in the local community. She grew up with the idea that you could start something from nothing and make everyone better off. But whatever early instincts she had, she had to set aside. When Ossete was a teenager, she won a scholarship to a boarding school in the United States. She tried to nurture that opportunity in the responsible way, hoping to become a doctor. She was talented enough to win another scholarship, to Earlham College, a liberal arts school founded by Quakers in Indiana. She started with a heavy load of science classes. But sitting through them felt like chewing sand. "I think I always knew I was made for business," she said. The difference in her business courses was this sense that the world really was just like her grade school playground. No one told you what to do. You had to figure it out on your own and do it. So, when she heard about a million-dollar social-innovation prize open to student entrepreneurs, she thought, They should be coming to us. We should be a part of all that.[1]

The Hult Prize was framed around a provocation: What could you invent to double the income of 10 million people by 2022, in a crowded city, simply by connecting people to the services they needed? Ossete went about finding a team of other students. She and two of her classmates had grown up in the developing world where buses were how most everyone got around. But the buses themselves were terrible—hot and dusty and slow. So the first idea that the students had was to start a business with better buses, with Wi-Fi and nice seats for working. The idea was to transform wasted hours into man-hours.

On the back of their carefully detailed plans, not to mention their personal stories, the team of four climbed past the early rounds of the prize, making it all the way up to the national round of the competition. But their idea still had the trappings of a dorm-room brainstorm: It was obvious, and obviously expensive. To grow this bus business at all meant that you'd have to buy more and more buses. It didn't scale. The judges at the Hult Prize gently told them as much. Ossete took that not as an honorable end to a class project, but as an encouraging beginning. Next time, instead of entering just the student portion of the competition—the well-meaning kids' table—they'd enter the main part, to vie against the very best ideas people had for winning $1 million to change the world.

It was about that time that Wycliffe Onyango Omondi, Ossete's right hand in this enterprise, started to think about his own experience with buses back home, and the most notable bus ride of his life. He'd also gotten a scholarship to tiny Earlham College, and the only big thing left to do was get there. He had to secure his student visa for the United States, which meant paying $150 and setting up an interview at the embassy in Nairobi, Kenya, a few miles from where he lived with his grandmother. The morning of his interview finally arrived. He was due at 10:00 a.m. And amazingly, he'd woken up late.

It was unlike him. He caught a bus with an hour to go. But in Kenya, setting out on a bus with an hour until you're due at an interview that could alter the course of your life isn't like sitting on a bus with an hour to spare in America. It's more like sitting in a cab in Manhattan, trying to cross midtown traffic at 5:00 p.m., when you're due someplace in ten minutes. Omondi was terrified the entire trip. Terrified that he'd miss his interview, lose his $150, and lose a chance to change his life. "What if the journey takes more than an hour?" asked Omondi. *Journey.* That was his word, to describe riding a few miles into the city. "I had this fear that I'm going to miss my interview and miss my scholarship."

When Omondi thought back to the experience, he started to wonder why the buses were always late. Most people who hadn't lived in Africa, and even some who had, assumed that it was because there weren't enough buses. And in fact, this is what he had assumed as well—that you could solve the transportation problem with bigger and better buses. Yet somewhere along the line Ossete had dug up a paper about urban transport, where some researchers had found that most of the world's transportation problems weren't about congestion. They were about organization. For Omondi, what had been a few disconnected memories from his life in Kenya snapped together into a story.

The reason the buses ran late wasn't that there weren't enough of them. It was because the system had no way to sense who was in need of a ride. The system had no feedback loops built into it. It wasn't planned by anyone. Instead, it was a hodgepodge of tiny companies, renting their buses out to driver crews. When a crew would take a bus out for the day, they started off in the hole. When it was time to return the bus at the end of the day, it didn't matter if they'd made any money—same fee. And so the bus crews would drive to a stop . . . and just wait. They'd wait until enough people came aboard so they could be sure that they'd at least make their money back. They waited and waited until it happened. They waited for hours if they had to.

This was a disaster if you were someone like Omondi trying to make it someplace in an hour. It was a catastrophe if you were any one of millions of Kenyans trying to make your way to a better place. Say a bus made you two hours late to school. Well then, you got two hours less schooling. If a bus made you two hours late in getting home to do family chores, then maybe you stopped going to school at all. And so on and so on, throughout the whole country: Late buses meant less health care and less work and fewer scholarships and less of anything you might strive for. Viewed from a certain angle, it was as if the bus drivers waiting around at bus stops weren't just a big problem for Africa. They were *the* problem. "So I thought, Oh, this is something I have to face," said Omondi.

Omondi and Ossete set about trying to understand the problem better, using a human-centered design toolkit published by IDEO in collaboration with Acumen. They went to Nairobi and talked to people who took buses every day. They realized that most people, women especially, were aghast at the risks. Before you ever got on the bus, it was common to get robbed. And once you did get on the bus, it was common to be cheated with the wrong change. In Kenya's male-dominated world of ad hoc small-business hustles, women were often scared to ask for what they were due back. It wasn't so unusual for a mother, going into town for a clinic visit or her monthly shopping, to look at the possibility of spending hours in line for a bus, and the possibility of being cheated out of her money, and decide she'd rather walk five miles. Omondi and Ossete, along with two classmates, figured that to solve the problem of bus drivers waiting around for fares and making everyone late, they needed to create some way for bus drivers to know how many people farther down wanted rides. And to solve the problem of cash serving as both a siphon for petty crime and a disincentive to try the bus altogether, they needed to get rid of cash.

They called the solution they hit upon Magic Ticketing. It was simple: Using a mobile phone, anyone could buy their ticket in advance. The idea took advantage of a mental model already ubiquitous in Kenya thanks to M-Pesa, which routes half the country's GDP and remains one of the world's most advanced mobile money systems. Yet Magic Ticketing didn't merely copy the pattern—it adapted it. First, you'd send an SMS to a number. That number would bring up a simple menu, allowing you to buy a ticket. The bus drivers would get their money, and also a real-time sense of where their passengers actually were and an incentive to ply their entire route. In other words, those drivers would have feedback that hadn't ever existed before: the total value of completing their route. For passengers, the same system would provide a way to check on where the bus was and an easier way to buy tickets.

By the time I talked to Omondi and Ossete, it had been a year since they'd won the prize they'd set out to capture—$1 million. Their first thought after getting the money during their senior year in college wasn't "How on earth are we going to spend all this." It was "This money is going to run out with all the plans we have." They had already tested their design with two thousand riders; together, that group had booked more than five thousand tickets. They still had plenty to figure out and plenty more to build—the back end for all those bus rides, a mapping system for routing everyone efficiently, a matching engine to tabulate demand.

Somewhere along the way, an adviser, who was also a consultant at the World Bank, had told them: You know, this problem isn't just in Kenya; it's everywhere. And so they had also started looking beyond Nairobi. Once all the technology was ready, the idea was to bring their new service, now called Magic Bus Ticketing, to twenty-nine cities across eleven nations. One of those cities? Richmond, Indiana, home to Earlham College, a city that had plenty of problems expanding its own bus routes. Just like so many others we've met in this book, these budding entrepreneurs had found a problem by zooming in close to one market—and then created a solution that had far greater reach. They, a couple of young immigrants hoping to make their home countries better, had ended up inventing something sorely needed back in Indiana. It was as hopeful a boomerang as you could imagine.

Consider all the things that made Magic Bus Ticketing possible. It couldn't have existed but for the ubiquity of the user-friendly cell phone. It couldn't work but for the ubiquitous behavior of texting, and the familiarity of pop-up menus. Without the mental model that people already had for sending payments via text message, and the simple interfaces that make it possible, the service would never have become one that manages to tacitly explain its inner workings. These patterns were the tools that would allow their idea to find its audience, and that would let the audience understand it without having to be taught.[2]

As a result, Omondi and Ossete weren't merely able to make something new. They were able to make something that couldn't exist otherwise. Kenya doesn't have the long history of governmental management that, in the West, has yielded the services we take for granted, such as reliable bus schedules. But instead of that infrastructure, there were user-friendly gadgets, which could allow the fruits of top-down government to bubble up from below. Magic Bus Ticketing represented an altogether new approach to building a civil society, built upon the affordances and mental models created elsewhere. The ease of readapting user-friendly patterns is the single biggest reason that design now dwells in so many places we wouldn't expect.

Henry Dreyfuss had the timing and wherewithal to fill the home with a mountain of gadgets previously unknown—things such as vacuum cleaners and self-cleaning ovens and washing machines, which brought greater ease to millions of women in postwar America by automating the manual labor of everyday life. Today, after eighty years of thrumming consumer progress, those in the West have come to a point where the new gadgets being introduced are solving smaller and smaller problems—to an extent that is increasingly absurd, whether it's ovens that beam video of cooking food to our smartphones, or beds that tell us how well we slept. (Has anyone ever had a problem knowing whether they slept well?) That's why the user-friendly things that designers now find themselves creating are, less and less frequently, physical things—which, after all, were easiest to imagine in the days of Dreyfuss, for their very thingness. But as the Magic Bus Ticketing system proves, this doesn't mean that the opportunities for design have grown smaller. Rather, they've grown larger, as technology creates the ability to smooth out the friction in the systems that the user-friendly world has made available to us. Today, you don't need to design a different bus to design an entirely new bus system; moreover, you don't need to remake a government in order to deliver the *structures* people need to improve their lives.

Harry West, who was, at the time we talked, CEO of Frog Design, is an heir to Henry Dreyfuss's vision of placing good design at the center of modern life. West, with a clipped English accent and fantastically arched eyebrows that can convey surprise, attentiveness, and skepticism with the tiniest change, is a roboticist by training. And over lunch, he delivered the message that carries through much of Frog's work today: design, as it was imagined for nearly a century, is over. "The transition from agrarian economies to metropolitan ones brought with it choice," West said, his fantastic eyebrows rising. "Now that choice is being democratized. You don't just get your insurance and your financial adviser from the company roster."[3] For example, with health care, the prospect of open exchanges has made people the direct consumers of something that was always bought for them, and made the companies themselves rethink who their users actually are. West pointed out that the mobile phone quickened the trend exponentially. Banks and insurance companies don't reach us through their stores and sales reps—their services arrive in hand, on our mobile phones, where we evaluate them in whatever context we like. The choices we make are increasingly based on nothing more than the pixels and user experience those companies create.

Dreyfuss saw the birth of that dynamic. Consumer choice has now come to include not just digital goods but the services we depend upon. West went on: "Don Norman thought about design mechanistically, as a top-down solution. But the problem wasn't that people didn't know how to design a door that was easy to open"—as in, a door with the proper affordances for telling which way it swung. "Rather, the problem is that having a door that was easy to open wasn't important to the person selling the door. Today, things happen from the ground up. Nothing you advertise will make a difference if you're not designing a different experience to support it." For so many industries, the customer is finally starting to become the user, and the goods they offer have to sell themselves for the first time. Mobile phones and social media have put companies directly in contact with the end user in ways they've never been before; the fate of their products lies in the social proof of how well those things work, whether tracked through word of mouth or a mere app rating in the App Store. Companies now can't merely focus on striking the right deal with an HR manager or insurance agent. They have to deliver services knowing that they'll be compared with Uber and Airbnb, because they all exist in hand and in comparison, one tap away.

In the arc of moving industries from things to pixels, it took a hundred years to codify what it meant to make something easy to use. By now, we know what usability means—it's feedback, mental models, and all the other nuances we've seen in this book. The biggest accomplishment of user-friendly design lies in making so many different types of things we might want to do understandable with the same tools. You can now access almost anything you'd ever want, if you know how an app works. And designers are assuming that new services need to fit into that same paradigm. User-friendly design is being applied to greater swaths of everyday life—and design itself is coming to encompass things we hardly think of as design at all. We might demand that an app be easy to understand, without an explanation needed. So why shouldn't we demand the same from government, from our food supply, from our health care?

Frog had recognized this need, and proposed a radical solution for Cigna, one inspired in part by the Disney MagicBand. It imagined an app and chatbot that would tell you, as soon as you walked into a health-care clinic, your coverage and what kind of treatment to expect. Birthed from an intensive study of how people wanted their health care to behave, that assistant was designed to demystify insurance by remodeling it around the metaphor of an adviser.

Moreover, the tools of design itself are being applied to higher-order problems. The Gates Foundation, one of the most consequential funders in the world, was built upon the premise of sensing the right problems to solve through the process of design thinking. (In fact, the foundation was for years one of IDEO's most prolific and high-profile clients.[4] More recently, it hired my collaborator Robert Fabricant's team at Dalberg Design to bring greater integration of human-centered design into its global health portfolio.) In Finland, the government had set up a department of design thinking—the so-called experimentation unit, which had spun twenty-six initiatives that ranged from which languages to teach in schools to how best to administer childcare. Each would be prototyped, tested with users, prototyped again, and then retested. To allow for the creation of a cohort of users who could test better services, the Finnish government passed a law allowing an exemption from a constitutional provision mandating equal treatment to every citizen.[5]

It is Pollyannaish to think that design will solve the world's problems. But it is self-evident that the methods of design will play a role in helping us understand, accept, and then make use of whatever solutions we're able to create. In helping people understand their world better, in creating the incentives and feedback loops for us to achieve better things, user-friendliness will be an assumed part of whatever comes next. The paradox of design in the twenty-first century will be the same one we face in society. A hundred years of exploding consumer choice have pulled us apart, blinding us to the costs of what we consume, in the name of making that consumption easier. The problem now is how to design for individual happiness while aiming us all toward higher ends that we can't accomplish on our own. We can no longer assume that a better world will come merely as a by-product of making more people comfortable. Whether the problem is climate change or fake news, design must now help us make decisions based not just on what's easy to use, but on what we should be using in the first place.

I once talked to a designer who'd spent nearly two decades at Apple, working first on desktop computers and later playing an integral role in creating the first iPhone. Out of a sense of duty, his entire extended family had bought the first generation of the iPhone. He came from a sprawling South Asian family that always got together during the Christmas holidays, when all the far-flung sons and daughters could take off work. That year, when he arrived at his parents' house and rang the bell, no one rushed to the door as they usually did. Wondering if they'd all stepped out, he walked in to find them all busily tapping on their iPhones. It was but a few months since it had launched, and he was still in a contented daze at having been part of it. Now his first thought was, *What have I done?*

Almost every designer I've ever met has come to a point in their career when they've wondered whether they actually made the world better by making more things—a consequence of the design industry's founding belief that consumption was the path to human progress. This question arises across generations. In 1971, Victor Papanek published *Design for the Real World*, which exhorted designers to stop focusing on making goods for the world's richest people. Even Henry Dreyfuss, with his heartfelt belief that social progress came down to better-designed products, had his doubts. In later years, he admitted that his role was to make the rich even richer—a startling observation for someone who'd lived through the great middle-class boom of the twentieth century. By the 1960s, he had quietly revised his three-paragraph design credo. He deleted the part mentioning that a designer had succeeded if he made people more eager to purchase. It was a public admission, however small, of a profound unease that lives on in the present day. But when today's designers grapple with their own effects on society, they have to contend with a scale of impact of which Dreyfuss could never have dreamed, thanks to how easy it is to use brand-new things. Dreyfuss worried about the small class of manufacturers who benefited wildly, and the broader class of people who didn't always have better lives—just lives with more stuff in them. Today's designers have to wrestle with that too, but also with a different concern. The effects their products have on society can be difficult to gauge because these effects are so wholly unpredictable and so utterly vast. After you've designed the Facebook Like button, how do you deal with the fact that in a mere ten years a new system of feedback loops rewired how information was spread? If you've designed the iPhone, how do you make peace with its marketing, which every year strives to convince us that our old phones aren't good enough anymore—thus enshrining planned obsolescence not merely as the cost of doing business, but as the ideal state of technology's progress?

Perhaps one way is to make something entirely different. Justin Rosenstein, the software genius who had helped invent the Like button, now dedicates his time to a new company, Asana, whose name references the yogic state of being both utterly alert and profoundly calm. Asana makes software for helping teams organize their work. In this, Rosenstein thinks he's found an answer to a world of distractions. His hope was to make collaboration toward a higher goal into "the path of least resistance." When he left Facebook, he and his cofounder had an aspiration of developing software that could make every project in the world 5 percent faster. A few years after they launched, they surveyed users and asked how much quicker Asana had made their teams. The average answer was 45 percent.

Today, Rosenstein carries that number around like a talisman. "It sounds cliché, but we've gotten pictures of people helped by aid organizations, saying, 'This person is well because of Asana.'" At a talk he gave to a gathering of biotech companies, a chief scientist at one of them told him that Asana was helping them create new antibiotics. "If all I was doing was helping any one of those teams, I would feel like this is worth doing," said Rosenstein. I asked whether it could also be helping teams make the next atomic bomb. Rosenstein nodded. He'd thought about that, too: "You have to have faith that humans are doing good things. I used to have more faith. But then, at the moment, I can look at our actual customers."[6]

I asked Rosenstein whether Silicon Valley really was capable of designing something that wasn't incentivized to distract us, to draw our attention to ends that suited a company rather than the person. After all, the App Store metaphor had created a literal field of competition in a person's hand, where every app was incentivized to fight for our limited attention using only the most distracting means possible—the pop-up notification. Rosenstein brought up the idea of a Hegelian dialectic—the idea that society creates a thesis that's met with a reaction, then an antithesis that amends that prior paradigm, and finally a synthesis, which resolves the tension between the two. To take one example, the industrial revolution—in which it seemed like machines made men into merely another raw input—spawned the idea of bending machines around the lives of men. Social media itself is another. August de los Reyes, the Microsoft designer who transmuted his paralysis into a new design ethos, once pointed out to me that social networking was the product of a generation of latchkey kids who grew up isolated in the suburbs; Rosenstein also pointed out that the hyperconnected internet was a response to the isolating effect of TV. We are still waiting for some more humane way of remaking the commons, one that combines our urges to be both sovereign and highly connected.

It will likely take a new generation to invent that synthesis, and there are signs that generation is already being made, thanks to social media. Leah Pearlman, Justin Rosenstein's collaborator on the Like button, had a startling insight when we talked: that the Like button couldn't have been designed anywhere but America, where so much of your personal identity is tied up in what you *do*.[7] That you can make yourself happy by doing more. But in trying to connect every single person in the world, Facebook also made us all keenly aware of what we were missing: the parties we weren't invited to, the smiles we weren't smiling. A growing body of research shows that it's fear of missing out—FOMO—that drives the unhappiness that seems to spring from social networking.[8] But interestingly, that unhappiness seems also limited to the generations that *didn't* have social networking from their very earliest years. Somehow, kids who grew up with social networking found a way to inoculate themselves from the danger of overconnection. Researchers detected in them a self-knowledge about how much was too much. They knew how to stay away when they needed to. I don't think it's a fool's hope that one of those kids will go on to make something that embodies that reflexive self-control. After all, there probably isn't any way to design the FOMO out of Facebook. Facebook *is* FOMO. A better Facebook means something that is nothing like Facebook, but which can fulfill the same need for connection. For now, we can only imagine what a product meant to make our world both smaller and more manageable might look like.

Where Dreyfuss assumed that greater good would come of giving people greater ease and the wherewithal to use the time they saved in pursuit of higher goals, we know now that higher goals have to be designed into the things we make. It's not just that objects can make our lives easier—it's that the objects in our lives can in fact change us. This is a more rigorous idea than it sounds like at first. We presume that our minds end inside our heads, but Andy Clark, a cognitive scientist and perhaps today's most influential and highly cited philosopher of mind, argues instead that mind and world are melded in an alloy. Consider a mathematician: On her own, she can make logical leaps and connections, yet she could not imagine her way to every nuance and callback required to prove Fermat's last theorem. But, if she has merely a pen and paper, and perhaps some journals to thumb through for reference, she can. You can see this in your own life: Consider what your day would be like if you had no access to a calendar; you'd be so much less capable, and so many things would slip through the cracks. Clark believes that what separates our minds from those of animals is the miraculous power to draft the artifacts around us into our own thoughts, to use them as tools to think ideas we'd have no access to any other way.[9]

If this is true—and there are reasons to believe it is, drawn from not only logic but neuroscience as well—then when a designer creates something new, she is giving form to a thought that allows other people to become more than they were. In a profoundly literal way, those new designs build new minds—just as Steve Jobs suggested when he called the computer a "bicycle for the mind," a device that would allow the power of thought to travel further, and as Doug Engelbart hoped for when he dreamed of using computers to accelerate human potential. This vein of thinking places a new ethical weight upon the act of design—and those ethics happen to connect to a striking number of ideas in this book. Clark, for example, sees a strong connection between his work and that of embodied cognition as well as inclusive design, which was founded on the assumption that disability isn't a limitation of the user but a mismatch between the user and the world we've designed. In that sense, we are all disabled in some ways, because the world can never be perfectly fitted to our needs. Becoming better, more capable people requires us to find the needs that may inspire new designs.

This was where industrial empathy started—what we saw before as Jane Fulton Suri's attempt to find the undercurrent of opportunity beneath everyday life. But today, the modern test-and-learn method—best exemplified in places such as Google and Facebook—has come to emphasize the creation of things that can be tested quickly, rather than those that require a far longer timescale to observe. To take one example, it is easy enough for us to tell our phones what we like in micro-detail: whether we want our notifications on or off, whether we like this or that story on our feed.

These interactions have been optimized to a fine point. And yet what we cannot tell our phone is what kind of overarching experience we'd like in our digital lives. It is bizarre that we accept this. If you were to go to a personal trainer, you wouldn't start by telling her how many biceps curls you'd like to be doing. You'd start with your goals; you might say something like "I just want to feel better, and in a year I'd like to be toned and trim, not swollen." That's not how we interact with our phones, because our phones were founded on the metaphor that they are tools to be used for tasks that we've already defined. As a result, it can be impossible to set forth our broader goals—to be happier, or to be closer with the people we care about.

Over time, our society puts more and more of ourselves into the objects we create; we invest them with a greater and greater sense of who we are, and who we want to become. Those artifacts, in turn, allow us to become more than we were before. This work isn't done. The next phase in user experience will be to change our founding metaphors so that we can express our higher needs, not just our immediate preferences. This will require users to resolve tensions that may seem impossible to resolve: how to connect people to more things while making their world easier to understand; to offer fewer, better choices in a world constantly filling up with more of them. It starts with remaking the assumptions that hide in plain sight.

Among the hundreds of interviews that I did for this book, I took the most inspiration from the people making the wildest bets on new ecosystems. Their efforts were all tiny compared with the vastness of Facebook and Apple. But they were inspiring, too. One was a young, bullheaded Canadian entrepreneur who had this new idea for a computer. Even in his bedroom, still living with his parents, he wondered: What if, instead of always having to buy new devices with new screens, you instead bought one device, a kind of digital amulet, that was simply a brain that held all the data you needed—the apps you used, the services you'd signed up for. And what if all the screens around you were just dumb commodities for accessing all the information in your digital amulet, when and if you needed to? It was a vision not so dissimilar from that of Carnival's Ocean Medallion—or, for that matter, Mark Weiser's field of ubiquitous computing, which he founded in the late 1980s, that tried to build ambient screens that might sense who was in the room and what they needed.

The point that this entrepreneur was making: Companies such as Apple are built to sell us more and more boxes, all of which do the same things. iPhone, iPad, iMac: Why do we need three sets of computer chips, all so that each device can roughly approximate the others? Of course, from Apple's perspective, the fact that all those boxes do the same thing as all the other boxes means that they can each justify their own expense. The redundancy is a feature, not a bug. The hyperactive connectivity that results was a necessary by-product. But what if we could cut the Gordian knot and do away with every assumption about how the gadget ecosystem works today? What if you simply carried around your digital amulet while all the screens around you were just dumb vessels waiting to be filled, ones that were cheap and actually unworthy of being constantly updated and thrown out? Why couldn't a world like that exist? "We're going to take on Samsung and Apple!" the young entrepreneur told me. His words seemed both inspiring and also unmoored. Nonetheless, he'd hustled together $2 million to start working on his idea. After meeting him half a dozen times, I couldn't tell if he was insane. But it didn't mean he was wrong. The proliferation of personal screens each reflecting a similar version of who we are is a hall of mirrors, obscuring a more humane way of living in the digital world, in which we see ourselves more clearly. While the principles of user-friendliness will persist, we might need new mental models and metaphors to better manage our digital lives.

I saw a hint of that possibility in the form of a startup that had raised $63 million in venture capital, on the hope of becoming the bedrock for the Internet of Things. The founder, Linden Tibbets, had been an engineer and designer working at IDEO when he came across Jane Fulton Suri's book *Thoughtless Acts*, which documented all the ingenious ways we make tools from the environment around us: how we tuck pencils behind our ears, or use a stray cork to prop open a door. "We're surrounded by things whose usages we've overridden," said Tibbets. "We live and breathe with them, and they're invisible until someone shows you them." Jane Fulton Suri had shown him a truth that was hiding in plain sight: "Once you see the world like this, you can't unsee it. You don't have to go far to have a brand-new experience of the world you live in."[10]

We naturally see the objects around us not just for what they're meant to do, but for what they might become. It's an essential feature of our human imaginations. A fire poker doesn't just poke fires. It's also a long, heavy rod with an end that's kind of pointy but not too pointy—so maybe you could fish something out from under the couch with it. And yet this essentially human capacity for remaking our world is almost wholly missing from digital life. We see an app or a website or a digital service, and it is nothing but the functional use that we expect from it in that moment. We don't understand what other functions these digital objects might perform; it's a world filled with fire pokers that only poke fires.

Tibbets thought this was an obvious and obviously human need—the ability to readily hack our world to suit whatever requirement arises in the moment. He wondered how a product built around that idea might work. And then, one day, he was in an Indian restaurant watching a waiter take an order. If the waiter sees you've ordered a drink, then he stops by the bar on his way to the kitchen. It was just like computer programming, really: *If* this happens, *then* do that. "I have this weird tendency to extrapolate an entire product starting from the name," he said. "There's something about being able to tie the thread from what you'd call something to how someone would emotionally connect to something." Which is another way of saying the metaphor came to him first, just as we've seen in so many other places throughout this book.

After quitting his job and tinkering in his living room for a year, he had a new company that he called If This Then That, or IFTTT. The service lets you connect one digital service to another by a drag-and-drop interface. One action will automatically spur another. There are now "recipes" that will brew coffee when your Fitbit senses that you've just woken up, turn off the lights when your thermostat senses that you're not home, or even make your house lights blink when you appear in someone else's Instagram photo. Some of these uses might sound absurd, but they sound absurd only because you are not the inventor. The point, said Tibbets, is to create something we've never had before for the digital world: an actual affordance, a way of looking at a service and saying, "Sure, that's fine. What if I could use it for that instead?" Tibbets wants to turn companies into mere verbs in a sentence that people write for themselves.

To date, there have been millions of IFTTT scripts created; there are hundreds more created every day. The company has millions of users. And yet it was still a precarious startup nursed by cheap venture-capital money. It was no more certain to last than any number of companies that had broken out to great success but were still looking for a path to permanence. Nonetheless, it represented a new kind of company, one that employed user-friendliness not to bundle more things together seamlessly but rather to break them apart. It was a new metaphor for the world we've left behind, and an intimation that there are more out there to be found.[11]

These possibilities are hidden beneath a thin varnish that makes the user-friendly world look more finished than it should. At almost every major Apple product announcement after the iPhone, until his retirement from the company in 2019, Jony Ive, the company's storied design guru, would lend his dulcet London accent to a video talking about how the miraculous new thing was designed. He has always been an oracular proponent of the inevitable in design. "So much of what we try to do is get to a point where the solution seems inevitable: you know, you think, 'Of course it's that way, why would it be any other way?'" he said in a rare interview.[12] But none of the things we make are ever inevitable. They only feel that way because someone buffed away everything that called attention to itself for the wrong reasons—a button that didn't make sense or a menu that was hard to understand. They only feel inevitable because someone designed them, and in doing so buffed away the clues of what might have been otherwise. That doesn't mean those clues don't exist, or that the gadgets themselves can't be undone. The things we make reflect the things we value. Those values can change. Even if the user-friendly world is straining to understand us better, that doesn't mean it cannot.

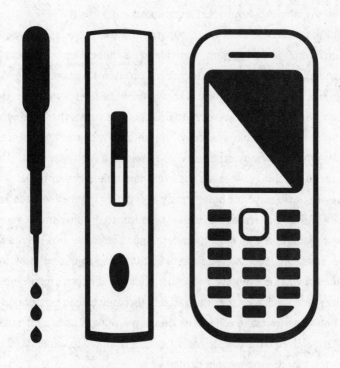

HIV self-test kit (2014)

Afterword:
Seeing the
World Through
User-Friendly Eyes

by Robert Fabricant

The easy and the simple are not identical. To discover what is really
simple and to act upon the discovery is an exceedingly difficult task.
—John Dewey, *Experience and Education*

In 2014, when Cliff and I conceived of this book, our vision was not
just to lift the veil on a bunch of important but little-known stories
about design. Rather, it was to help make the book's readers into in-
formed, critical consumers of design—and, in particular, the user-
experience design that bleeds into new facets of our lives every day.
As a designer, I believe that a user-centered ethos should be applied
to all our experiences. We should never expect less. So this book
is meant to be a user experience thoughtfully crafted around your
needs as a reader: You are this book's user, and the user at the center of the user-friendly world.

Now that you've read the story of how user-friendly design came to be and the principles that underlie it, my goal is to provide you with a brief look at how design works from the perspective of a day-to-day practitioner. This approach to creating user-friendly experiences, developed over twenty-five years of design practice, can be applied not just to the sparkly new things in your life, such as apps or wearables, but also to the really mundane stuff, such as the statements from your health insurance company. When I first began working as a designer, I saw these outputs as vastly different design challenges. They do require some different, specialized skills to fully execute, but they can—and should—be approached with the same user-centered mind-set.

While the added detail in this section may not turn you into a designer, I hope you will be able to take away a few things that you might consider testing out in your own work, whatever that might be. And I hope, most of all, that you become more critical of the myriad user-friendly experiences designed with you in mind. After all, when did you first become aware of the pervasive role of marketing and advertising in your daily life? Back in the 1950s and '60s, public understanding of the influence of marketing on consumer culture was just beginning to emerge. In today's world we take that understanding for granted, doing our best to make sure that our children grow up savvy and discriminating in their response to marketing, instead of taking these messages at face value. We are at a similar inflection point in the user-friendly world, as Cliff has so beautifully articulated.

One way to get there is to try seeing the world as a series of experiences ready to be remade. Like Donald Norman, and Henry Dreyfuss before him, I have always viewed my environment through user-friendly eyes, constantly aware of how things could be made to work better for people and better reflect their values. I am always impatient with how many experiences still fall short of this basic promise. Consider the self-service checkout experience at your grocery store, with its mishmash of poorly engineered interactions: touchscreen menus for selections, sensors for scanning items, card readers for payment, keypads for entering your PIN, and a stylus for signing your name (a legacy interaction that goes back thousands of years but is meaningless today). Like me, you may have finally learned how to successfully orchestrate each of these disparate interactions in the proper sequence, only to be chastised for not placing your items in the bagging area. It is obvious that each of these interactions was developed separately and designed in a vacuum. I feel those seams, and they motivate me. As a designer, I want to work on every piece of a puzzle, not just one part, whether it's the keypad, touchscreen, or store layout.

This is a significant shift from what I imagined a design career to be when I began working as a graphic designer in the mid-1980s. I started out designing logos for big companies like the New York City Health and Hospitals Corporation. Working in a team of designers, we would spend weeks exploring the current state of the health-care system, developing a new perspective on how hospitals might change in the future based on our own experiences—all just to produce an abstracted brand identity. I found this process both inspiring and profoundly frustrating. Why bring so much creative thinking to the table for a logo, even a beautiful one, that doesn't improve the way the system works for people? I could say the same thing about designing a new hospital bed, waiting room, or digital bedside monitor. To improve something as complex as a health-care system requires not only a host of different skills—from industrial design to service design to environmental design—but also the wherewithal to combine them.

That is what I and many of my peers desperately wanted the chance to do, particularly after the original dot-com boom and bust in 2001, when so many digital-only businesses disappeared overnight. I was lucky to land at Frog Design, one of the few places that had a broad range of design capabilities under one roof. Bringing those capabilities together was exhilarating. It opened up new frontiers for user-friendly design, as well as a host of new responsibilities (as demonstrated by Frog's work on Disney's MagicBand, discussed in chapter 8). To what ends should these capabilities be deployed? Answering that question became a personal obsession. But the only way I could find an answer was to stop focusing on *what* we were making. As the acclaimed Japanese industrial designer Naoto Fukasawa—an early IDEO employee—eloquently put it, the best designs "dissolve into behavior" so that they become invisible rather than stand out for their artistry. In other words, the success of our work was not to be found in the beauty of the result, but rather in observing how it fit into and supported people's actual behavior.[1] That lesson, though perhaps obvious to you after having read this book, nonetheless goes unheeded quite often. Consider, for example, the spectacular failure of Google Glass, despite its being backed by a brilliant team of designers and engineers.

I am fond of telling new designers on my team that "behavior is our medium," not products or technologies. This idea couldn't be more different from where I started, fiddling with fonts and colors (which wasn't my greatest talent anyway) and building user interfaces. It represents a shift that can be both liberating and frustrating, because "good design" turns out not to depend on any singular talent. Instead, it can only be found in the way people react and respond to a design. This shift also means that designers must accept the consequences of their work in the world, not just the intentions that went into designing them or the beauty of the result. These consequences can encompass environmental concerns (for example, not wanting to produce more disposable junk) as well as the broader societal impacts that come with influencing people's behavior.

To address issues at this level, more and more designers like me are seeking out different clients and partners to work with, particularly the public-sector organizations making up the core of the practice that I began with my partner, Ravi Chhatpar, at Dalberg Design in 2014. But what makes us qualified to tackle broad societal challenges? After all, what we do is not without risk. Tucker Viemeister, one of the founders of Smart Design, whose father designed the Tucker automobile, is fond of quipping that design is "the most dangerous profession in the world." Designers are not medical doctors or electrical engineers—we do not go through any form of certification before jumping into the design of a self-driving car or an HIV self-testing kit. But we are highly trained tinkerers, with a robust set of prototyping skills that make up for our lack of formal credentials. We find ways to identify user needs, rapidly develop and test solutions, and gather user feedback while relying on the principles found within this book. I hope that these design principles are beginning to seem like common sense—start with the user, gather feedback, try again. But how do you leap from a set of principles to create a satisfying user experience, whether that user is a customer in a drugstore looking for cold meds or an aging family member trying to stay connected to her family and friends?

What does it feel like to follow a user-centered design process, step-by-step?

1. Start with the User

Imagine you've been asked to design a home appliance or a personal-health app. How would you know which users and which needs are worth designing for? You could always start with yourself, but this can quickly become a trap, as you will naturally assume that your needs are the most important ones. The better thing might be to start with a group of people who are like you in some way, such as your coworkers, friends, family members, or people who also shop at your local pharmacy. That is a reasonable point of entry, since you will be able to relate to the situations and expectations of those users. But even with that common ground, individual needs often diverge quickly once you start observing what people actually do. Just look at the different ways that people order something as prosaic as a cup of coffee. In today's hyperpersonalized culture, how do you uncover the sort of insights that reflect the needs of more than one person?

When I worked as a designer at Frog, we developed a number of approaches to help our teams avoid these biases. When conducting research in a new context or situation—whether that was a trading desk on Wall Street or a savings-and-loan group in Rwanda—we often worked with users to visually map each of the links in their decision trees to get a better understanding of whom they turn to first and trust the most. This sort of exercise often leads to unexpected insights. For example, when we were asked to redesign the customer experience for a large U.S. health-care company, I would never have predicted that my team at Frog would end up speaking with a group of hairdressers in Pensacola, Florida. But one of our first activities was to ask typical customers, "Who do you turn to for advice when your child is sick?" A number of women we interviewed mentioned that they frequently discussed personal health issues with their hairdressers. Unlike a pharmacist or even a doctor, a hairdresser has nothing at stake in selling health products, which makes her at once trustworthy to her clients and a potentially very valuable resource for exactly the sort of user insights that the health-care industry lacks—as well as a source for inspiration. Unlike doctors, hairdressers generally spend a little extra time making their customers feel comfortable and taken care of in very basic ways, such as shampooing their hair or massaging their scalps before they get started. We found that consumers were much more willing to listen to health advice when it was paired with suggestions for other, more appealing ways to treat themselves, such as a certificate for a massage or pedicure. This insight shaped our recommendations for how to redesign a program offering health coaches to support patients with expensive chronic diseases such as diabetes and rheumatoid arthritis.

Once you identify an interesting group of people to learn from, you have to meet them on their own terms. One mistake that marketing-led organizations often make is to start by developing a new product and then try to make it attractive to their customers. It rarely succeeds; this is the main reason so many new products seem immediately superfluous. Companies should instead start by understanding the needs of their users and then work backward to develop the right product, feature, or message. This is why you should always meet users on their turf, and why you should also conduct research in a way that puts them in the lead. They should be the guide to their own world. (The Stanford design professor Dev Patnaik calls this the "Grand Tour.") Very often, it is the mundane objects in their lives that prompt the most illuminating stories and lessons, whether at home or at work.

Designers have developed a number of clever techniques to open up fresh windows into users' lives. For example, you might try asking someone to unpack their handbag, backpack, or satchel while narrating the reasons they choose to keep certain objects with them at all times—from the practical, like keys or lip balm, to the sentimental, like a trinket from a recent trip. One of my former colleagues at Frog, Jan Chipchase, dubbed this technique "bag-mapping," which he perfected in his days as a globe-trotting researcher for Nokia. "Bag-mapping is a useful exercise to become acquainted with the norms of a society," he said. "What we do or don't decide to carry is a reflection of ourselves and the environment in which we live and work." In other words, we use these techniques not to learn about the objects themselves (though that can be interesting) but to get at the deeper motivations behind people's choices, particularly their habitual ones. It is one way to explore the gaps between what people say matters to them and what they do in their day-to-day lives. In many ways the apps on our smartphones are an alternate version of similar choices, which is why Jan perfected bag-mapping for Nokia, at the time the largest mobile phone company in the world.

2. Walk in the User's Shoes

One of the basic premises of user-friendly design is that the best work starts with a clear understanding of user needs—and not with the desire to produce a cool product or interface.[2] Henry Dreyfuss was the first designer to truly live by this design ethos. Dreyfuss loved to "walk in the shoes" of his customers, which could mean driving a tractor, sewing in a factory, or pumping gas. For today's designers, Dreyfuss-style immersion in the day-to-day experience of a typical user is a given. The challenge for the designer is to see the routine with fresh eyes, a practice that may sound easy but actually takes a great deal of patience, particularly given the range of distractions in our overstimulated world. You might find yourself, for example, observing how commuters navigate a bus stop or train station, paying special notice to people who seem the most lost and confused. How do they find their way when the station is packed during rush hour? Whom do they ask for help? This sort of observation, which we often conducted in pairs at Frog, can go on for many hours a day over the course of several weeks in multiple cities. And it might be equally important to observe the situation both during late-night hours, when the station is virtually empty, and at rush hour, when it's humming.

Designers often begin by testing out new experiences—say, an exercise routine or an online food-delivery service like Blue Apron—for themselves, to better empathize with user needs and behaviors. We pay close attention to the highs and lows, the moments when we feel most confident as well as our hiccups and failures.[3] Though it sounds obvious, it is amazing how few executives have experienced their own product from end to end, whether that means signing up for a new 401(k) account or trying out a new form of contraception. The former CEO of the stylish budget airline JetBlue, David Neeleman, was well known for taking time to work as a flight attendant several times a year. He did it to be closer to his customers and his staff and understand their day-to-day needs and pain points. Unfortunately, in my experience, these sorts of executives are rare.

In 2017, my team at Dalberg partnered with a group of organizations developing a new reproductive health product for young women in southern Africa. During an initial workshop with the client team, our creative lead was curious to know how many people had given the placebo version a test-drive. She had, but the only other person to raise her hand was the CEO of the company. This provided us with an important insight, as our client didn't seem to fully understand how strange the first-time experience with this product would be for the young women they were trying to serve. Among other things, our follow-up research identified a series of metaphors that could make the product easier to understand. For example, we encouraged users to chew gum during our sessions and reflect on how the flavor dissolved over time in their mouths, the same way that the antiretroviral medicine to prevent HIV would dissolve in their bodies and eventually run out and need to be replaced.

As in the above example, designers often have valuable perspective as a new user, someone who is not already accustomed to the way things are supposed to work. When they can't test a product or experience it themselves, it may make sense to go "shopping" for fresh perspectives. I often encourage designers to experiment with radical shifts in context. For example, if we were asked to improve the waiting experience at a CVS MinuteClinic, we might begin by observing the experience in a crowded emergency waiting room at midnight and then check into a high-end spa. Our designers would try switching roles where possible. As Jane Fulton Suri noted: "The critical component is to not just notice what people are doing, but to really try to understand what's driving it," which can be best understood from a variety of perspectives. Sometimes you might even get behind the sales counter and see people's behavior from the other side. Dreyfuss frequently did this as a pastime, visiting stores and shopping centers whenever he was in a new city, regardless of what he was working on at the time.

Underlying these design practices is a larger truth about the user-friendly age: The world is not chaotic or random, even if it appears that way at first. People's behavior and choices follow certain patterns and routes that do not always appear logical when you first encounter them. But if you tune in to their patterns and truly walk in their shoes, you can get at the hidden truths that drive their daily routines, whether they live in Pensacola, Florida, or Kigali, Rwanda.

3. Make the Invisible Visible

As Cliff observes, feedback surrounds us every moment of every day, helping us to make sense of the user-friendly world. If feedback is well designed, we generally take it for granted. Head out to work in the morning and you step into a series of habitual feedback loops that guide your daily routine. You feel the satisfying click as you lock the front door before heading out to your car. Your phone buzzes with an alert about an email as you walk across the yard and down the block to where you are parked. Press your key fob and your car chirps to let you know that it is exactly where you left it and ready to go. Feedback is the fundamental language of user-friendly design. But the big challenge with designing feedback is figuring out when and where to provide it.

I am awed by the ever-expanding universe of ways designers provide feedback. And yet feedback is often a nuisance—just think of the phone alerts that always seem to appear at the wrong time. It turns out that appropriate feedback is a harder design problem to solve than you think, and we are all intuitively aware when it misses the mark. Try walking into the New York City subway system and swiping a MetroCard. For daily commuters like me, this gesture has become habitual, almost unconscious; the motion of swiping and stepping through the turnstile have become one. However, if your swipe is not smooth and self-assured, the turnstile will lock up and you will slam your thighs into a cold stainless-steel bar. Who designed that? You probably didn't notice that your motion was accompanied by a faint tone to confirm that your swipe went through. The noise probably worked perfectly when it was tested in a design studio, but no one can realistically hear it in a loud Brooklyn subway station.[4]

When I started out as a user-experience designer back in the early 1990s, most of the experiences I worked on were self-contained, such as the interfaces for early ATMs. They were not unlike those boxes invented by Dr. Skinner (see chapter 9) with simple feedback loops between the machine and the user. The design challenge came down to very basic mappings to get the physical buttons and the information on-screen to support a single, fluid interaction. This challenge is not unlike the sort of problems described by Donald Norman in *The Design of Everyday Things*. Action and reaction. Satisfying solutions that could be developed once and applied over and over again. But feedback has slipped out of simple Skinner boxes and into the user-friendly world, where it needs to be tested extensively, or millions of commuters will suffer the results.[5]

This sounds like a daunting amount of work, but it doesn't have to be. Many designers I know are fond of a technique called "Wizard of Oz," in which we use smoke and mirrors to simulate the behavior of a smart system to see if it makes sense to users long before our clients invest in building it. This is a technique both Padgett and Holmes relied on when developing new user experiences for Carnival and Microsoft, as described earlier. The basic idea is quite simple: Figure out how you and your colleagues can perform the feedback that is missing, maybe by flashing a light or making a more effective sound to confirm an action. Then test it. Timing, placement, and sensory feedback can all be approximated without any fancy design tools. One of our teams at Frog got quite skilled at using this approach for the design of voice recognition services such as the ones you experience when using Siri to search your iPhone. The Wizard of Oz technique allowed us to simulate the artificial intelligence component of the service and responded with different screens of information based on queries from our user research participants.

How do designers stay sharp and develop a "second ear" for

fine-tuning this critical layer of the user experience? We've each developed our own tricks. I always pay particular attention to the mechanics of new experiences when I am traveling (just as Patricia Moore did during her visit to Russia for Loewy Design, as described in chapter 7). I can remember the first time I visited a hotel in Europe or Asia and the lights in my room wouldn't turn on. I flipped the switch and the feedback was missing—nothing happened. Eventually, someone showed me how to insert my card key into the slot by the door with a satisfying thunk, and miraculously the entire room was lit. Even better, I didn't need to worry about turning the lights off when I left. I just grabbed the card key from the slot and walked out. This time, the missing feedback (the lights stayed on momentarily as I walked out) was somehow liberating. Why couldn't we do this at home, say, with a smart controller? A whole new way of thinking about personalized spaces can open up with a shift in feedback from the micro (the physical affordance of a light switch) to the macro (environments that adapt to your needs). It is precisely the little differences between what you expect to happen and a slightly new experience that can radically shift our assumptions of what a product (or smart environment) should be.

I often use travel for inspiration, but there are plenty of opportunities at home. Switch between an iPhone and Android or between Google Maps and a competing app like Waze, and all the little design decisions are thrown into relief—just like visiting a foreign country.[6] As Michael Margolis, a user-experience partner at Google Ventures, is fond of saying, "Treat your competitors as your first prototypes." Take advantage of all the effort that some designers have put into their work and learn from it. This is a great way to understand the choices that various designers have made when faced with the exact same challenge: designing feedback.

4. Build on Existing Behavior

I often encourage the designers I work with to observe a situation as if they were cinematographers, zooming in and out from small details (the way someone folds a napkin or splits the check) to the larger scene as it unfolds around them (the flow of people, particularly those who manage and run the restaurant), looking for patterns that emerge at each level. What objects are people using? Where do they seem completely confident and engaged versus hesitant or frustrated? Where do groups gather and why? I instruct my teams to make careful note of what is surprising or confusing. Patterns of behavior will emerge naturally.[7]

Using this approach, you will start to notice behaviors that stand out from the norm. Designers are always delighted to stumble upon these outliers in the course of user observation. If you watch six or seven people in a given situation, often one or two will stand out in the way they behave or respond. The beauty of this approach is that it only takes one outlier to give you a fresh perspective, but you have to follow up and engage the outlier one-on-one (without judgment) to better understand how his or her needs or motivations veer from the norm. Perhaps this person has evolved a different mental model for celebrating special occasions with family or entertaining clients that could be a valuable insight for OpenTable, LinkedIn, or American Express.

Designers generally prefer to build on existing behaviors we can observe in the world today—even if they might seem pretty unusual at first—rather than potential future behaviors dreamed up by marketing executives. Are people likely to order their groceries by talking to a fridge? Who knows. These can be difficult questions to answer, particularly when there might not be existing users you can easily observe. For that reason, user research often involves looking beyond the target customers for a given product or service. You might turn to a family with ten or more children for insights into new meal-planning services. Or you might speak with immigrants who are baffled by health insurance to better understand how to design concierge services for hospitals. The key is to consider users who have an outsized or pronounced need that would require them to develop behaviors outside the norm. Underlying this approach is yet another key principle of user-friendly design: Today's niche markets will become tomorrow's mass markets. Small investments in studying the behavior of outliers today can drive future adoption on a large scale. At Frog, we viewed extreme or outlier research as an important point of competitive differentiation, because it often inspired solutions that wouldn't occur to our clients who were too deeply immersed in their fields to see them.

At Dalberg, where we work across many different cultures, unexpected patterns of behavior surface all the time. One thing we often notice, particularly in resource-constrained environments (like that of Renuka, the woman in Delhi discussed in chapter 5): People often string together several products or services to meet their needs. Working with the Office of Innovation at UNICEF, we engaged users in three cities—Jakarta, Nairobi, and Mexico City—to better understand how they manage their health or get their kids to school safely. We spoke with a woman named Jessica who supported her family by selling meals to customers across one of the largest slums in Nairobi. She used YouTube to look up new recipes online and then posted lunch options to her growing network of local customers via WhatsApp. You may do the very same thing in parts of your life—switching among several apps to plan a night out with friends, for example. While you may feel that each app does its job perfectly, designers will see an opportunity for a more integrated solution whose value is greater than the sum of its parts. Consider your exercise routine, which might involve a mash-up of gear, apps, and classes. The fitness company Peloton saw an opportunity to create a premium experience that seamlessly integrated home exercise equipment, streaming media, and virtual instructors. Each of these elements could easily be found elsewhere, but through clever design the result is much more convenient and user friendly—a value proposition that users are more than happy to pay for and investors are rewarding, with Peloton having achieved a $4 billion valuation as of 2018.

Some users are not satisfied with everyday jury-rigging and will go one step further by adapting or augmenting their world to better suit their needs. Most designers are trained to pay particular attention to work-arounds and augmentations to existing experiences, even when these so-called hacks have become invisible to the users themselves. In such situations, you will observe a host of interesting bespoke adaptations, which Fulton Suri refers to as our "little systems." A common example is the Post-it notes people place on their computer screens at work or the list of instructions next to their DVR or set-top box. I was recently delayed at JFK and watched a fellow business traveler transform his rolling suitcase into a mini movie theater by using the adjustable handle to prop up his iPad in a perfect viewing position. People will often apologize for their hacks as if they are a sign of weakness, a gap in their own abilities, rather than a resourceful way to make their world a bit more accommodating. Users tend to be surprised when you show interest in their work-arounds and mental assists, but they are invaluable sources of insight. They might even help a designer identify a major gap in the current experience that can be filled by a whole new product or service (see Apple Shortcuts, page 151, and IFTTT, page 298). Find a few hundred Jessicas and you may have found the opportunity to launch a one-stop home-cooked meal-delivery service, as the founders of Holachef have done in Mumbai, building on the long tradition of *dabbawalas*[8] in India. Or you may see an opening to provide a new income source for refugees who can offer meals out of their homes showcasing their unique culinary traditions, as the founders of League of Kitchens are pioneering in New York and Los Angeles.

5. Climb the Ladder of Metaphors

As George Lakoff explained (see chapter 5), we all use metaphors to understand our world. They are a powerful tool for designers. Inspiration for metaphors can come from almost anywhere, even the candy aisle. According to one of my former Frog colleagues, Cordell Ratzlaff, who was in charge of the OS design group at Apple for many years, Steve Jobs once taped a Life Saver to the computer monitor used by one of his user-experience designers as a metaphor for the colorful, glossy buttons that would delight end users of Apple's newest operating system, OS X. The difference today is that metaphors have gone beyond surface personality to shape the way products behave and to suggest how we might interact with them over time—the "ladder" described in chapter 5. Designers are always looking for metaphors that can help organize and guide a broader set of relationships. For example, you might think that the metaphor for the Disney MagicBand came from jewelry, given that it is worn like a bracelet. But that was just the physical shape of the band. The guiding concept for Frog's Disney work came from the biblical metaphor of "the keys to the kingdom," in which the visitor has been given special privileges (like royalty) to enjoy the park in exactly the way they see fit. This metaphor encapsulates a host of qualities and behaviors that are embodied throughout the park, with the potential to elevate the user's experience to a whole new level of "magic."

In some cases, the designer's job is much easier once a dominant metaphor has emerged within a product category—such as the widespread adoption of the feed metaphor, established by RSS and later popularized by Twitter, to organize the flow of information that we receive through our social networks (see page 134). Individual designers at a place like Snap will typically look to improve upon the way that Facebook or Twitter have designed their feeds—but they are unlikely to abandon the metaphor entirely. The noted usability guru Jakob Nielsen, Donald Norman's partner in Nielsen Norman Group, has described this effect, which is now known as Jakob's law: "Users spend most of their time on other sites. This means that users prefer your site to work the same way as all the other sites they already know."[9]

We can see this effect well beyond the digital world. Automobiles still owe much of their familiar form to the metaphor of the "horseless carriage" that originally emerged at the turn of the century and was eventually adopted by all the major automotive manufacturers. As we have seen in chapter 4, the role of the car in our lives is fundamentally changing.[10] What is the most useful metaphor for a self-driving car? I worked with an executive at DaimlerChrysler who saw the future of the automobile through the metaphor of a workspace, not a carriage—a combination of office and lounge where productivity, not just moving from one place to another as efficiently as possible, is the goal. As designers, we are often brought in to help bridge the transition as familiar products morph into something new and different. At Frog, we experienced this firsthand working for the leading provider of jukeboxes in the United States. What is the point of a physical jukebox when we walk into the bar with a complete library of our favorite music in our pocket? How might these two devices communicate? What metaphor might help support the transition to that new experience?

Luckily, metaphors tend to surface organically through the normal course of user research—you just have to pay close attention to what people say and do. Our design team at Dalberg recently interviewed potential customers for a mobile savings service in Indonesia, and found that they understood and appreciated the value of their savings if it were converted into more familiar units, such as kilograms of rice or liters of cooking oil. This is particularly true for the digital savings accounts that our client, a mobile operator, was bringing to market. Digital money is much less tangible than physical currency, so the metaphor of oil or rice increased confidence for new users of the service. You might be tempted to see this shift as merely a bit of slick consumer marketing, but the metaphor reveals a much deeper truth about customer behavior. If you are poor, then your stored wealth must always work hard for you. It must do more than one thing. Our Western mental model of "locking things up" is clearly not the right metaphor for these and the billions of other unbanked people throughout the developing world. It's not that they don't understand the purpose of "storing funds"—it just has very little value in their day-to-day lives when money can be put to much more active use in the form of a cow, or a dowry, or a loan to a friend who is starting a small business.

6. Expose the Inner Logic

The title of this book was inspired by my father, Richard Fabricant, who is an extremely sharp and active eighty-eight-year-old with little patience for technology. Whenever he gets frustrated with something new, he turns to me and remarks, "I thought the iPhone was supposed to be so user friendly!" Never has "user friendly" sounded so cutting. These days, whenever we get together, he hands me his Kindle with a set of clippings from *The New York Times Book Review* so that I can purchase and download whatever caught his eye, for him to read at his leisure. I have walked him through the steps of searching for titles any number of times, but the mental model just won't stick. He has a hard time understanding the switch between searching on his device and searching the digital store. These can be very challenging conversations to sort through, as language quickly breaks down. We think we're talking about the same thing, but we are not.

Mental models live below the surface. Users generally have neither the self-awareness nor the language to articulate their deeper, conceptual understanding of how a product or service works. Yet we rely on unconscious mental models to function every day. We feel our way through the world by constructing our own inner logic, particularly when faced with new experiences. For that reason, most designers have developed techniques to expose a user's inner logic through guided exercises that test the boundaries of their mental model. As with any of the activities I have described above, the designer should not assume that there is a correct mental model for a product or service. People usually blame themselves for not understanding something. It is the designer's job to take the user's side and blame any flaws on the product—or the product designer—whenever possible. This can be tricky, particularly when you are the one who designed the thing in the first place![11]

The fact is that we are all pretty confused at times. How did my exercise routine become an app? How did my coffee grinder become a pod? In the user-friendly world, products are being redefined less by what they can do and more by the novel, often digitally enhanced ways we interact with them. The very concept of a product is becoming much more confusing than it used to be, whether we're talking about a book, a TV, or an automobile.[12] What does it mean when a product can talk back to you, follow you, or send you recommendations for how to use it better? In this new era, we build mental models as we go, largely through feedback loops. The job of the designer is to surface these mental models so that products can be better tuned to user expectations and easier to integrate into our lives.

One common approach that I have used throughout my work is to ask the user to sketch the way something works from memory. This exercise can be particularly good for dense interfaces such as a television remote control. Most users will remember the basics, such as the volume and channel buttons, but their mental models diverge from there. More complex tasks, such as managing the amount of available recording space on a DVR, can expose interesting variations in the mental models among different users within the same family, for example. How many episodes of *SpongeBob* should we keep? Should we always keep the most recent ones at the top of the list? And what about *Game of Thrones*? The key is to ask the user to draw and label the various options and choices from memory so that you can get a deeper window into their understanding (remember, the user-friendly world does not come with captions). I try to pay particular attention to what is left out of the picture, not just what is included. I then ask the users to narrate the steps they go through to complete a simple task (something designers call a "think-aloud"). And I ask the users to narrate a series of actions, the ones they are accustomed to as well as ones they might not have tried, like searching their TV for shows that star Kevin Bacon. (Yes, your cable box can probably do this!)

Exercises like these can reveal the limits of the mental model the user has constructed for how and why something works the way it does. You will come to understand why tailored features on a car (cruise control) or microwave (the "baked potato" button) or television remote control (picture in picture) are so rarely used despite their practical benefits. These features may not be intended for everyone, though they have become standardized. But even those people who might benefit greatly from their use can find it hard to bolt them onto their existing mental models, and they ultimately forget they are there. They become invisible. You will also come to understand why there is tremendous resistance against any significant shift in our understanding of how something works. Take, for example, the transition from a standard car to an electric vehicle, which can lead to unintended emotional consequences like "range anxiety"—a fear of being stranded by a dead battery—which a number of designers are actively working on addressing through improved dashboard visualizations and other forms of feedback.

Back in 1958, the cognitive psychologist George Miller was one of the first to document the concept of cognitive load, based on his studies of the limits of short-term memory. This led to the popularization of Miller's law: The average person can keep only seven (plus or minus two) items in their working memory. There is some controversy as to whether seven is or is not a magic number. But most designers have an intuitive appreciation of the principle behind this law, and they "chunk" related options together to reduce cognitive load and reinforce a more coherent mental model. You probably wish this design strategy were more consistently applied to a number of bewildering products in your life, including remote controls, with their dizzying array of strangely labeled, shaped, and colored buttons. I know I do.

7. Extend the Reach

One of the principles our book highlights is that user-friendly products should build stronger connections with users over time. How do designers anticipate and plan ahead to create satisfying experiences across a product journey that could last years or decades, such as owning a car or managing an online collection of family photos? Extending your design task can feel very challenging, as it introduces so many more variables. Even in a product journey of a few hours, users are often distracted, juggling many different needs and goals at one time. Companies lose sight of this basic fact and assume that their users remain focused on one task or activity at a time. This is why it is important for user-friendly designs to connect the dots for their customers, over both the short and long term. Unresolved or disconnected elements of any experience can undermine our confidence in a brand or service provider. Why did I type in my account number when I called customer service only to have the agent ask for it again? This observation is not just a feature of the design process but ties deeply into cognitive psychology. In the 1920s, the Soviet psychiatrist Bluma Wulfovna Zeigarnik conducted a study in which she found that uncompleted tasks are easier to remember than successful ones, a discovery known as the Zeigarnik effect.

User experience should support the entire user journey, not just a single moment or interaction.[13] Consider everything that happens between reserving a hotel room online and touching your head on the pillow, then checking out a few days later. Each step should be interlinked through a series of feedback loops that propel you forward, like a daisy chain, while providing a consistent feeling of comfort, confidence, and ease. Even successful consumer-driven companies such as Marriott and Disney can find it difficult to step back and look objectively from the customer's point of view across every step of their journey, given how their businesses are typically organized into functional silos such as marketing, product management, and customer support, and channels like retail and digital. It is always an eye-opening experience when you map out in detail all the different hoops that the average user must jump through. These blind spots can be a huge barrier to an effective user-friendly experience, which is why John Padgett (see chapter 8) is such a strong voice in this book. It is tempting to think that one simple medallion or wristband can make up for many shortcomings. But it is rarely that easy, given the fact that different parts of an organization are typically in control at different steps, as Padgett's story illustrates.

One of the most important issues we try to address as designers is when the user's journey actually starts and ends. This is not always obvious. Your client might assume that it all starts when the customer walks into their store or opens their app, when in fact there might be many factors, and earlier experiences, that shape the user experience long before any direct point of engagement. These neglected spaces—before, between, or after direct product touch-points—are often the best design opportunities, as they can be strengthened with feedback to better connect the dots across the entire journey in unexpected and often delightful ways. Sometimes user journeys can extend across many years, even a lifetime. I do a lot of design work in global health, where there is an increasing focus on tracking progress across the entire health journey of a newborn child or an adolescent mother. What does that look like?

One answer is, not too dissimilar from the story about Carnival Cruise Line, but extended over a much longer period of time and designed around personal rituals and life events. I recently served as a mentor to an organization called Khushi Baby, which has developed a low-cost wearable amulet to store a baby's unique identifier and capture the baby's health-care data across multiple events during the early years of life. The product is currently undergoing its first deployment and randomized controlled trial in more than seventy villages in Udaipur, India. The key to its appeal does not come from any technical innovation—all the technologies are remarkably basic—but rather from a novel design mothers can relate to. The approach started with talking to hundreds of mothers in villages and observing children wearing amulets on a black thread to ward off disease. The cultural fit of the necklace strengthens its potential for long-term sustainability, as a ritual and habit that can be passed down from one generation to another within families. How do you extend these cultural insights across the health journey for a mother and child? Ritual-based, habit-forming design is a frontier for our work at Dalberg and a long-term goal for many designers tackling broad social issues.

8. Form Follows Emotion

Designers are often surprised by how much user satisfaction is driven by the emotional rather than functional benefits of an experience. But the right emotional connection with a user can make up for many of the challenges I describe above, from poor feedback to a convoluted mental model. (The connection between emotional aesthetics and perceived ease of use was first documented in 1995 by researchers from the Hitachi Design Center who tested variations of an ATM user interface with more than 250 participants.)[14] Our job as designers is not just to make things work better so that users can get on with their lives. It is to surprise, delight, and build a meaningful relationship over time. Consider all of the effort that companies like Starbucks put into fine-tuning the aesthetic and emotional experience around what is a relatively brief encounter each morning. The emotional payoff of the perfect cappuccino is pretty clear. But what about preparing our income taxes, something we do once a year and would rather avoid entirely?

Brad Smith, the CEO of Intuit, has become a vocal advocate for emotional design, which may be surprising given that his company is best known for tax-preparation software. Adopting a user-friendly approach to research, his team at Intuit discovered a great deal about the emotional layers driving user perceptions of their product: "Consumers spend 6 billion hours each year using software to prepare their income taxes; anything we can do to reduce that time will be a gift. At the end of the process, most taxpayers are owed a refund—and for 70 percent of them, that refund is the single largest check they'll receive during the year. In this context we began to think less about the pure functionality of our software and more about the emotional payoff of reducing drudgery and speeding the way toward a big windfall." Under his direction, the Intuit product development team spent tens of thousands of hours "working alongside customers to see how they actually use our products." Smith said, "As we did, we made notes with smiley faces next to elements that customers enjoyed and sad faces at places where they hit a snag—an example of using design to simplify the feedback mechanism. We've emphasized to engineers, product managers, and designers that functionality isn't enough anymore. We have to build emotion into the product."[15]

I sometimes ask my designers to think of the product journey as a form of romance, complete with emotional highs and lows. We even ask users to write breakup letters to products and services that no longer work for them. What you learn from these letters is that user-friendly design is about much more than usability.

Frog's founder and my former boss, Hartmut Esslinger, was one of the first product designers to truly celebrate the power of emotion to drive positive user experiences,[16] and his motto, "Form follows emotion," still sets the bar for the design team at Frog.[17] Even Don Norman has come around to this sort of thinking, despite his emphasis on the scientific nature of design, writing an entire book on the topic in 2003 called *Emotional Design*. But few companies have truly embraced this mind-set, which is why it is so surprising to see a financial services software company lead the charge. It is equally surprising that a company such as Apple, which crafts products that inspire such deep emotions from its users, will occasionally drop the ball. Consider how long it took Apple to recognize the power of emojis and build them directly into iOS. I will never forget when I bought my daughter, Evie, her first iPhone at the age of thirteen. We took it home and set it up, and she immediately went to text her best friend, Isola. Yet when she began to type her message, there were no emojis available, as we hadn't installed any special keyboards. She looked at me, crestfallen, and said, "Daddy, you bought the wrong phone!" Her moment of truth was a major fail.

The Designer's Moment of Truth

While user-friendliness has become orthodoxy within the design world and institutionalized within corporate America, there is no guarantee that you will create a great product by following my advice. In many ways, the approach that I have described above is just the entry point into the world of user-friendly design. Much of the most critical and arduous work is in the details, tested and prototyped repeatedly until they come together.

The moment of truth will come sooner than you think: when you first put your design in front of someone, with no direction or explanation. As most designers will tell you, time slows down as you wait to see what this first user will do. How will they engage? How will they respond to the elements that you have so carefully crafted? I always find that in the seconds before the first user even responds, I can see aspects of our design clearly for the first time. Perhaps it is empathy at work. The first moment when you see your work through the user's eyes is priceless. You are confronted with so many tiny problems that somehow remained hidden, despite your best efforts. You often wish you could stop time and take your prototype back to the shop to change just a few small things. Soon enough, you can, and you will continue to refine the design . . . over and over again. The feedback cycle between designer and user is the beating heart of the user-friendly world.[18]

Each time you put something in front of a user, you will notice different things. Back in my Frog days we were designing a micro-dermabrasion device for a large consumer products company. It was simple from an engineering perspective, so we had freedom to test out different form factors as well as subtle placements for the controls. During multiple rounds of user research, we set the table with about a dozen different prototypes and paid special attention to which ones our young female users picked up first and which they held on to the longest. At first, there didn't seem to be an obvious logic to their preferences. But our user research lead, who was a young woman, noticed how these users looked at their often nicely manicured hands while they held the different models we had created. They were drawn to the products with a form that flattered their hands, making them look more elegant and graceful.[19] This became an easy test that our industrial design team could apply as we further refined and finalized the physical shape and surface textures of the product.[20] The positive response to the design among younger women gave our client the confidence to shift its strategy for the product toward a different audience, which resulted in a bestselling device when it was introduced to the market.[21]

Such insights sound clear in hindsight, even obvious at times. But it doesn't feel that way when you are in the thick of it. The design process can be arduous for long stretches with no easy answers in sight. Teams frequently get frustrated and demoralized. So it is incredibly satisfying when the pieces finally start to fall into place, particularly when you are tackling the social issues that are at the core of my current design practice.

In some cases, it may take years and years before you see any sort of real progress. In 2008, I began working with a team of designers, as well as a local NGO partner in South Africa, to create a self-service experience that would allow anyone (particularly someone young who will not visit a sexual health clinic for fear of being judged) to test themselves for HIV in a private and discreet manner. Four years later, I found myself sitting in the office of a large public hospital in Edendale, a small city in KwaZulu-Natal with some of the highest HIV infection rates in the world. In the next room a nervous young woman opened a package containing an HIV self-test kit. We had carefully designed the kit, along with a service that offers access to a trained HIV counselor via cell phone. The combined experience was meant to work as simply as a home pregnancy test. We had stayed up two nights in a row, making dozens of minor adjustments to how the test packet was folded and how exactly three drops of blood, not two, were represented in the printed instructions on the inside cover of the kit.

The woman opened the packet and slowly went through the instructions, printed in Zulu. At one point she picked up the cell phone and considered connecting to remote support, but she decided against it and completed the process herself, correctly determining her status, which was negative. We breathed a huge sigh of relief, and follow-up tests revealed that her self-diagnosis was as accurate as the one she subsequently received from a trained HIV counselor at the hospital. This successful result was repeated hundreds of times over the subsequent months, with countless refinements to improve the ease and accuracy of the experience. Slowly and painstakingly, we took a dreadful experience that failed 64 percent of the time and redesigned it to be 98 percent accurate in a clinical study.[22] As Joshua Porter, cofounder of 52 Weeks of UX, is fond of saying, "the behavior you are seeing is the behavior you designed for." The next time we ran a self-testing session in this community, youths were lined up outside for the chance to participate.

I share the story of this young woman so that you don't come away with the false impression that user-friendly design is simple to achieve. It is not, and many within the design world feel understandably frustrated when they watch a complex design process being taught with a formulaic problem-solving approach to business and engineering students around the world at places like the Stanford d.school. But we also cannot treat design as some sort of alchemy, a black box that is opaque to the world around us, to users like you. The beliefs and assumptions underlying user-friendly design must be exposed to the light of day for examination and questioning by a broad audience, considering the risk of massive unintended consequences, particularly given the breadth of the issues we are tackling now. Ultimately, it is you—the user—who must hold us accountable to the principles outlined here. How else can we take on the vast sweep of user experiences surfaced in this book and make them work better for us and society at large?

Appendix:

A Brief History

of "User Friendly"

It seems like new technologies are popping up every day that tantalize us with the promise of greater ease, comfort, and convenience in our daily lives. But what makes one product succeed while others fail? History can be a good guide. It is helpful to place these new experiences within a broader lineage that extends back many centuries, long before the rise of computers and digital technology. The core principles of user-friendly design can be traced back to iconic products from ancient Greece. Included below is a partial list of significant milestones.

1716: LOUIS XV ARMCHAIR SEATING

Louis XV introduced a radical shift in the concept of authority by abandoning the formality of a stiff, upright throne at Versailles in favor of more comfortable lounge seating—showing that ease was the ultimate projection of power and privilege.

1874: QWERTY TYPEWRITER KEYBOARD, Christopher Latham Sholes

The QWERTY layout was devised in the early 1870s by Christopher Latham Sholes and popularized by E. Remington and Sons to slow down typing speeds and thereby avoid mechanical malfunctions. Remington's decision not to monopolize his design led to the widespread adoption of a standard that today seems unkillable.

1894: "MAKESHIFT," William Morris

William Morris coined the term "makeshift" to describe the poor quality and usability of cheap factory goods that flooded the European market during the early years of the industrial revolution.

1898: STEERING WHEEL, Charles Rolls

After an early period of divergence and experimentation with a range of different levers and tillers, several automotive manufacturers converged on a boating metaphor to explain how users might control a car. Charles Rolls (of Rolls-Royce) was the first to take this design into broader production.

1900: KODAK BROWNIE CAMERA, Eastman Kodak and Walter Dorwin Teague

Eastman Kodak sold its famous cameras largely on their ease of use, with the motto "You push the button and we do the rest." To achieve this goal, George Eastman reconfigured an entire supply chain around film development, transforming photography from an expert hobby (just like the early PCs) into a true consumer technology.

1907: AEG CONSUMER APPLIANCES, Peter Behrens

The first wave of technology adoption in the home emerged in the early twentieth century with a host of electrical appliances, such as hot-water kettles, intended to be convenient and time-saving for homemakers. Peter Behrens, considered by many to be the first modern industrial designer, recognized the power of design to make these devices iconic, delightful, and easy to use, informing the Bauhaus's later faith in the promise of modern industry.

1909: SELFRIDGE DEPARTMENT STORE, Harry Gordon Selfridge

Selfridge was the first department store to move products out from under the counter and onto open shelving where customers could touch and feel them directly, without asking for a shopkeeper's help.

1911: *THE PRINCIPLES OF SCIENTIFIC MANAGEMENT,* Frederick Winslow Taylor

Taylor's rigorous observation of factory worker efficiency led to a focus on ergonomics and usability to minimize wasted effort and boost productivity. His time-saving approach was based on optimizing human behavior to suit the capabilities of the machines before them and to minimize human error.

1915: FORD ASSEMBLY LINE, Henry Ford

The Ford assembly line was the definitive application of Taylor's principles of scientific management. Ford optimized his assembly line to make the Model T as cheaply and uniformly as possible, with no room for customization or consumer taste, thereby reducing the cost of an automobile from $825 to $260 by 1924.

1920s: HOME ECONOMICS, Christine Frederick

Home economics attempted to free up leisure time for women so that they might pursue their own betterment. The pursuit of efficiency in the home laid the groundwork for a wave of appliances, such as washing machines, that became a sustaining source of work for Behrens, Dreyfuss, Loewy, and many other early industrial designers.

1921: MODERN ETHNOGRAPHY, Franz Boas

In the 1920s, during his studies of Native Americans in the Pacific Northwest, the anthropologist Franz Boas developed detailed methods for observing daily life and practices that provided the foundation for modern ethnography as practiced by Alphonse Chapanis, Henry Dreyfuss, Jane Fulton Suri, Donald Norman, Jan Chipchase, and others.

1925: "L'ESPRIT NOUVEAU," Le Corbusier

Le Corbusier introduced a modernist lifestyle aesthetic that stripped away decorative and ornamental touches in favor of simplified, mass-produced products to create a "machine to inhabit." His groundbreaking exhibition embodied the Bauhaus belief that beauty can be found at the intersection of aesthetics and engineering.

1927: MODEL A, Henry Ford

Henry Ford, who for years resisted offering variations on the Model T, was finally forced by rising competition from General Motors and others to introduce the Model A, which offered a range of options and colors in a Ford automobile for the first time.

1927: MASCHINENMENSCH ROBOT FROM *METROPOLIS*, Fritz Lang and Walter Schulze-Mittendorff

Fritz Lang's dystopian vision for the societal impact of technology took iconic form in the character of a female robot who served as the ambassador for a more advanced world—brought to life by the sculptor Walter Schulze-Mittendorff.

1930: RKO THEATER, SIOUX CITY, IOWA, Henry Dreyfuss

Henry Dreyfuss spent three days observing the behavior of patrons of RKO's new but unpopular movie house in Sioux City. He noticed that the local farmers and laborers were uncomfortable entering the richly carpeted lobby in their dirty work boots—which he quickly corrected by adding some cheap rubber mats. That idea presaged the modern recognition of how social mores guide the adoption of new products, particularly those that incorporate technology.

1930: SKINNER BOX, Burrhus Frederic Skinner

By isolating how an animal responded to a controlled input, the Skinner box revealed the way feedback loops guide behavior. Though Skinner's reductionist view of psychology fell out of favor, it spawned landmark studies of the power of feedback and rewards in the human brain.

1933: SEARS TOPERATOR WASHING MACHINE, Henry Dreyfuss

Dreyfuss's first great hit, the Toperator washing machine, featured a streamlined, art deco design that avoided any hard-to-clean joints—an early nod to the user's lifestyle that would be echoed widely. Another detail considered the user's psychology and anticipated the rationale that governs the design of modern apps and gadget interfaces: Dreyfuss bunched the controls together at the top, so that the user could readily understand all its functions at once. Hence the name Toperator.

1936–45: B-17 FLYING FORTRESS LANDING FLAP CONTROLS, Alphonse Chapanis

Based on extensive user research into the causes of pilot error in World War II, Alphonse Chapanis introduced airplane levers that could be identified in the pilot's hand by their shapes. Chapanis's system of shape-coding remains in use in all commercial aircraft today.

1947: POLAROID INSTANT CAMERA, Edwin Land and William Dorwin Teague

At a time when Kodak dominated photography, Polaroid upended the business by collapsing the entire messy process of film development into a user-friendly format that provided immediate gratification to consumers. Instagram's original logo depicted a Polaroid OneStep camera.

1950: *THE HUMAN USE OF HUMAN BEINGS: CYBERNETICS AND SOCIETY,* Norbert Wiener

Cybernetics, which began by formalizing how machines might approximate the responsiveness of humans, eventually influenced modern computer science. Wiener, the field's founding father, popularized the social implications of cybernetics, drawing analogies between the role of feedback in control systems (such as a computer) and social systems (such as an amusement park or social network).

1950s: DISNEYLAND, Walt Disney

Disneyland was Walt Disney's first attempt to translate his imagination into real life, in the form of an exactingly designed theme park. Disneyland presaged the end-to-end experience design that has become commonplace today.

1953: HONEYWELL ROUND THERMOSTAT, Henry Dreyfuss

The Honeywell thermostat was one of Dreyfuss's most successful and iconic designs, in which form and interaction are seamlessly blended together for ease of use. The Honeywell thermostat later inspired the Nest smart thermostat.

1954: FITTS'S LAW, Paul Fitts

With his eponymous law governing the relationship between button size and ease of use, Fitts helped invent the cross-disciplinary study of human-computer interaction.

1956: MILLER'S LAW, George Miller

The cognitive psychologist George Miller was one of the first to document the concept of cognitive load, based on his studies of the limits of short-term memory. His research led to the widespread adoption of Miller's law as a rule of thumb by designers to reduce complexity and resist the pressure to lard products with more features.

1959: PRINCESS PHONE, Henry Dreyfuss

Dreyfuss's Princess phone was an ergonomic design inspired by the way young girls would squirrel away in bed with their clunky AT&T phones. Available in a range of colors, the Princess phone was a groundbreaking example of a communication device tailored to social context.

1960: *THE MEASURE OF MAN,* Henry Dreyfuss and Alvin Tilley

The Measure of Man was the first book to systematically lay out the proportions of the average man and woman—referred to as Joe and Josephine—so that products might be designed around them. NASA would later follow with the *Anthropometric Source Book*, which would become a standard reference for product designers.

1960s: ELIZA CONVERSATIONAL BOT, Joseph Weizenbaum

Developed at MIT, Eliza was the first chatbot—a language program meant to behave like a therapist, asking questions of users simply based on what they'd typed. To Weizenbaum's surprise, participants at times chatted with Eliza for hours—showing that people readily lend emotional weight to their interactions with machines.

1968: "THE MOTHER OF ALL DEMOS"—HYPERTEXT, CURSOR, MOUSE, INTERNET, Doug Engelbart

This live demonstration introduced many of the core design concepts that would shape personal computing. Engelbart developed the demo while at Stanford Research Institute, which would later license its mouse patent to Apple for approximately $40,000.

1970s: TEN PRINCIPLES OF GOOD DESIGN, Dieter Rams

Over a thirty-four-year career as the chief design officer of Braun, Rams created a host of iconic appliances and consumer electronics based on his belief in simplicity (as opposed to decoration) as a core value of user-friendly design. In the 1970s Rams laid down a set of ten principles that summed up his philosophy, which today are held sacred by many designers. Under Jony Ive, several of Apple's products echoed Rams's iconic designs: the first iPod and the Braun T3 radio; the original iPhone calculator app and the Braun ET44 calculator; and the G5 Mac Pro and the Braun T1000 radio, to give just three examples.

1972: "USER FRIENDLY," Harlan Crowder

One of the first documented uses of the term "user friendly" being applied to software design appeared in an obscure programming white paper that Crowder wrote while working in operations research at IBM. But the broader notion of user-friendly design truly bloomed twelve years later when Apple introduced its Macintosh computer, which was marketed as a computer "for the rest of us."

1979: THREE MILE ISLAND ACCIDENT

The cognitive psychologist Donald Norman's groundbreaking research into the cause of the largest nuclear meltdown in U.S. history revealed a host of design flaws that demonstrated the fatal mismatch between engineering models and the way our brains actually work, particularly under pressure. He went on to expand on many of these concepts in his groundbreaking work *The Design of Everyday Things*.

Early 1980s: LAWN MOWER USABILITY, Jane Fulton Suri

Fulton Suri was hired by the U.K. government to better understand consumer mishaps with lawn mowers, chain saws, and other consumer goods. Her research, with its emphasis on understanding the nuanced, everyday context in which people experienced product design, would become a pillar of IDEO's design practice and the design industry at large.

1982: GRID COMPASS LAPTOP COMPUTER, Bill Moggridge

Not only the first laptop computer, but the first to bear a clamshell case with a screen that could be readily adjusted for any sitting position, the Grid Compass presaged a world of portable, convenient, and user-friendly high technology. Moggridge went on to help found IDEO and coin the term "interaction design" to refer to the myriad ways users engage with technology.

1984: CYCLONIC VACUUM CLEANER (PROTOTYPE), James Dyson

On his way to creating the first cyclonic vacuum cleaner, Dyson produced more than five thousand prototypes. Inspired by industrial methods for filtering dirt, the prototype couldn't clog and didn't need a dust bag. Dyson's first production design, the DA001, was finally released in 1993, and bore a crucial improvement: a clear plastic dust bin, which showed users just how much dust they'd removed, creating a feedback loop that made people want to use the product more.

1984: MACINTOSH COMPUTER, Steve Jobs

Apple's first masterpiece worked on many levels, making new technology palatable and desirable in ways it had never been before. The Macintosh introduced myriad new concepts through metaphor (the desktop and windows); sought to convey approachability through a case that tilted up to the user, like a face; and made interacting with digital objects almost physically intuitive by allowing them to be directly manipulated with a mouse and cursor. Apple deliberately marketed the Mac as being first and foremost for "the rest of us"—the users. An early ad asked: "Since computers are so smart, wouldn't it make sense to teach computers about people, instead of teaching people about computers?" Apple's investment in design spurred the industry's ascendance in Silicon Valley with Frog, IDEO, and others contributing to the success of the original Mac.

1985: ELDERLY AUGMENTATION SUIT, Patricia Moore

As a young designer, Moore questioned the premise of designing for the average user, exemplified in Dreyfuss's *Measure of Man*. Wearing a restrictive costume that simulated both the look and experience of being elderly, Moore sought both to faithfully represent and to design for an underserved demographic. In doing so, she pioneered the idea of inclusive design and its ethos of designing better products by thinking first of the underserved.

1988: *THE DESIGN OF EVERYDAY THINGS,* Donald Norman

Norman's pioneering work connecting design to cognitive principles has been a bible for product and user-experience designers for decades. Norman took a bit longer to recognize the importance of emotion and delight in user-friendly design, releasing *Emotional Design* as a follow-up in 2003.

1990: OXO PEELER, Sam Farber and Dan Formosa

OXO, the ubiquitous kitchenware brand, was born from a peeler with a simple handle akin to a bike handlebar grip, chunky and easy to use. That product also became an archetype for inclusive design—the ethos that Pat Moore helped articulate. Sam Farber, OXO's founder, was inspired to create the peeler with a thick, rubber-finned handle after he watched his wife, Betsey, who had arthritis, struggle while peeling an apple.

1990s: PERSONA, Alan Cooper

Cooper invented a process for doing primary user research, then representing users' unmet needs in the form of composited personas. The goal was to help designers empathize with needs other than their own—and in doing so, avoid the natural trap of assuming too much about an idealized user, as exemplified by Dreyfuss's *Measure of Man*. Personas remain ubiquitous in design today.

1992: AERON CHAIR, Don Chadwick and Bill Stumpf

The signature mesh material for the Aeron chair was first developed to prevent bedsores in the elderly but turned out to be equally valuable in enhancing comfort for legions of office workers—spawning one of the most profitable office products in history.

1996: "THE COMING AGE OF CALM TECHNOLOGY," Mark Weiser and John Seely Brown

In their pioneering paper, Mark Weiser and John Seely Brown introduced a new vision for computing in which technology blends seamlessly into the periphery—one that Spike Jonze would bring to life in the movie *Her* and Amazon would introduce to millions of homes with Alexa. Today, in an era of constant smartphone distraction, that vision grows in urgency.

1997: ONE-CLICK PURCHASE, Amazon

Amazon turned user-friendly design into a decisive competitive advantage by patenting its one-click feature, which removed nearly all checkout friction and brought instant gratification to the web. It was the single most valuable button ever created—until the invention of Facebook's Like button in 2009.

1997: GOOGLE, Larry Page and Sergey Brin

Page and Brin revolutionized the web with a novel algorithm that ranked pages not just by their content but by the actual humans linking to that content. Google's signature "one box" design was meant to translate the push-button simplicity of a Polaroid camera to a monumental task: finding any given piece of information amid a limitless universe of knowledge.

1999: EMOJI

Emojis were first introduced in Japan by NTT Docomo as a feature of i-mode—the most advanced mobile internet platform of its time—to increase the use and frequency of messaging by adding a new, evocative layer into conversations. Today, as many linguists argue, emojis are redefining the way we communicate.

1999: TWO-SECOND REWIND, Paul Newby

TiVo heralded a new era for TV and digital video, and, in addition to ad skipping, one of its earliest and most loved features was the two-second rewind. Its invention sprang from observing users watching TV and wondering what someone had just said.

2001: APPLE IPOD, Jony Ive, Tony Fadell, and Phil Schiller

Just like the Sony Walkman in the late 1970s, the iPod ushered in a wave of gadget adoption that was driven by user-experience innovations rather than new functionality. The iPod click wheel embodied Apple's long-held belief in the seamless integration of hardware and software. Though its design was first inspired by a Bang & Olufsen phone, it also echoed Dreyfuss's Honeywell Round thermostat and a Dieter Rams masterpiece, the Braun T3 personal radio.

2003: ITUNES STORE, Apple

In addition to creating an easy alternative to music piracy that stabilized the industry, the iTunes Store showed how user-friendly design could reshape an entire business ecosystem. The ease with which iPod (and later iPhone) users could browse, purchase, download, and manage music created a self-reinforcing cycle of use and adoption.

2004: FUSION DASHBOARD, IDEO and Smart Design

Hoping to mold driving behavior, Ford introduced a radical metaphor in the user interface of the dashboard for its mainstream hybrid vehicle, the Ford Fusion. The interface, which depicted green leaves sprouting when drivers went easy on the gas and brakes, provided positive, emotional reinforcement of environmentally friendly driving practices—an early attempt to fuse user-friendly design and sustainability.

2007: IPHONE MULTI-TOUCH SCREEN, Apple

Before the iPhone was announced, Apple was worth $74 billion; by 2018, it was worth over $1 trillion. Steve Jobs had always dreamed of increasingly natural ways of interfacing with computers. In the iPhone, which served the functions of at least half a dozen different devices, his company finally hit on one that made computers not only personal but ever present. But in doing so, Apple brought forth a world of constant access and distraction whose consequences are still unfolding.

2008: APP STORE, Apple

The iPhone may have been the first, most important step, but it was the App Store that unleashed the mobile revolution. Mobile apps delivered possibilities for convenience, ease, amusement, connection, and abuse that have reshaped expectations for nearly every industry one can name—while also leading to an explosion in the demand for and relevance of user-experience designers.

2009: BEHAVIOR MODEL FOR PERSUASIVE DESIGN, B. J. Fogg

B. J. Fogg, founder of the Behavior Design Lab at Stanford University, introduced a simple model for influencing user behavior—motivate users, prompt them at the right time, and make it easy to act on the prompt—that would inspire a generation of app designers and developers, including the founders of Instagram. Today, tech companies have at times used Fogg's insights to make their products habit-forming for billions of users. It's an open question whether we can wean ourselves off them, and whether we want to.

2009: LIKE BUTTON, Justin Rosenstein, Leah Pearlman, Aaron Sittig, Mark Zuckerberg, and others

The most successful button in history, the Like button made it almost frictionless for users to act on even the faintest twinge of affection or animosity; multiplied, that signal would shape the information diet of billions. The Like button introduced a new layer of social exchange that society hadn't seen before; and it proved once again the power of feedback to shape our psyches.

2011: NEST LEARNING THERMOSTAT, Tony Fadell, Ben Filson, and Fred Bould

The Nest Learning Thermostat represented a milestone in applying the sort of user-friendly design approach we associate with high-end devices such as the iPhone to the mundane appliances we take for granted. Like the Ford Fusion dashboard, the Nest thermostat incorporates subtle behavioral nudges intended to make the product more convenient to use as well as more environmentally sustainable. Its interface was a direct descendant of Dreyfuss's Honeywell Round thermostat.

2012: DESIGN PRINCIPLES, U.K. Government

Intended to ensure that public services would be accessible while responding to user needs, the U.K. was a pioneer in adopting user-centered design principles. That process—understanding user needs, prototyping solutions for them, then iterating upon feedback—would soon be adopted by other governments, including those of Finland, France, New York City, and Spain.

2013: HER, Spike Jonze

Both a love story and a cautionary tale for how user-friendly technology might become embedded in our emotional lives, *Her* portrays a future in which computers have blended into the world around us, becoming both invisible and ubiquitous.

2013: DISNEY MAGICBAND/MYMAGIC+, John Padgett, Frog Design

Disney's MagicBand system augured a future in which the physical world would respond to our needs before we were even aware of them. The system was meant to be magical, eliminating the regular friction of daily life—keys, checkouts, lines—and in so doing, fulfill the expectations of a new generation weaned on smartphones.

2013: GOOGLE GLASS, Google

Google, in a rush to bring augmented reality to market, failed to consider the embarrassment of wearing a computer wrapped around your face. Though its features were wonky, slow, and limited, the project of creating a digital overlay to the real world continues apace, in efforts such as Instagram's face filters and Google Lens, which allows your smartphone camera to conduct information searches overlaid upon the real world.

2014: ALEXA, Amazon

Quietly launched in 2014, Amazon's smart speaker was a surprise consumer hit, quickly selling millions of devices and sparking a race among technology giants to make new conversational interfaces. Along the way, it raised a question at least as old as Eliza, the first chatbot: Just how anthropomorphic should technology be?

2014: MODEL S AUTOPILOT FEATURE, Tesla

Tesla introduced its supposed self-driving feature to the mass market through a simple overnight software upgrade. In the user-friendly era, in which it is assumed that new products and apps shouldn't require much instruction, Autopilot conveyed a muddy sense of what it could and could not do—with sometimes fatal consequences.

2016: INSTAGRAM STORIES

In 2016, after noticing that users were becoming more self-conscious about posting to Instagram, the company copied the disappearing-messages feature of Snapchat, to spectacular success. Just a few years before, the iPod click wheel had proved that a user-experience innovation could ignite widespread adoption; Snapchat did the same. But in an era of digital products, those innovations are nearly impossible to defend from copycats for long.

2016: GENERAL DATA PROTECTION REGULATION, European Union

EU decision makers opened up a new frontier in user-friendly design by enacting a set of laws intended to give users control over their personal data. Left unsaid was a larger design problem that seems poised to grow in importance: allowing users to understand where all their data has gone, and what benefits they're actually getting in exchange.

Notes

1. CONFUSION

1. Mike Gray and Ira Rosen, *The Warning: Accident at Three Mile Island* (New York: W. W. Norton, 1982), 73.
2. Ibid., 84; Daniel F. Ford, *Three Mile Island: Thirty Minutes to Meltdown* (New York: Viking, 1982), 17.
3. Gray and Rosen, *Warning*, 85.
4. Ibid., 74.
5. Ibid., 77.
6. Ibid., 43.
7. Ibid., 87.
8. Ibid., 90.
9. Ibid., 91.
10. Ibid., 111–12.
11. Ibid., 187–88.

12. Ibid., 188–89.

13. Elian Peltier, James Glanz, Mika Gröndahl, Weiyi Cai, Adam Nossiter, and Liz Alderman, "Notre-Dame Came Far Closer to Collapsing Than People Knew. This Is How It Was Saved," *New York Times*, July 18, 2019, www.nytimes.com/interactive/2019/07/16/world/europe/notre-dame.html.

14. Sheena Lyonnais, "Where Did the Term 'User Experience' Come From?," *Adobe Blog*, https://theblog.adobe.com/where-did-the-term-user-experience-come-from.

15. For more context on the history, see Donald A. Norman, "Design as Practiced," in *Bringing Design to Software*, ed. Terry Winograd (Boston: Addison-Wesley, 1996), https://hci.stanford.edu/publications/bds/12-norman.html.

16. Interviews with Donald Norman, December 11–12, 2014.

17. Ford, *Three Mile Island*, 101.

18. Gray and Rosen, *Warning*, 104.

19. Ford, *Three Mile Island*, 133.

20. Jon Gertner, "Atomic Balm?," *New York Times Magazine*, July 16, 2006, www.nytimes.com/2006/07/16/magazine/16nuclear.html.

21. Cam Abernethy, "NRC Approves Vogtle Reactor Construction—First New Nuclear Plant Approval in 34 Years," *Nuclear Street*, February 9, 2012, http://nuclearstreet.com/nuclear_power_industry_news/b/nuclear_power_news/archive/2012/02/09/nrc-approves-vogtle-reactor-construction-_2d00_-first-new-nuclear-plant-approval-in-34-years-_2800_with-new-plant-photos_2900_-020902.

22. Marc Levy, "3 Mile Island Owner Threatens to Close Ill-Fated Plant," AP News, May 30, 2017, www.apnews.com/266b9aff54a14ab4a6bea903ac7ae603.

23. Gray and Rosen, *Warning*, 260.

24. Mitchell M. Waldrop, *The Dream Machine: J.C.R. Licklider and the Revolution That Made Computing Personal* (New York: Viking, 2001), 54–57.

25. Or, as the behavioral economist Daniel Kahneman writes, "The absence of definite information concerning the outcomes of actions one has not taken is probably the single most important factor that keeps regret in life within tolerable bounds. We can never be absolutely sure that we would have been happier had we chosen another profession or another spouse . . . Thus, we are often protected from painful knowledge concerning the quality of our decisions." Quoted in Michael Lewis, *The Undoing Project: A Friendship That Changed Our Minds* (New York: W. W. Norton, 2016), 264.

26. Tim Harford, "Seller Feedback," *50 Things That Made the Modern Economy*, BBC World Service, August 6, 2017, www.bbc.co.uk/programmes/p059zb6n.

27. Waldrop, *Dream Machine*, 57–58.
28. Interview with Robby Stein, November 11, 2016.
29. Gray and Rosen, *Warning*, 19–21.
30. To be clear, TMI 2 and TMI 1 were always a little bit different in their designs; TMI 2 was more problematic owing to its being a rush job.
31. The second thing you find at TMI is more subtle. There is an approach to what the workers do when anything goes wrong. At the time of TMI 2, the workers were trained to follow a rote list of procedures when an accident loomed. Today, they begin not with procedures but with symptoms, methodically following a checklist of things to monitor. Instead of trying to tease apart a web of conflicting information, they systematically close down branches of possibility. The procedure is meant to immerse them in what is going on now, rather than what usually goes right.

    Put another way, they have a new mental model of how an accident even occurs. The former method created, in the minds of Velez and Hauser and everyone at TMI 2, a fog of possibilities that stood outside all the procedures they'd been given. The new method, of methodically following lines on a flowchart, constrains how many things the workers would have to consider at any one time so that they can better isolate what's gone wrong. The power of mental models is that they help us anticipate how something should behave; they let us deduce what should be true.
32. One of the chief reasons that some products aggravate us is that the mental model is nonexistent or confusing. Consider one of the worst features that Apple has ever introduced, iCloud, which is supposed to be a simple way to back up all the files on your computer. But what is it? Who knows? Sometimes it's an option in a drop-down menu: "Backup to iCloud." Sometimes it's a website. Sometimes it's a form you have to sign in to. And still other times it's a baffling warning, prompting you to take action for a feature you don't remember signing up for. Nowhere is it actually a *thing* that you're able to picture. It is, quite literally, a cloud of options. It suffers in comparison to Dropbox, which is also a way to back up your files. Dropbox is only ever a folder on your computer. The mental model is simple: Folders store things. Put things in the folder, they're stored. The entirety of Dropbox's success—its explosive user growth, thousands of employees, a company valued at nearly $10 billion—lay in providing a mental model where none had existed before.
33. Sometimes mental models break down alongside their mappings. Consider your TV: There was a time you clicked the channels up and down, like a radio, which made sense because the TV got its signal over the airwaves and each channel was a segment of radio frequency. Today—in the world of Netflix and HBO Go and Amazon Prime—the TV has become an

awful thing to use, because flipping the channels doesn't map to an eco-system of the television anymore.

34. This trend is otherwise known as the "consumerization of IT," a phrase so sleep-inducing that it elides just how big a change it portends.

2. INDUSTRY

1. Interview with Mladen Barbaric, August 11, 2015.
2. Interview with Bo Gillespie, October 31, 2015.
3. Reporting and interviews with Mladen Barbaric, June 30, 2015.
4. In her career, Johnstone has focused on prevention of sexual assault, as opposed to resistance or defense. Imagine a scene at a bar: A woman who's had more to drink than she thought, who suddenly finds herself the object of attention from a guy who'd been clinging to their group all night. Maybe someone knows him from a class, or he's a friend of a friend. And then, when her friends have gone, he's still there offering to take care of her. Johnstone began to wonder: What would it take for a bystander to step in, to check in on that woman, to ask her if she was okay? (Interview with Dusty Johnstone, February 18, 2016.)
5. Interview with Mladen Barbaric, September 15, 2015.
6. Bill Davidson, "You Buy Their Dreams," *Collier's*, August 2, 1947, 23.
7. Henry Dreyfuss, "The Industrial Designer and the Businessman," *Harvard Business Review*, November 6, 1950, 81.
8. Russell Flinchum, *Henry Dreyfuss, Industrial Designer: The Man in the Brown Suit* (New York: Rizzoli, 1997), 22.
9. Beverly Smith, "He's into Everything," *American Magazine*, April 1932, 150.
10. Gilbert Seldes, "Artist in a Factory," *New Yorker*, August 29, 1931, 22.
11. Smith, "He's into Everything," 151.
12. I saw a hint of this, perhaps from Dreyfuss's own hand, when I went to rummage through his papers at the Cooper Hewitt design museum's archive in New Jersey. In a typed-out list of all Dreyfuss's projects, someone had drawn a decisive "X" through all the theater work.
13. Flinchum, *Henry Dreyfuss, Industrial Designer*, 48.
14. That dynamic is what caused the designer William Morris, a forefather of the industrial design industry, to coin the word "makeshift." William Morris, "Makeshift," speech given at a meeting sponsored by the Ancoats Recreation Committee at New Islington Hall, Ancoats, Manchester, November 18, 1894, www.marxists.org/archive/morris/works/1894/make .htm.
15. Alva Johnston, "Nothing Looks Right to Dreyfuss," *Saturday Evening Post*, November 22, 1947, 132.
16. Ibid., 20.

17. Ibid.

18. Arthur J. Pulos, *American Design Ethic: A History of Industrial Design* (Cambridge, MA: MIT Press, 1986), 261.

19. Ibid., 304.

20. Ibid.

21. Ibid., 305.

22. Jeffrey L. Meikle, *Design in the USA* (New York: Oxford University Press, 2005), 91.

23. Ibid.

24. Pulos, *American Design Ethic*, 331–32.

25. David A. Hounshell, *From the American System to Mass Production, 1800–1932* (Baltimore: Johns Hopkins University Press, 1985), 280–92.

26. Pulos, *American Design Ethic*, 330.

27. Johnston, "Nothing Looks Right to Dreyfuss," 21.

28. Ibid.

29. Ibid.

30. Smith, "He's into Everything," 151.

31. Johnston, "Nothing Looks Right to Dreyfuss," 135.

32. Seldes, "Artist in a Factory," 24.

33. Her father was a rich businessman who retired to devote himself to social causes; her mother was a suffragist and birth-control advocate who had been instrumental in bringing daylight savings time to the United States, to better take advantage of working hours.

34. Smith, "He's into Everything," 151; Johnston, "Nothing Looks Right to Dreyfuss," 135.

35. Meikle, *Design in the USA*, 108.

36. Ibid., 107.

37. Johnston, "Nothing Looks Right to Dreyfuss," 135.

38. Meikle, *Design in the USA*, 114.

39. It isn't a coincidence that the very first evidence of user-centered kitchens is found in the Netherlands in the seventeenth century, where women were expected to be the captains of their own homes. The architecture reflected this. As opposed to upper-class houses in England and France, where the kitchen was either separated from the main rooms or hidden in the basement, Dutch kitchens were the home's beating heart. Dutch women made those kitchens a part of family life. They designed the space, making it easier to use for themselves, with amenities such as copper cookware hung along the walls, running hot water, and cabinetry to display prized housewares. For more, see Witold Rybczynski, *Home: A Short History of an Idea* (New York: Viking, 1986).

40. Dreyfuss, "The Industrial Designer and the Businessman," 79.

3. ERROR

1. S. S. Stevens, "Machines Cannot Fight Alone," *American Scientist* 34, no. 3 (July 1946): 389–90.
2. Francis Bello, "Fitting the Machine to the Man," *Fortune*, November 1954, 152.
3. Stevens, "Machines Cannot Fight Alone," 390.
4. Ibid.
5. Ibid.
6. Donna Haraway, *Simians, Cyborgs, and Women: The Reinvention of Nature* (New York: Routledge, 1990), 47–50.
7. Today, Fitts is best known in the world of human-computer interaction as the discoverer of Fitts's law, which undergirds the buttons we use in computer interfaces. The law provides a mathematical formulation of an intuitive truth: buttons are easier to find when they're bigger and closer at hand. Therefore, the more important a button is, the bigger it should be—a pattern you can see in any piece of modern software. One nuanced example of this is the sticky task bar at the top of most desktop programs. Task bars are so quick and easy to find because your cursor simply stops as soon as it reaches them. They're effectively infinite in size: It doesn't matter if you overshoot a task bar by a lot or a little. You've still reached it.
8. Alphonse Chapanis, "Psychology and the Instrument Panel," *Scientific American*, April 1, 1953, 75.
9. Bello, "Fitting the Machine to the Man," 154.
10. Chapanis, "Psychology and the Instrument Panel," 76.
11. Stevens, "Machines Cannot Fight Alone," 399.
12. Ibid., 394.
13. Ibid., 76.
14. Ibid., 399.
15. Chapanis, "Psychology and the Instrument Panel," 76.
16. Bello, "Fitting the Machine to the Man," 135.
17. Bill Davidson, "You Buy Their Dreams," *Collier's*, August 2, 1947, 68.
18. Russell Flinchum, *Henry Dreyfuss, Industrial Designer: The Man in the Brown Suit* (New York: Rizzoli, 1997), 89–90.
19. Russell Flinchum, "The Other Half of Henry Dreyfuss," Design Criticism M.F.A. Lecture Series, School of Visual Arts, New York, October 25, 2011, https://vimeo.com/35777735.
20. Henry Dreyfuss, "The Industrial Designer and the Businessman," *Harvard Business Review*, November 6, 1950, 80.
21. Dreyfuss, "The Industrial Designer and the Businessman," 135.
22. Henry Dreyfuss, *Designing for People*, 4th ed. (New York: Allworth, 2012), 20.

23. Eventually, Joe and Josephine would evolve into some two hundred drawings, showing all types of human beings, from the first to the ninety-ninth percentile.

24. Dreyfuss, "The Industrial Designer and the Businessman," 78.

25. Jorge Luis Borges, "On Exactitude in Science," in *Collected Fictions* (New York: Viking, 1998).

26. This idea of not letting your own hand obscure the action on-screen is actually behind one of the design details that fueled Uber's rise. Initially, the app had you drop a pin with your fingertip to mark your location. But that meant your fingertip actually obscured the location you were trying to mark. Uber soon revamped its app, so that you moved the map while the pin stayed centered on the screen.

27. Dreyfuss, "The Industrial Designer and the Businessman," 79.

28. Flinchum, *Henry Dreyfuss, Industrial Designer*, 168.

29. Interview with Ralph Kaplan, April 29, 2016.

30. This is a point that's been made steadily in the last decade by Robert Fabricant. See Fabricant, "Behavior Is Our Medium," presentation at the Interaction Design Association conference, Vancouver, 2009, https://vimeo.com/3730382.

4. TRUST

1. Alex Davies, "Americans Can't Have Audi's Super Capable Self-Driving System," *Wired*, May 15, 2018, www.wired.com/story/audi-self-driving-traffic-jam-pilot-a8-2019-availability.

2. Victor Cruz Cid, "Volvo Auto Brake System Fail," YouTube, May 19, 2015, www.youtube.com/watch?v=_47utWAoupo.

3. RockTreeStar, "Tesla Autopilot Tried to Kill Me!" YouTube, October 15, 2015, www.youtube.com/watch?v=MrwxEX8qOxA.

4. Andrew J. Hawkins, "This Map Shows How Few Self-Driving Cars Are Actually on the Road Today," *The Verge*, October 23, 2017, www.theverge.com/2017/10/23/16510696/self-driving-cars-map-testing-bloomberg-aspen.

5. There is an irony in this: Audi is owned by Volkswagen, which at the same time was embroiled in a scandal over untrustworthy emissions performance. The engineers and designers in this story had no involvement in that.

6. Interview with Brian Lathrop, January 8, 2016.

7. Asaf Degani, *Taming HAL: Designing Interfaces Beyond 2001* (New York: Palgrave Macmillan, 2004).

8. Interview with Yves Béhar, June 22, 2017.

9. Clifford Nass, *The Man Who Lied to His Laptop: What Machines Teach Us About Human Relationships* (New York: Current, 2010), 12.

10. Ibid., 6–7.

11. William Yardley, "Clifford Nass, Who Warned of a Data Deluge, Dies at

55," *New York Times*, November 6, 2013, www.nytimes.com/2013/11/07 /business/clifford-nass-researcher-on-multitasking-dies-at-55.html.

12. Byron Reeves and Clifford Nass, *The Media Equation: How People Treat Computers, Television, and New Media Like Real People and Places* (New York: CSLI Publications, 1996), 12.

13. H. P. Grice, "Logic and Conversation," *Syntax and Semantics*, vol. 3, *Speech Acts* (Cambridge, MA: Academic Press, 1975), 183–98.

14. Nass, *Man Who Lied to His Laptop*, 8.

15. Interview with Erik Glaser, October 20, 2016.

16. Frank O. Flemisch et al., "The H-Metaphor as a Guideline for Vehicle Automation and Interaction," National Aeronautics and Space Administration, December 2003; Kenneth H. Goodrich et al., "Application of the H-Mode, a Design and Interaction Concept for Highly Automated Vehicles, to Aircraft," National Aeronautics and Space Administration, October 15, 2006.

17. William Brian Lathrop et al., "System, Components and Methodologies for Gaze Dependent Gesture Input Control," Volkswagen AG, assignee, Patent 9,244,527, filed March 26, 2013, and issued January 26, 2016, https://patents.justia.com/patent/9244527.

18. Interview with Brian Lathrop, July 10, 2016.

19. Interviews with Brian Lathrop, February 22 and 25, 2016.

20. Lathrop et al., "System, Components and Methodologies."

21. Rachel Abrams and Annalyn Kurtz, "Joshua Brown, Who Died in Self-Driving Accident, Tested Limits of His Tesla," *New York Times*, July 1, 2016, www.nytimes.com/2016/07/02/business/joshua-brown-technology -enthusiast-tested-the-limits-of-his-tesla.html; David Shepardson, "Tesla Driver in Fatal 'Autopilot' Crash Got Numerous Warnings: U.S. Government," Reuters, June 19, 2017, www.reuters.com/article/us-tesla-crash/tesla -driver-in-fatal-autopilot-crash-got-numerous-warnings-u-s-government -idUSKBN19A2XC; "Transport Safety Body Rules Safeguards 'Were Lacking' in Deadly Tesla Crash," *Guardian*, September 12, 2017, www.theguardian .com/technology/2017/sep/12/tesla-crash-joshua-brown-safety-self-driving -cars.

22. "Transport Safety Body Rules Safeguards 'Were Lacking.'"

23. Ryan Randazzo et al., "Self-Driving Uber Vehicle Strikes, Kills 49-Year-Old Woman in Tempe," AZCentral.com, March 19, 2018, www.azcentral.com /story/news/local/tempe-breaking/2018/03/19/woman-dies-fatal-hit -strikes-self-driving-uber-crossing-road-tempe/438256002/.

24. Carolyn Said, "Exclusive: Tempe Police Chief Says Early Probe Shows No Fault by Uber," *San Francisco Chronicle*, March 26, 2018, www.sfchronicle .com/business/article/Exclusive-Tempe-police-chief-says-early-probe -12765481.php.

25. Jared M. Spool, "The Hawaii Missile Alert Culprit: Poorly Chosen File Names," *Medium*, January 16, 2018, https://medium.com/ux-immersion -interactions/the-hawaii-missile-alert-culprit-poorly-chosen-file-names -d30d59ddfcf5; Jason Kottke, "Bad Design in Action: The False Hawaiian Ballistic Missile Alert," Kottke.org, January 16, 2018, https://kottke.org /18/01/bad-design-in-action-the-false-hawaiian-ballistic-missile-alert.

26. Eric Levitz, "The Hawaii Missile Scare Was Caused by Overly Realistic Drill," *New York*, January 30, 2018, http://nymag.com/intelligencer/2018 /01/the-hawaii-missile-scare-was-caused-by-too-realistic-drill.html; Nick Grube, "Man Who Sent Out False Missile Alert Was 'Source of Concern' for a Decade," *Honolulu Civil Beat*, January 30, 2018, www.civilbeat.org/2018 /01/hawaii-fires-man-who-sent-out-false-missile-alert-top-administrator -resigns; Gene Park, "The Missile Employee Messed Up Because Hawaii Rewards Incompetence," *Washington Post*, February 1, 2018, www .washingtonpost.com/news/posteverything/wp/2018/02/01/the-missile -employee-messed-up-because-hawaii-rewards-incompetence.

27. A. J. Dellinger, "Google Assistant Is Smarter Than Alexa and Siri, but Honestly They All Suck," *Gizmodo*, April 27, 2018, https://gizmodo.com /google-assistant-is-smarter-than-alexa-and-siri-but-ho-1825616612.

28. For a good list of these, see Tubik Studio, "UX Design Glossary: How to Use Affordances in User Interfaces," *UX Planet*, https://uxplanet .org/ux-design-glossary-how-to-use-affordances-in-user-interfaces -393c8e9686e4.

29. Interview with Sameer Saproo, May 5, 2016.

5. METAPHOR

1. Interview with Renuka, July 3, 2016.
2. Jessi Hempel, "What Happened to Facebook's Grand Plan to Wire the World?," *Wired*, May 17, 2018, www.wired.com/story/what-happened-to -facebooks-grand-plan-to-wire-the-world.
3. Ibid.
4. Researcher transcripts, February 24–28, 2015.
5. Klaus Krippendorff, *The Semantic Turn: A New Foundation for Design* (Boca Raton, FL: CRC, 2005), 168.
6. Researcher transcripts, February 24–28, 2015.
7. George Lakoff and Mark Johnson, *Metaphors We Live By*, 2nd ed. (Chicago: University of Chicago Press, 2003), 15.
8. Ibid., 158.
9. Ibid., 7–8.
10. Perhaps the first instance of an information feed in the digital world was the RSS feed, originally developed by Apple's Advanced Technology Group.
11. Micheline Maynard, "Waiting List Gone, Incentives Are Coming for

Prius," *New York Times*, February 8, 2007, www.nytimes.com/2007/02/08 /automobiles/08hybrid.html.

12. Interviews with David Watson, July 12, 2016; Ian Roberts, November 28, 2016; Jeff Greenberg, May 26, 2016; Richard Whitehall, May 10, 2016; and Dan Formosa, May 10, 2016.

13. There was one problem, dealing with the very feedback of driving. How could you connect the thing that you do in the moment with what good you could do over time? One of the reasons that we don't do well with long-term behavior change is that we lack an ability to see things working. To get people to change their behavior, they'd need to get feedback that showed them, immediately, the longer-term effects of driving better. It wasn't enough to drive better for a few minutes. Those few minutes had to add up.

14. Jane Fulton Suri, "Saving Lives Through Design," *Ergonomics in Design* (Summer 2000): 2–10.

15. Interview with Bill Atkinson and Andy Hertzfeld, May 14, 2018.

16. Interview with Bruce Horn, May 9, 2018.

17. Interview with Atkinson; Michael A. Hiltzik, *Dealers of Lightning: Xerox PARC and the Dawn of the Computer Age* (New York: HarperCollins, 1999), 332–45.

18. Interview with Hertzfeld.

19. Hiltzik, *Dealers of Lightning*, 340.

20. Alan Kay, "A Personal Computer for Children of All Ages," Proceedings of the ACM National Conference, Xerox Palo Alto Research Center, 1972, Viewpoints Research Institute, http://worrydream.com/refs/Kay%20 -%20A%20Personal%20Computer%20for%20Children%20of%20All%20 Ages.pdf.

21. As of 2010, the license plate on Tesler's Subaru read NO MODES.

22. One of the first people to notice the vital role that metaphors play in allowing us not just to describe things but to invent them was Donald Schon, a peripatetic academic philosopher who became obsessed with the inner workings of creativity. Schon, hoping to see the spark as it formed, eventually found a company willing to let him observe the invention process. The company made paintbrushes, and was trying to design a new one made with cheaper, synthetic bristles. For months, all the prototypes had failed, producing a gloopy mess instead of a continuous smear of color—until one day, while Schon watched, one of the researchers blurted out a metaphor: "A paintbrush is like a pump!"

That leap of logic made no sense at first. But that researcher was trying to explain that a paintbrush wasn't merely about its bristles. A paintbrush carried paint *between* its bristles, thanks to capillary forces. When a brush's bristles bend against a wall, the spaces between those bristles flare out. They create channels that allow the paint to flow and smear evenly. On the back of that insight, the researchers began anew with a different mental model. They began reengineering how the artificial bristles *bent*, rather than how thick they were or how many there were. As Schon describes it, "Paintbrush-as-pump was a generative metaphor for the researchers in the sense that it generated new precautions, explanations, and inventions."

23. R. Polk Wagner and Thomas Jeitschko, "Why Amazon's '1-Click' Ordering Was a Game Changer," Knowledge@Wharton by the Wharton School of the University of Pennsylvania, September 14, 2017, http://knowledge .wharton.upenn.edu/article/amazons-1-click-goes-off-patent.

24. The earliest steering wheels appeared in motorized tractors and sleds. Their precursor was the tiller, a steering technology borrowed from boats. And on boats, a tiller turns the rudder left. In response, the ship turns right. Therefore, proto-steering-wheels actually moved a vehicle in the *opposite* direction that you steered. But the car evolved to become familiar in its own right. The metaphorical reference to boating was lost. And so, it became "natural" to turn a wheel right, and have the car turn right.

25. To take another example of a shifting metaphor: If you use an Apple laptop, you may have noticed that sometime around 2010, the scrolling direction of the trackpad changed from moving a page down when you scrolled *up*, to "natural"—meaning that when you swipe down, the page moves down. The former works like a spyglass would: As you move, the spyglass stays trained on what's in view; the bit you're reading moves *up* onto the screen. Natural scrolling is different. It's as if you're pushing a physical page upward as you read. The first metaphor made sense in the era of desktops, when windows functioned like spyglasses onto the content of a page. The later metaphor makes sense only with touchscreens, and the idea that the thing you previously thought was a screen had in fact become something like paper. I've asked people how they set their computers, and their answers break on generational lines: Only people who came of age with desktop computers turn natural scrolling off. Younger people, who came of age with smartphones, leave it on.

26. Research transcripts, February 17–21, 2015.

27. Ellis Hamburger, "Where Are They Now? These Were the 10 Best iPhone Apps When the App Store Launched in 2008," *Business Insider*, May 17, 2011, www.businessinsider.com/the-best-iphone-apps-when-the-app-store -launched-2011-5.

28. Lindy Woodhead, *Shopping, Seduction and Mr. Selfridge* (New York: Random House, 2013); Tim Harford, "Department Store," *50 Things That Made the Modern Economy*, BBC World Service, July 2, 2017, www.bbc.co.uk /programmes/p056srj3.

29. Ari Weinstein and Michael Mattelaer, "Introduction to Siri Shortcuts," presentation at the Apple Worldwide Developers Conference, McEnery

Convention Center, San Jose, June 5, 2018, https://developer.apple.com/videos/play/wwdc2018/211/.

30. Cliff Kuang, "Fuchsia, Google's Experimental Mobile OS, Solves Glaring Problems That Apple Doesn't Get," *Fast Company*, May 10, 2017, www.fastcompany.com/90124729/fuchsia-googles-experimental-mobile-os-solves-glaring-problems-that-apple-doesnt-get.

31. Descartes imagined that he was in thrall to some demon who held him asleep in a dream, controlling everything he experienced. Modern philosophers call this the "brain in a vat" thought experiment; you might also imagine *The Matrix*.

32. Some experiments in the field of embodied cognition have come under scrutiny in the broader psychological community, owing to the so-called replication crisis that has rocked the entire profession. But "grounded cognition" remains a live vein of research.

33. Samuel McNerney, "A Brief Guide to Embodied Cognition: Why You Are Not Your Brain," *Scientific American*, November 4, 2011, https://blogs.scientificamerican.com/guest-blog/a-brief-guide-to-embodied-cognition-why-you-are-not-your-brain.

34. Interview with Philippa Mothersill, March 22, 2016.

35. As early as 1921, psychologists had already shown that people associate angled lines with being "furious," "serious," and "agitating," while curved lines were "sad," "quiet," and "gentle."

36. Recently, an academic tried to understand why the fascia of cars tend to be wide; after studying both wider watches and wider cars, she concluded that those designs seemed more dominant because we're primed to read aggression into wider human faces. See Mark Wilson, "The Reason Your Brain Loves Wide Design," *Fast Company*, August 24, 2017, www.fastcodesign.com/90137664/the-reason-your-brain-loves-wide-products.

6. EMPATHY

1. *The Simpsons*, season 2, episode 28, "O Brother Where Art Thou," aired February 21, 1991, www.dailymotion.com/video/x6tg4a5.

2. Tony Hamer and Michele Hamer, "The Edsel Automobile Legacy of Failure," *ThoughtCo.*, January 6, 2019, www.thoughtco.com/the-edsel-a-legacy-of-failure-726013.

3. Interview with Bob McKim, November 29, 2016.

4. Julia P. A. von Thienen, William J. Clancey, and Christoph Meinel, "Theoretical Foundations of Design Thinking," in *Design Thinking Research*, ed. Christoph Meinel and Larry Leifer (Cham, Switzerland: Springer Nature, 2019), 15, https://books.google.com/books?id=-9hwDwAAQBAJ.

5. William J. Clancey, introduction to *Creative Engineering: Promoting Innova-*

tion by Thinking Differently, by John E. Arnold (self-pub., Amazon Digital Services, 2017), 9.

6. John E. Arnold, *The Arcturus IV Case Study*, edited and with an introduction by John E. Arnold, Jr. (1953; repr., Stanford University Digital Repository, 2016), https://stacks.stanford.edu/file/druid:rz867bs3905/SC0269 _Arcturus_IV.pdf.

7. Morton M. Hunt, "The Course Where Students Lose Earthly Shackles," *Life*, May 16, 1955, 188.

8. Arnold, *Arcturus IV Case Study*, 139.

9. Interview with Larry Leifer, April 22, 2016.

10. Hunt, "Course Where Students Lose Earthly Shackles," 195–96.

11. William Whyte, Jr., "Groupthink," *Fortune*, March 1952.

12. Clancey, *Creative Engineering*, 8.

13. Ibid.

14. See also Barry M. Katz, *Make It New: The History of Silicon Valley Design* (Cambridge, MA: MIT Press, 2015).

15. Interview with David Kelley, December 15, 2016.

16. Katherine Schwab, "Sweeping New McKinsey Study of 300 Companies Reveals What Every Business Needs to Know About Design for 2019," *Fast Company*, October 25, 2018, www.fastcompany.com/90255363/this -mckinsey-study-of-300-companies-reveals-what-every-business-needs -to-know-about-design-for-2019.

17. Jeanne Liedtka, "Why Design Thinking Works," *Harvard Business Review*, September/October 2018, https://hbr.org/2018/09/why-design-thinking -works.

18. Interview with Jane Fulton Suri, June 30, 2016.

19. Interview with Dan Formosa, May 20, 2016.

20. Interview with Tim Brown, January 7, 2016.

21. Later, for that reason, Moggridge would coin the term "interaction design" to encompass not just the physical features of a product but the digital ones as well—the experience of the entire thing.

22. Cooper was already famous among software designers for inventing Visual Basic, a graphical tool later bought by Microsoft that allowed programmers to build new programs from systems of widgets. When Cooper was setting out to understand his early users, he noticed commonalities that reached across them—say, a harried programmer who couldn't find a piece of code that someone else had developed, or a product manager who didn't understand why the coders always missed their deadlines. Personas were his way of simplifying all those nuances into a summary that could be readily explained. For more, see Alan Cooper et al., *About Face: The Essentials of Interaction Design*, 4th ed. (New York: Wiley, 2014).

23. These snapshots eventually became a tiny book written by Jane Fulton Suri and IDEO, *Thoughtless Acts?* (San Francisco: Chronicle, 2005).

24. After six years, that experiment yielded Mayo's "Jack and Jill" consultation rooms, which remain a gold standard in medical care. The insight was that better clinical care wasn't about delivering more tests and technology, but rather better conversations between doctor and patient. As a result, the Jack and Jill conversation rooms are oriented around a "kitchen table." They don't have a medical bed or exam tools; those sit in a separate exam room shared among conversation rooms.

25. Avery Trufelman, "The Finnish Experiment," *99% Invisible*, September 19, 2017, https://99percentinvisible.org/episode/the-finnish-experiment.

26. Pagan Kennedy, "The Tampon of the Future," *New York Times*, April 1, 2016, www.nytimes.com/2016/04/03/opinion/sunday/the-tampon-of-the-future.html.

7. HUMANITY

1. John Markoff, *What the Dormouse Said: How the Sixties Counterculture Shaped the Personal Computer Industry* (New York: Penguin, 2005), 148–50.

2. "Military Service—Douglas C. Engelbart," Doug Engelbart Institute, www.dougengelbart.org/about/navy.html.

3. Markoff, *What the Dormouse Said*, 48.

4. John Markoff, *Machines of Loving Grace: The Quest for Common Ground Between Humans and Robots* (New York: Ecco, 2016).

5. Matthew Panzarino, "Google's Eric Schmidt Thinks Siri Is a Significant Competitive Threat," *The Next Web*, November 4, 2011, https://thenextweb.com/apple/2011/11/04/googles-eric-schmidt-thinks-siri-is-a-significant-competitive-threat.

6. Interview with Derrick Connell, May 20, 2016.

7. Alex Gray, "Here's the Secret to How WeChat Attracts 1 Billion Monthly Users," World Economic Forum, March 21, 2018, www.weforum.org/agenda/2018/03/wechat-now-has-over-1-billion-monthly-users/.

8. Even before computers trickled into the popular imagination, we dreamed of creating machines that we could speak with. Fritz Lang's classic film from 1927, *Metropolis*, was made while the industrial design profession was just being born in the States. In it, there's a class war between an arrogant overclass that lives aboveground and a restive underclass that toils in the machine-dominated bowels of the city. A scientist hoping to bring the haves and have-nots together builds a robot as the ideal mediator—one that speaks for the new industrial world, but also speaks in ways humans can understand. Spoiler: The robot turns out to be murderous.

9. Interview with Ronette Lawrence, May 13, 2018.

10. Interviews with Kat Holmes, November 17, 2015; February 12, 2016; May 19, 2015.

11. For example, when the characters in sci-fi movies ranging from *Minority Report* to *Iron Man* to *Prometheus* use computers, they navigate a holographic universe of data, swiping though impossibly complex readouts that whiz by too fast for us to read. What they're doing is meant to say, Humans can't do this yet, but someday they will. Someday they'll be able to process all this information in a flash. Someday, humans will become superhuman. As it happens, this is a vision that would have appealed to Doug Engelbart, creator of the Mother of All Demos, who thought that the way forward was to make people experts in a new way of computing so that they might leave their old lives behind. (In fact, he wanted to create a virtual world in which people could fly through data.)

12. Interview with K. K. Barrett, November 18, 2014.

13. Interview with August de los Reyes, February 12, 2016.

14. Interviews with de los Reyes, November 17 and December 2, 2015.

15. Interview with Pat Moore, October 16, 2015.

16. Pat Moore and Charles Paul Conn, *Disguised: A True Story* (Waco, TX: Word, 1985), 63.

17. Cliff Kuang, "The Untold Story of How the Aeron Chair Was Born," *Fast Company*, February 5, 2013, www.fastcompany.com/1671789/the-untold -history-of-how-the-aeron-chair-came-to-be.

18. "Microsoft AI Principles," Microsoft, www.microsoft.com/en-us/ai/our -approach-to-ai.

19. Interview with Jon Friedman, February 9, 2018.

20. James Vincent, "Google's AI Sounds Like a Human on the Phone— Should We Be Worried?," *The Verge*, May 9, 2018, www.theverge.com/2018 /5/9/17334658/google-ai-phone-call-assistant-duplex-ethical-social -implications.

21. Nick Statt, "Google Now Says Controversial AI Voice Calling System Will Identify Itself to Humans," *The Verge*, May 10, 2018, www.theverge.com /2018/5/10/17342414/google-duplex-ai-assistant-voice-calling-identify -itself-update.

22. Interview with Steph Hay, May 23, 2017.

23. Interview with Audra Koklys, May 23, 2017.

8. PERSONALIZATION

1. Austin Carr, "The Messy Business of Reinventing Happiness," *Fast Company*, April 15, 2015, www.fastcompany.com/3044283/the-messy -business-of-reinventing-happiness.

2. Interview with Meg Crofton, August 1, 2014.

3. Carr, "The Messy Business of Reinventing Happiness."

4. Interview with John Padgett, December 21, 2016.

5. Rachel Kraus, "Gmail Smart Replies May Be Creepy, but They're Catching On Like Wildfire," *Mashable*, September 20, 2018, https://mashable.com/article/gmail-smart-reply-growth/.

6. John Jeremiah Sullivan, "You Blow My Mind. Hey, Mickey!," *New York Times Magazine*, June 8, 2011, www.nytimes.com/2011/06/12/magazine/a-rough-guide-to-disney-world.html.

7. See Jill Lepore, *These Truths: A History of the United States* (New York: W. W. Norton, 2018), 528; and for a superb breakdown of Walt Disney's aesthetic sensibilities, see Sullivan, "You Blow My Mind. Hey, Mickey!"

8. Interviews with John Padgett, October 31, November 8, and December 28, 2016; July 31 and August 1, 2017.

9. Interview with Tom Staggs, August 1, 2014.

10. Interview with Nick Franklin, August 1, 2014.

11. Interview with Staggs.

12. Interview with Crofton.

13. Brooks Barnes, "At Disney Parks, a Bracelet Meant to Build Loyalty (and Sales)," *New York Times*, January 7, 2013, www.nytimes.com/2013/01/07/business/media/at-disney-parks-a-bracelet-meant-to-build-loyalty-and-sales.html.

14. Carr, "The Messy Business of Reinventing Happiness."

15. Ibid.

16. Scott Kirsner, "The Biggest Obstacles to Innovation in Large Companies," *Harvard Business Review*, July 30, 2018, https://hbr.org/2018/07/the-biggest-obstacles-to-innovation-in-large-companies.

17. Interviews with Padgett, July 31 and August 1, 2017.

18. Ibid.

19. Currently, the company closest to this ideal isn't American. It's the Chinese conglomerate Tencent, whose messaging platform, QQ, serves as a portal for accessing the company's litany of subsidiaries. These offer services akin to nearly every American tech company you can imagine, including Amazon, Google, Facebook, PayPal, Uber, and Yelp—all under the aegis of a single brand.

20. For a listing of the world's largest cruise ships, see Wikipedia, "List of largest cruise ships," accessed March 12, 2019, https://en.wikipedia.org/wiki/List_of_largest_cruise_ships.

21. Interview with Jan Swartz, July 31, 2017.

22. Interviews with Padgett, July 31 and August 1, 2017.

23. Interviews with Michael Jungen, July 31 and August 1, 2017.

24. Interviews with Padgett, July 31 and August 1, 2017.

25. Interviews with Swartz, July 31 and August 1, 2017.

26. Tim Wu, "The Tyranny of Convenience," *New York Times*, February 16, 2018, www.nytimes.com/2018/02/16/opinion/sunday/tyranny-convenience.html.

27. Luke Stangel, "Is This a Sign That Apple Is Serious About Making a Deeper Push into Original Journalism?," *Silicon Valley Business Journal*, May 9, 2018, www.bizjournals.com/sanjose/news/2018/05/09/apple-news-journalist-hiring-subscription-service.html.

28. Sam Levin, "Is Facebook a Publisher? In Public It Says No, but in Court It Says Yes," *Guardian*, July 3, 2018, www.theguardian.com/technology/2018/jul/02/facebook-mark-zuckerberg-platform-publisher-lawsuit.

29. Nathan McAlone, "Amazon Will Spend About $4.5 Billion on Its Fight Against Netflix This Year, According to JPMorgan," *Business Insider*, April 7, 2017, www.businessinsider.com/amazon-video-budget-in-2017-45-billion-2017-4.

30. Interviews with Nick de la Mare, January 13 and August 29, 2017.

9. PERIL

1. Interview with Leah Pearlman, May 2, 2017.

2. Interview with Justin Rosenstein, March 16, 2017.

3. The actual graphic was created by Aaron Sittig.

4. Justin Rosenstein, "Love Changes Form," Facebook, September 20, 2016, www.facebook.com/notes/justin-rosenstein/love-changes-form/10153694912262583; and Wikipedia, "Justin Rosenstein," https://en.wikipedia.org/wiki/Justin_Rosenstein.

5. See Facebook's filing to go public: United States Securities and Exchange Commission, Form S-1: Registration Statement, Facebook, Inc., Washington, D.C.: SEC, February 1, 2012, www.sec.gov/Archives/edgar/data/1326801/000119312512034517/d287954ds1.htm.

6. Nellie Bowles, "Tech Entrepreneurs Revive Communal Living," *SFGate*, November 18, 2013, www.sfgate.com/bayarea/article/Tech-entrepreneurs-revive-communal-living-4988388.php; Oliver Smith, "How to Boss It Like: Justin Rosenstein, Cofounder of Asana," *Forbes*, April 26, 2018, www.forbes.com/sites/oliversmith/2018/04/26/how-to-boss-it-like-justin-rosenstein-cofounder-of-asana/.

7. Daniel W. Bjork, *B. F. Skinner: A Life* (Washington, D.C.: American Psychological Association, 1997), 13, 18.

8. Ibid., 25–26.

9. Ibid., 54–55.

10. Ibid., 81.

11. Ibid., 80.

12. XXPorcelinaX, "Skinner—Free Will," YouTube, July 13, 2012, www
   .youtube.com/watch?v=ZYEpCKXTga0.

13. Natasha Dow Schüll, *Addiction by Design: Machine Gambling in Las Vegas*
   (Princeton, NJ: Princeton University Press, 2014), 108.

14. Lesley Stahl, *Sixty Minutes*, "Slot Machines: The Big Gamble," CBS News,
   January 7, 2011, www.cbsnews.com/news/slot-machines-the-big-gamble
   -07-01-2011/.

15. Interview with David Zald, January 20, 2017.

16. Alexis C. Madrigal, "The Machine Zone: This Is Where You Go When You
   Just Can't Stop Looking at Pictures on Facebook," *The Atlantic*, July 31, 2013,
   www.theatlantic.com/technology/archive/2013/07/the-machine-zone
   -this-is-where-you-go-when-you-just-cant-stop-looking-at-pictures-on
   -facebook/278185.

17. For a more detailed look at how interfaces use not only variable rewards
   but also "dark patterns" such as social reciprocity and fear of missing out,
   see Tristan Harris's essay "How Technology Is Hijacking Your Mind—from
   a Magician and Google Design Ethicist" (*Medium*, May 18, 2016), which
   kicked off much of the debate in the UX community about tech addiction.

18. Sally Andrews et al., "Beyond Self-Report: Tools to Compare Estimated
   and Real-World Smartphone Use," *PLoS ONE* (October 18, 2015), https://
   journals.plos.org/plosone/article?id=10.1371/journal.pone.0139004.

19. Julia Naftulin, "Here's How Many Times We Touch Our Phones Every
   Day," *Business Insider*, July 13, 2016, www.businessinsider.com/dscout
   -research-people-touch-cell-phones-2617-times-a-day-2016-7.

20. Sara Perez, "I Watched HBO's Tinder-Shaming Doc 'Swiped' So You Don't
   Have To," *TechCrunch*, September 12, 2018, https://techcrunch.com/2018/09
   /11/i-watched-hbos-tinder-shaming-doc-swiped-so-you-dont-have-to/.

21. Betsy Schiffman, "Stanford Students to Study Facebook Popularity," *Wired*,
   March 25, 2008, www.wired.com/2008/03/stanford-studen-2/.

22. Miguel Helft, "The Class That Built Apps, and Fortunes," *New York Times*,
   May 7, 2011, www.nytimes.com/2011/05/08/technology/08class.html.

23. B. J. Fogg, "The Facts: BJ Fogg and Persuasive Technology," *Medium*,
   March 18, 2018, https://medium.com/@bjfogg/the-facts-bj-fogg-persua
   sive-technology-37d00a738bd1.

24. Simone Stolzoff, "The Formula for Phone Addiction Might Double as a
   Cure," *Wired*, February 1, 2018, www.wired.com/story/phone-addiction
   -formula/.

25. Noam Scheiber, "How Uber Uses Psychological Tricks to Push Its Drivers'
   Buttons," *New York Times*, April 2, 2017, www.nytimes.com/interactive
   /2017/04/02/technology/uber-drivers-psychological-tricks.html.

26. Taylor Lorenz, "17 Teens Take Us Inside the World of Snapchat Streaks,
   Where Friendships Live or Die," *Mic*, April 14, 2017, https://mic.com

/articles/173998/17-teens-take-us-inside-the-world-of-snapchat-streaks
-where-friendships-live-or-die#.f8S7Bxz4i.

27. Alan Cooper, "The Oppenheimer Moment," lecture delivered at the Interaction 18 Conference, February 6, 2018, https://vimeo.com/254533098.

28. Max Read, "Donald Trump Won Because of Facebook," *New York*, November 9, 2016, http://nymag.com/intelligencer/2016/11/donald-trump-won
-because-of-facebook.html.

29. Joshua Benton, "The Forces That Drove This Election's Media Failure Are
Likely to Get Worse," *Nieman Lab*, November 9, 2016, www.niemanlab.org
/2016/11/the-forces-that-drove-this-elections-media-failure-are-likely
-to-get-worse/.

30. Tom Miles, "U.N. Investigators Cite Facebook Role in Myanmar Crisis," Reuters, March 12, 2018, www.reuters.com/article/us-myanmar
-rohingya-facebook/u-n-investigators-cite-facebook-role-in-myanmar
-crisis-idUSKCN1GO2PN.

31. Amanda Taub and Max Fisher, "Where Countries Are Tinderboxes and
Facebook Is a Match," *New York Times*, April 21, 2018, www.nytimes.com
/2018/04/21/world/asia/facebook-sri-lanka-riots.html.

32. Amy B. Wang, "Former Facebook VP Says Social Media Is Destroying Society with 'Dopamine-Driven Feedback Loops,'" *Washington Post*, December 12, 2017, www.washingtonpost.com/news/the-switch/wp/2017/12
/12/former-facebook-vp-says-social-media-is-destroying-society-with
-dopamine-driven-feedback-loops/.

33. Taub and Fisher, "Where Countries Are Tinderboxes and Facebook Is a
Match."

34. Matthew Rosenberg, "Cambridge Analytica, Trump-Tied Political Firm, Offered to Entrap Politicians," *New York Times*, March 19, 2018, www.nytimes
.com/2018/03/19/us/cambridge-analytica-alexander-nix.html.

35. Interviews with Michal Kosinski, April 25, May 18, July 7, and December 4,
2017.

36. Michal Kosinski, David Stillwell, and Thore Graepel, "Private Traits and
Attributes Are Predictable from Digital Records of Human Behavior,"
Proceedings of the National Academy of Sciences 110, no. 15 (April 13, 2013):
5802–805, www.pnas.org/content/110/15/5802.full.

37. Sean Illing, "Cambridge Analytica, the Shady Data Firm That Might Be
a Key Trump-Russia Link, Explained," *Vox*, April 4, 2018, www.vox.com
/policy-and-politics/2017/10/16/15657512/cambridge-analytica-facebook
-alexander-nix-christopher-wylie.

38. Joshua Green and Sasha Issenberg, "Inside the Trump Bunker, with Days
to Go," *Bloomberg News*, October 27, 2016, www.bloomberg.com/news
/articles/2016-10-27/inside-the-trump-bunker-with-12-days-to-go.

39. Kendall Taggart, "The Truth About the Trump Data Team That People

Are Freaking Out About," *BuzzFeed News*, February 16, 2017, www
.buzzfeednews.com/article/kendalltaggart/the-truth-about-the-trump
-data-team-that-people-are-freaking.

40. Sam Machkovech, "Report: Facebook Helped Advertisers Target Teens
Who Feel 'Worthless,'" *Ars Technica*, May 1, 2017, https://arstechnica.com
/information-technology/2017/05/facebook-helped-advertisers-target
-teens-who-feel-worthless/.

41. Elizabeth Kolbert, "Why Facts Don't Change Our Minds," *New Yorker*,
February 27, 2017, www.newyorker.com/magazine/2017/02/27/why
-facts-dont-change-our-minds.

42. Mark Newgarden and Paul Karasik, *How to Read* Nancy: *The Elements of
Comics in Three Easy Panels* (Seattle: Fantagraphics, 2017), 98.

43. Thomas Wendt, "Critique of Human-Centered Design, or Decentering Design," presentation at the Interaction 17 Conference, February 7,
2017, www.slideshare.net/ThomasMWendt/critique-of-humancentered
-design-or-decentering-design.

44. Tim Wu, "The Tyranny of Convenience," *New York Times*, February 16, 2018,
www.nytimes.com/2018/02/16/opinion/sunday/tyranny-convenience
.html.

45. Nellie Bowles, "Early Facebook and Google Employees Form Coalition to
Fight What They Built," *New York Times*, February 4, 2018, www.nytimes
.com/2018/02/04/technology/early-facebook-google-employees-fight
-tech.html.

10. PROMISE

1. Interview with Leslie Saholy Ossete, November 18, 2016.

2. This dynamic is happening all across the developing world: The mobile
phone has led to innovative, design-led transportation experiments underway in Mexico City, Jakarta, and Delhi. Meanwhile, the spread of
M-Pesa, the world's most popular mobile money system, has yielded a
platform for dozens of new services, such as Digifarm, a farmers' marketplace (which was created by Safaricom, working with Dalberg Design).

3. Interview with Harry West, March 3, 2016.

4. See "How We Work Grant: IDEO.org," Bill and Melinda Gates Foundation,
www.gatesfoundation.org/How-We-Work/Quick-Links/Grants-Database
/Grants/2010/10/OPP1011131; "Unlocking Mobile Money," IDEO.org, www
.ideo.org/project/gates-foundation; and "Giving Ed Tech Entrepreneurs a
Window into the Classroom," IDEO.org, www.ideo.com/case-study/giving
-ed-tech-entrepreneurs-a-window-into-the-classroom.

5. Avery Trufelman, "The Finnish Experiment," *99% Invisible*, September 19,
2017, https://99percentinvisible.org/episode/the-finnish-experiment/.

6. Interview with Justin Rosenstein, March 16, 2017.

7. Interview with Leah Pearlman, May 2, 2017.

8. Jean M. Twenge, "Have Smartphones Destroyed a Generation?," *The Atlantic*, September 2017, www.theatlantic.com/magazine/archive/2017/09/has-the-smartphone-destroyed-a-generation/534198/.

9. Larissa MacFarquhar, "The Mind-Expanding Ideas of Andy Clark," *New Yorker*, April 2, 2018, www.newyorker.com/magazine/2018/04/02/the-mind-expanding-ideas-of-andy-clark.

10. Interview with Linden Tibbets, January 20, 2015.

11. Tibbets's point of view bears some resemblance to that of Mark Weiser. Ubiquitous computing anticipated much of what we see today in places ranging from Google to Disney World. Weiser argued that seamless design was a trap, and that the better goal was "seamful" design that would surface the handoffs between devices.

12. Marcus Fairs, "Jonathan Ive," *Icon* 4 (July/August 2003), www.iconeye.com/404/item/2730-jonathan-ive-%7C-icon-004-%7C-july/august-2003.

AFTERWORD

1. As Henry Dreyfuss discovered when observing the moviegoers at the RKO theater in Sioux City (see pages 55–56).

2. This principle is now encoded in the inner workings of the U.K. government and adopted by most UN agencies through the Digital Principles for Development, which were inspired, in part, by a collaboration that I led between Frog Design and the UNICEF Office of Innovation.

3. "The word 'experience' traces back . . . to the Latin *experientia*, which means 'a test or attempt.' It's related to both 'experiment' and 'expert,' connoting both repeated trials and eventual mastery. 'Experience' is acquired over time, via direct contact with the world; it is firsthand, unmediated and always, inherently, embodied." Carina Chocano, "Why Suppress the 'Experience' of Half the World?," *New York Times*, November 28, 2018, www.nytimes.com/2018/10/23/magazine/why-suppress-the-experience-of-half-the-world.html.

4. Robert Fabricant, "Why Does Interaction Design Matter? Let's Look at the Evolving Subway Experience," *Fast Company*, September 19, 2011.

5. As discussed in chapter 1, Wiener was a pivotal figure in the study of feedback in large-scale information systems, which he popularized in 1950 with the publishing of his bestselling *The Human Use of Human Beings: Cybernetics and Society*.

6. iPhone users were rudely awakened to the importance of these subtle yet powerful design differences when Apple swapped out Google Maps for its own map application with the release of the iPhone 5.

7. Thom Erickson from Apple and IBM Research eloquently described how

to observe these patterns of interaction in his seminal 2005 essay "Five Lenses: Towards a Toolkit for Interaction Design," http://tomeri.org/5Lenses.pdf.

8. The *dabbawalas* constitute a 125-year-old, self-organizing lunch-box delivery and return system that moves hot lunches from homes and restaurants to 200,000 people at work in India, especially in Mumbai. A color-coding system identifies the destination and recipient.

9. Jon Yablonski, "Jakob's Law," Laws of UX, https://lawsofux.com/jakobs-law.

10. Helen Fisher, chief scientific adviser to Match.com, has observed that, for the baby-boomer generation, the automobile actually represented nothing more than a "rolling bedroom." Fisher, "Technology Hasn't Changed Love. Here's Why," filmed June 2016 in Banff, Canada, TED video, www.ted.com/talks/helen_fisher_technology_hasn_t_changed_love_here_s_why.

11. Firms like Frog generally task a designer who didn't work on the product to lead any user feedback sessions, as they are more likely to be impartial.

12. As the design educator and author Jon Kolko has noted in his book *Well-Designed: How to Use Empathy to Create Products People Love* (Boston: Harvard Business Review, 2014).

13. As John Dewey so eloquently captured in his seminal work *Experience and Education* (New York: Touchstone, 1938).

14. In 1983, Jonathan Grudin and Allan Maclean published similar research showing that users sometimes choose a slower interface for aesthetic reasons even when they are familiar with more efficient alternatives. Their paper was met with resistance from colleagues at Microsoft, who viewed a scientific approach to efficiency as the ultimate goal of successful user-interface design.

15. Brad Smith, "Intuit's CEO on Building a Design-Driven Company," *Harvard Business Review*, January/February 2015, https://hbr.org/2015/01/intuits-ceo-on-building-a-design-driven-company.

16. Peter Behrens also recognized the power of emotion and delight, even in the design of industrial products: "Don't think that even an engineer, when he buys a motor, takes it to bits in order to scrutinize it. Even he as a specialist buys from the external appearance. A motor ought to look like a birthday present." Dreyfuss also aspired to create lowly household appliances, like vacuum cleaners, that would not look out of place under a Christmas tree.

17. Esslinger's motto was a pointed departure from the Bauhaus ethos of "form follows function" as exemplified in the iconic work of Dieter Rams, who dominated German product design at the time. The saying "form fol-

lows function" purportedly dates back to the American architect Louis Sullivan, who was a mentor to Frank Lloyd Wright.

18. This is a process that is increasingly data-enabled with the profusion of new technologies for tracking user behavior on a more and more granular level.

19. Our observation is not unlike the inspiration for Philippa Mothersill's work for Gillette as described on pages 154–55.

20. Recent research from the Delft Institute of Positive Design has shown that we unconsciously communicate the positive emotions we associate with a product based on how we hold it in our hands.

21. This story is not dissimilar from Dreyfuss's experience designing the best-selling "Princess phone" for AT&T in 1959 after watching the way young women cradled telephones in their laps for long periods when lying in bed and chatting with their friends.

22. As documented in Mary Dong et al., "Can Laypersons in High-Prevalence South Africa Perform an HIV Self-Test Accurately?," presented at the 2014 International AIDS Conference, Melbourne, Australia, July 20–25, 2014, http://pag.aids2014.org/EPosterHandler.axd?aid=10374.

Bibliography

Abernethy, Cam. "NRC Approves Vogtle Reactor Construction—First New Nuclear Plant Approval in 34 Years." *Nuclear Street*, February 9, 2012. http://nuclearstreet.com/nuclear_power_industry_news/b/nuclear_power_news/archive/2012/02/09/nrc-approves-vogtle-reactor-construction-_2d00_-first-new-nuclear-plant-approval-in-34-years-_2800_with-new-plant-photos_2900_-020902.

Abrams, Rachel, and Annalyn Kurtz. "Joshua Brown, Who Died in Self-Driving Accident, Tested Limits of His Tesla." *New York Times*, July 1, 2016. www.nytimes.com/2016/07/02/business/joshua-brown-technology-enthusiast-tested-the-limits-of-his-tesla.html.

Andrews, Sally, David A. Ellis, Heather Shaw, and Lukasz Piwek. "Beyond Self-Report: Tools to Compare Estimated and Real-World Smartphone Use." *PLoS ONE* 10 (October 18, 2015). Accessed August 28, 2018. https://journals.plos.org/plosone/article?id=10.1371/journal.pone.0139004.

Apple Computer, Inc. *Apple Human Interface Guidelines: The Apple Desktop Interface*. Boston: Addison-Wesley, 1987.

Arnold, John E. *The Arcturus IV Case Study*. Edited and with an introduction by John E. Arnold, Jr. Stanford University Digital Repository, 2016. Originally published 1953. https://stacks.stanford.edu/file/druid:rz867bs3905/SC0269 _Arcturus_IV.pdf.

Bargh, John. *Before You Know It: The Unconscious Reasons We Do What We Do*. New York: Touchstone, 2017.

Barnes, Brooks. "At Disney Parks, a Bracelet Meant to Build Loyalty (and Sales)." *New York Times*, January 7, 2013. www.nytimes.com/2013/01/07/business /media/at-disney-parks-a-bracelet-meant-to-build-loyalty-and-sales.html.

Bello, Francis. "Fitting the Machine to the Man." *Fortune*, November 1954.

Benton, Joshua. "The Forces That Drove This Election's Media Failure Are Likely to Get Worse." *Nieman Lab*, November 9, 2016. www.niemanlab.org /2016/11/the-forces-that-drove-this-elections-media-failure-are-likely-to -get-worse/.

Bill and Melinda Gates Foundation. "How We Work Grant: IDEO.org." Accessed December 9, 2017. www.gatesfoundation.org/How-We-Work/Quick-Links /Grants-Database/Grants/2010/10/OPP1011131.

Bjork, Daniel W. *B. F. Skinner: A Life*. Washington, D.C.: American Psychological Association, 1997.

Borges, Jorge Luis. "On Exactitude in Science." In *Collected Fictions*. New York: Viking, 1998.

Bowles, Nellie. "Early Facebook and Google Employees Form Coalition to Fight What They Built." *New York Times*, February 4, 2018. www.nytimes .com/2018/02/04/technology/early-facebook-google-employees-fight -tech.html.

———. "Tech Entrepreneurs Revive Communal Living." *SFGate*, November 18, 2013. www.sfgate.com/bayarea/article/Tech-entrepreneurs-revive -communal-living-4988388.php.

Buxton, William. "Less Is More (More or Less)." In *The Invisible Future: The Seamless Integration of Technology in Everyday Life*, edited by P. Denning (New York: McGraw-Hill, 2001), 145–79. www.billbuxton.com/LessIsMore.pdf.

Caplan, Ralph. *Cracking the Whip: Essays on Design and Its Side Effects*. New York: Fairchild Publications, 2006.

Carbon Dioxide Information Analysis Center, Environmental Sciences Division, Oak Ridge National Laboratory, Tennessee. "CO2 Emissions (Metric Tons per Capita)." World Bank. https://data.worldbank.org/indicator/en.atm .co2e.pc.

Carr, Austin. "The Messy Business of Reinventing Happiness." *Fast Company*, April 15, 2015. www.fastcompany.com/3044283/the-messy-business-of -reinventing-happiness.

Carr, Nicholas. *The Glass Cage: How Our Computers Are Changing Us*. New York: W. W. Norton, 2014.

CBS News. "Slot Machines: The Big Gamble." January 7, 2011. www.cbsnews.com/news/slot-machines-the-big-gamble-07-01-2011/.

Chapanis, Alphonse. "Psychology and the Instrument Panel." *Scientific American*, April 1, 1953.

Chocano, Carina. "Why Suppress the 'Experience' of Half the World?" *New York Times*, November 28, 2018. www.nytimes.com/2018/10/23/magazine/why-suppress-the-experience-of-half-the-world.html.

Cid, Victor Cruz. "Volvo Auto Brake System Fail." YouTube, May 19, 2015. www.youtube.com/watch?v=_47utWAoupo.

Clancey, William J. Introduction to *Creative Engineering: Promoting Innovation by Thinking Differently*, by John E. Arnold. Self-published, Amazon Digital Services, 2017. www.amazon.com/Creative-Engineering-Promoting-Innovation-Differently-ebook/dp/B072BZP9Z6.

Cooper, Alan. *The Inmates Are Running the Asylum: Why High-Tech Products Drive Us Crazy and How to Restore the Sanity*. Indianapolis: Sams, 2004.

———. "The Oppenheimer Moment." Lecture delivered at the Interaction 18 Conference, La Sucrière, Lyon, France, February 6, 2018. https://vimeo.com/254533098.

Cooper, Alan, Christopher Noessel, David Cronin, and Robert Reimann. *About Face: The Essentials of Interaction Design*. 4th ed. New York: Wiley, 2014.

Davidson, Bill. "You Buy Their Dreams." *Collier's*, August 2, 1947.

Davies, Alex. "Americans Can't Have Audi's Super Capable Self-Driving System." *Wired*, May 15, 2018. www.wired.com/story/audi-self-driving-traffic-jam-pilot-a8-2019-availablility/.

Degani, Asaf. *Taming HAL: Designing Interfaces Beyond 2001*. New York: Palgrave Macmillan, 2004.

Dellinger, A. J. "Google Assistant Is Smarter Than Alexa and Siri, but Honestly They All Suck." *Gizmodo*, April 27, 2018. https://gizmodo.com/google-assistant-is-smarter-than-alexa-and-siri-but-ho-1825616612.

Deutchman, Alan. *The Second Coming of Steve Jobs*. New York: Broadway, 2001.

Dewey, John. *Experience and Education*. New York: Touchstone, 1938.

Dong, Mary, Rachel Regina, Sandile Hlongwane, Musie Ghebremichael, Douglas Wilson, and Krista Dong. "Can Laypersons in High-Prevalence South Africa Perform an HIV Self-Test Accurately?" Presented at the 2014 International AIDS Conference, Melbourne, Australia, July 20–25, 2014. http://pag.aids2014.org/EPosterHandler.axd?aid=10374.

Doug Engelbart Institute. "Military Service—Douglas C. Engelbart." Accessed May 9, 2017. www.dougengelbart.org/content/view/352/467/.

Dourish, Paul. *Where the Action Is: The Foundations of Embodied Interaction*. Cambridge, MA: MIT Press, 2001.

Dreyfuss, Henry. *Designing for People.* 4th ed. New York: Allworth, 2012.

———. "The Industrial Designer and the Businessman." *Harvard Business Review,* November 6, 1950.

Erickson, Thom. "Five Lenses: Towards a Toolkit for Interaction Design." http://tomeri.org/5Lenses.pdf.

Eyal, Nir. *Hooked: How to Build Habit-Forming Products.* Self-published, 2014.

Fabricant, Robert. "Behavior Is Our Medium." Presentation at the Interaction Design Association conference, Vancouver, 2009. https://vimeo.com/3730382.

———. "Why Does Interaction Design Matter? Let's Look at the Evolving Subway Experience." *Fast Company,* September 19, 2011.

Fairs, Marcus. "Jonathan Ive." *Icon* 4 (July/August 2003). www.iconeye.com/404/item/2730-jonathan-ive-%7C-icon-004-%7C-july/august-2003.

Flemisch, Frank O., Catherine A. Adams, Sheila R. Conway, Michael T. Palmer, Ken H. Goodrich, and Paul C. Schutte. "The H-Metaphor as a Guideline for Vehicle Automation and Interaction." National Aeronautics and Space Administration, December 2003.

Flinchum, Russell. *Henry Dreyfuss, Industrial Designer: The Man in the Brown Suit.* New York: Rizzoli, 1997.

———. "The Other Half of Henry Dreyfuss." Design Criticism MFA Lecture Series, School of Visual Arts, New York, October 25, 2011. http://vimeo.com/35777735.

Fogg, B. J. "The Facts: BJ Fogg and Persuasive Technology." *Medium,* March 18, 2018. https://medium.com/@bjfogg/the-facts-bj-fogg-persuasive-technology-37d00a738bd1.

Ford, Daniel F. *Three Mile Island: Thirty Minutes to Meltdown.* New York: Viking, 1982.

Gertner, Jon. "Atomic Balm?" *New York Times Magazine,* July 16, 2006. Accessed July 16, 2017. www.nytimes.com/2006/07/16/magazine/16nuclear.html.

Goodrich, Kenneth H., Paul C. Schutte, Frank O. Flemisch, and Ralph A. Williams. "Application of the H-Mode, a Design and Interaction Concept for Highly Automated Vehicles, to Aircraft." National Aeronautics and Space Administration, October 15, 2006.

Gray, Alex. "Here's the Secret to How WeChat Attracts 1 Billion Monthly Users." World Economic Forum, March 21, 2018. www.weforum.org/agenda/2018/03/wechat-now-has-over-1-billion-monthly-users/.

Gray, Mike, and Ira Rosen. *The Warning: Accident at Three Mile Island.* New York: W. W. Norton, 1982.

Green, Joshua, and Sasha Issenberg. "Inside the Trump Bunker, with Days to Go." *Bloomberg News,* October 27, 2016. www.bloomberg.com/news/articles/2016-10-27/inside-the-trump-bunker-with-12-days-to-go.

Grice, H. P. "Logic and Conversation." In *Syntax and Semantics*. Vol. 3, *Speech Acts*, edited by Peter Cole and Jerry L. Morgan, 183–98. Cambridge, MA: Academic Press, 1975.

Grube, Nick. "Man Who Sent Out False Missile Alert Was 'Source of Concern' for a Decade." *Honolulu Civil Beat*, January 30, 2018. www.civilbeat.org/2018 /01/hawaii-fires-man-who-sent-out-false-missile-alert-top-administrator -resigns/.

Guardian. "Transport Safety Body Rules Safeguards 'Were Lacking' in Deadly Tesla Crash." September 12, 2017. www.theguardian.com/technology/2017 /sep/12/tesla-crash-joshua-brown-safety-self-driving-cars.

Hamburger, Ellis. "Where Are They Now? These Were the 10 Best iPhone Apps When the App Store Launched in 2008." *Business Insider*, May 17, 2011. www .businessinsider.com/the-best-iphone-apps-when-the-app-store-launched -2011-5.

Hamer, Tony, and Michele Hamer. "The Edsel Automobile Legacy of Failure." *ThoughtCo*. January 6, 2018. www.thoughtco.com/the-edsel-a-legacy-of-failure -726013.

Haraway, Donna. *Simians, Cyborgs, and Women: The Reinvention of Nature*. New York: Routledge, 1990.

Harford, Tim. "Department Store." *50 Things That Made the Modern Economy*. BBC World Service, July 2, 2017. www.bbc.co.uk/programmes/p056srj3.

———. *Messy: The Power of Disorder to Transform Our Lives*. New York: River-head, 2016.

———. "Seller Feedback." *50 Things That Made the Modern Economy*. BBC World Service, August 6, 2017. www.bbc.co.uk/programmes/p059zb6n.

Harris, Tristan. "How a Handful of Tech Companies Control Billions of Minds Every Day." Presented at TED2017, April 2017. www.ted.com/talks/tristan _harris_the_manipulative_tricks_tech_companies_use_to_capture_your _attention.

———. "How Technology Is Hijacking Your Mind—from a Magician and Google Design Ethicist." *Medium*, May 18, 2016.

Hawkins, Andrew J. "This Map Shows How Few Self-Driving Cars Are Actu-ally on the Road Today." *The Verge*, October 23, 2017. www.theverge.com /2017/10/23/16510696/self-driving-cars-map-testing-bloomberg-aspen.

Helft, Miguel. "The Class That Built Apps, and Fortunes." *New York Times*, May 7, 2011. www.nytimes.com/2011/05/08/technology/08class.html.

Hempel, Jessi. "What Happened to Facebook's Grand Plan to Wire the World?" *Wired*, May 17, 2018. www.wired.com/story/what-happened-to-facebooks -grand-plan-to-wire-the-world/.

Hiltzik, Michael A. *Dealers of Lightning: Xerox PARC and the Dawn of the Computer Age*. New York: HarperCollins, 1999.

Hounshell, David A. *From the American System to Mass Production, 1800–1932.* Baltimore: Johns Hopkins University Press, 1985.

Hunt, Morton M. "The Course Where Students Lose Earthly Shackles." *Life,* May 16, 1955.

Hutchins, Edwin. *Cognition in the Wild.* Cambridge, MA: MIT Press, 1995.

IDEO.org. "Giving Ed Tech Entrepreneurs a Window into the Classroom." Accessed October 11, 2017. www.ideo.com/case-study/giving-ed-tech-entre preneurs-a-window-into-the-classroom.

———. *The Field Guide to Human-Centered Design.* Self-published, 2015.

Illing, Sean. "Cambridge Analytica, the Shady Data Firm That Might Be a Key Trump-Russia Link, Explained." *Vox,* April 4, 2018. www.vox.com/policy-and -politics/2017/10/16/15657512/cambridge-analytica-facebook-alexander -nix-christopher-wylie.

Johnston, Alva. "Nothing Looks Right to Dreyfuss." *Saturday Evening Post,* November 22, 1947.

Katz, Barry M. *Make It New: The History of Silicon Valley Design.* Cambridge, MA: MIT Press, 2015.

Kay, Alan. "A Personal Computer for Children of All Ages." Proceedings of the ACM National Conference, Xerox Palo Alto Research Center, 1972. Viewpoints Research Institute. Accessed November 11, 2017. http://worrydream .com/refs/Kay%20-%20A%20Personal%20Computer%20for%20Children% 20of%20All%20Ages.pdf.

Kennedy, Pagan. *Inventology: How We Dream Up Things That Change the World.* New York: Eamon Dolan, 2016.

———. "The Tampon of the Future." *New York Times,* April 2, 2016. www.ny times.com/2016/04/03/opinion/sunday/the-tampon-of-the-future.html.

Kirsner, Scott. "The Biggest Obstacles to Innovation in Large Companies." *Harvard Business Review,* July 30, 2018. https://hbr.org/2018/07/the-biggest -obstacles-to-innovation-in-large-companies.

Kolbert, Elizabeth. "Why Facts Don't Change Our Minds." *New Yorker,* February 27, 2017. www.newyorker.com/magazine/2017/02/27/why-facts-dont -change-our-minds.

Kolko, Jon. *Well-Designed: How to Use Empathy to Create Products People Love.* Boston: Harvard Business Review, 2014.

Kosinski, Michal, David Stillwell, and Thore Graepel. "Private Traits and Attributes Are Predictable from Digital Records of Human Behavior." *Proceedings of the National Academy of Sciences* 110, no. 15 (April 13, 2013): 5802–805. Accessed June 6, 2018. www.pnas.org/content/110/15/5802.

Kottke, Jason. "Bad Design in Action: The False Hawaiian Ballistic Missile Alert." Kottke.org, January 16, 2018. https://kottke.org/18/01/bad-design -in-action-the-false-hawaiian-ballistic-missile-alert.

Kraus, Rachel. "Gmail Smart Replies May Be Creepy, but They're Catching On Like Wildfire." *Mashable*, September 20, 2018. https://mashable.com/article/gmail-smart-reply-growth/.

Krippendorff, Klaus. *The Semantic Turn: A New Foundation for Design*. Boca Raton, FL: CRC, 2005.

Kuang, Cliff. "Fuchsia, Google's Experimental Mobile OS, Solves Glaring Problems That Apple Doesn't Get." *Fast Company*, May 10, 2017. www.fastcompany.com/90124729/fuchsia-googles-experimental-mobile-os-solves-glaring-problems-that-apple-doesnt-get.

———. "The Untold Story of How the Aeron Chair Was Born." *Fast Company*, February 5, 2013. www.fastcompany.com/1671789/the-untold-history-of-how-the-aeron-chair-came-to-be.

Lacey, Robert. *Ford: The Men and the Machine*. 4th ed. New York: Ballantine, 1991.

Lakoff, George, and Mark Johnson. *Metaphors We Live By*. 2nd ed. Chicago: University of Chicago Press, 2003.

———. *Philosophy in the Flesh: The Embodied Mind and Its Challenge to Western Thought*. New York: Basic Books, 1999.

Lange, Alexandra. "The Woman Who Gave the Macintosh a Smile." *New Yorker*, April 19, 2018. www.newyorker.com/culture/cultural-comment/the-woman-who-gave-the-macintosh-a-smile.

Lathrop, William Brian, Maria Esther Mejia Gonzalez, Bryan Grant, and Heiko Maiwand. "System, Components and Methodologies for Gaze Dependent Gesture Input Control." Volkswagen AG, assignee. Patent 9,244,527, filed March 26, 2013, and issued January 26, 2016. https://patents.justia.com/patent/9244527.

Lepore, Jill. *These Truths: A History of the United States*. New York: W. W. Norton, 2018.

Levin, Sam. "Is Facebook a Publisher? In Public It Says No, but in Court It Says Yes." *Guardian*, July 3, 2018. www.theguardian.com/technology/2018/jul/02/facebook-mark-zuckerberg-platform-publisher-lawsuit.

Levitz, Eric. "The Hawaii Missile Scare Was Caused by Overly Realistic Drill." *New York*, January 30, 2018. http://nymag.com/intelligencer/2018/01/the-hawaii-missile-scare-was-caused-by-too-realistic-drill.html.

Levy, Marc. "3 Mile Island Owner Threatens to Close Ill-Fated Plant." AP News, May 30, 2017. www.apnews.com/266b9aff54a14ab4a6bea903ac7ae603.

Levy, Steven. *Insanely Great: The Life and Times of Macintosh, the Computer That Changed Everything*. 2nd ed. New York: Penguin, 2000.

Lewis, Michael. *The Undoing Project: A Friendship That Changed Our Minds*. New York: W. W. Norton, 2016.

Liedtka, Jeanne. "Why Design Thinking Works." *Harvard Business Review*, September/October 2018. hbr.org/2018/09/why-design-thinking-works.

Lorenz, Taylor. "17 Teens Take Us Inside the World of Snapchat Streaks, Where Friendships Live or Die." *Mic*, April 14, 2017. https://mic.com/articles /173998/17-teens-take-us-inside-the-world-of-snapchat-streaks-where -friendships-live-or-die#.f8S7Bxz4i.

Lupton, Ellen, Thomas Carpentier, and Tiffany Lambert. *Beautiful Users: Designing for People*. Princeton, NJ: Princeton Architectural Press, 2014.

Lyonnais, Sheena. "Where Did the Term 'User Experience' Come From?" *Adobe Blog*, August 28, 2017. https://theblog.adobe.com/where-did-the-term-user -experience-come-from/.

MacFarquhar, Larissa. "The Mind-Expanding Ideas of Andy Clark." *New Yorker*, April 2, 2018. www.newyorker.com/magazine/2018/04/02/the-mind -expanding-ideas-of-andy-clark.

Machkovech, Sam. "Report: Facebook Helped Advertisers Target Teens Who Feel 'Worthless.'" *Ars Technica*, May 1, 2017. https://arstechnica.com /information-technology/2017/05/facebook-helped-advertisers-target -teens-who-feel-worthless/.

Madrigal, Alexis C. "The Machine Zone: This Is Where You Go When You Just Can't Stop Looking at Pictures on Facebook." *The Atlantic*, July 31, 2013. www.theatlantic.com/technology/archive/2013/07/the-machine-zone-this -is-where-you-go-when-you-just-cant-stop-looking-at-pictures-on-facebook /278185/.

Markoff, John. *Machines of Loving Grace: The Quest for Common Ground Between Humans and Robots*. New York: Ecco, 2016.

———. *What the Dormouse Said: How the Sixties Counterculture Shaped the Personal Computer Industry*. New York: Penguin, 2005.

Maynard, Micheline. "Waiting List Gone, Incentives Are Coming for Prius." *New York Times*, February 8, 2007. www.nytimes.com/2007/02/08/automobiles /08hybrid.html.

McAlone, Nathan. "Amazon Will Spend About $4.5 Billion on Its Fight Against Netflix This Year, According to JPMorgan." *Business Insider*, April 7, 2017. www.businessinsider.com/amazon-video-budget-in-2017-45-billion-2017-4.

McCullough, Malcolm. *Digital Ground: Architecture, Pervasive Computing, and Environmental Knowing*. Cambridge, MA: MIT Press, 2004.

McNerney, Samuel. "A Brief Guide to Embodied Cognition: Why You Are Not Your Brain." *Scientific American*, November 4, 2011. https://blogs.scientificamerican .com/guest-blog/a-brief-guide-to-embodied-cognition-why-you-are-not -your-brain/.

Meikle, Jeffrey L. *Design in the USA*. New York: Oxford University Press, 2005.

———. *Twentieth Century Limited: Industrial Design in America, 1925–1939*. Philadelphia: Temple University Press, 1979.

Merchant, Brian. *The One Device: The Secret History of the iPhone*. New York: Little, Brown, 2017.

Mickle, Tripp, and Amrith Ramkumar. "Apple's Market Cap Hits $1 Trillion." *Wall Street Journal*, August 2, 2018. www.wsj.com/articles/apples-market -cap-hits-1-trillion-1533225150.

Microsoft. "Microsoft AI Principles." Accessed September 9, 2018. www .microsoft.com/en-us/ai/our-approach-to-ai.

Miles, Tom. "U.N. Investigators Cite Facebook Role in Myanmar Crisis." Reuters, March 12, 2018. www.reuters.com/article/us-myanmar-rohingya -facebook/u-n-investigators-cite-facebook-role-in-myanmar-crisis -idUSKCN1GO2PN.

Moggridge, Bill. *Designing Interactions*. Cambridge, MA: MIT Press, 2007.

Moore, Pat, and Charles Paul Conn. *Disguised: A True Story*. Waco, TX: Word, 1985.

Naftulin, Julia. "Here's How Many Times We Touch Our Phones Every Day." *Business Insider*, July 13, 2016. www.businessinsider.com/dscout-research -people-touch-cell-phones-2617-times-a-day-2016-7.

Nass, Clifford. *The Man Who Lied to His Laptop*. New York: Current, 2010.

Newgarden, Mark, and Paul Karasik. *How to Read Nancy: The Elements of Comics in Three Easy Panels*. Seattle: Fantagraphics, 2017.

Norman, Donald A. "Design as Practiced." In *Bringing Design to Software*, edited by Terry Winograd. Boston: Addison-Wesley, 1996. https://hci.stanford.edu /publications/bds/12-norman.html.

———. *The Design of Everyday Things*. New York: Doubleday, 1988.

———. *Emotional Design: Why We Love (or Hate) Everyday Things*. 2nd ed. New York: Basic Books, 2005.

———. "What Went Wrong in Hawaii, Human Error? Nope, Bad Design." *Fast Company*, January 16, 2018. www.fastcompany.com/90157153/don-norman -what-went-wrong-in-hawaii-human-error-nope-bad-design.

Panzarino, Matthew. "Google's Eric Schmidt Thinks Siri Is a Significant Competitive Threat." *The Next Web*, November 4, 2011. https://thenextweb .com/apple/2011/11/04/googles-eric-schmidt-thinks-siri-is-a-significant -competitive-threat/.

Park, Gene. "The Missile Employee Messed Up Because Hawaii Rewards Incompetence." *Washington Post*, February 1, 2018. www.washingtonpost.com /news/posteverything/wp/2018/02/01/the-missile-employee-messed-up -because-hawaii-rewards-incompetence/.

Peltier, Elian, James Glanz, Mika Gröndahl, Weiyi Cai, Adam Nossiter, and Liz Alderman. "Notre-Dame Came Far Closer to Collapsing Than People Knew. This Is How It Was Saved." *New York Times*, July 18, 2019. www.nytimes.com /interactive/2019/07/16/world/europe/notre-dame.html.

Perez, Sara. "I Watched HBO's Tinder-Shaming Doc 'Swiped' So You Don't Have To." *TechCrunch*, September 12, 2018. https://techcrunch.com/2018/09 /11/i-watched-hbos-tinder-shaming-doc-swiped-so-you-dont-have-to.

Petroski, Henry. *The Evolution of Useful Things: How Everyday Artifacts—from*

Forks and Pins to Paper Clips and Zippers—Came to Be as They Are. New York: Vintage, 1994.

Pulos, Arthur J. *American Design Ethic: A History of Industrial Design*. Cambridge, MA: MIT Press, 1986.

Rams, Dieter. "Ten Principles for Good Design." Vitsœ. Accessed November 2018. www.vitsoe.com/gb/about/good-design.

Randazzo, Ryan, Bree Burkitt, and Uriel J. Garcia. "Self-Driving Uber Vehicle Strikes, Kills 49-Year-Old Woman in Tempe." AZCentral.com, March 19, 2018. www.azcentral.com/story/news/local/tempe-breaking/2018/03/19/woman -dies-fatal-hit-strikes-self-driving-uber-crossing-road-tempe/438256002/.

Read, Max. "Donald Trump Won Because of Facebook." *New York*, November 9, 2016. http://nymag.com/intelligencer/2016/11/donald-trump-won-because -of-facebook.html.

Reeves, Byron, and Clifford Nass. *The Media Equation: How People Treat Computers, Television, and New Media Like Real People and Places*. New York: CSLI Publications, 1996.

RockTreeStar. "Tesla Autopilot Tried to Kill Me!" YouTube, October 15, 2015. www.youtube.com/watch?v=MrwxEX8qOxA.

Rose, David. *Enchanted Objects: Design, Human Desire, and the Internet of Things*. New York: Scribner, 2014.

Rosenberg, Matthew. "Cambridge Analytica, Trump-Tied Political Firm, Offered to Entrap Politicians." *New York Times*, March 19, 2018. www.nytimes .com/2018/03/19/us/cambridge-analytica-alexander-nix.html.

Rosenstein, Justin. "Love Changes Form." Facebook, September 20, 2016. Accessed April 30, 2018. www.facebook.com/notes/justin-rosenstein/love -changes-form/10153694912262583.

Rutherford, Janice Williams. *Selling Mrs. Consumer: Christine Frederick and the Rise of Household Efficiency*. Athens: University of Georgia Press, 2003.

Rybczynski, Witold. *Home: A Short History of an Idea*. New York: Viking, 1986.

Said, Carolyn. "Exclusive: Tempe Police Chief Says Early Probe Shows No Fault by Uber." *San Francisco Chronicle*, March 26, 2018. www.sfchronicle.com/business /article/Exclusive-Tempe-police-chief-says-early-probe-12765481.php.

Scheiber, Noam. "How Uber Uses Psychological Tricks to Push Its Drivers' Buttons." *New York Times*, April 2, 2017. www.nytimes.com/interactive/2017/04 /02/technology/uber-drivers-psychological-tricks.html.

Schiffman, Betsy. "Stanford Students to Study Facebook Popularity." *Wired*, March 25, 2008. www.wired.com/2008/03/stanford-studen-2/.

Schüll, Natasha Dow. *Addiction by Design: Machine Gambling in Las Vegas*. Princeton, NJ: Princeton University Press, 2014.

Schwab, Katherine. "Sweeping New McKinsey Study of 300 Companies Reveals What Every Business Needs to Know About Design for 2019." *Fast Company*, October 25, 2018. www.fastcompany.com/90255363/this-mckinsey-study

-of-300-companies-reveals-what-every-business-needs-to-know-about
-design-for-2019.

Seldes, Gilbert. "Artist in a Factory." *New Yorker*, August 29, 1931.

Shepardson, David. "Tesla Driver in Fatal 'Autopilot' Crash Got Numerous Warnings: U.S. Government." Reuters, June 19, 2017. www.reuters.com/article/us
-tesla-crash/tesla-driver-in-fatal-autopilot-crash-got-numerous-warnings-u-s
-government-idUSKBN19A2XC.

The Simpsons. Season 2, episode 28, "O Brother Where Art Thou." Aired February 21, 1991. www.dailymotion.com/video/x6tg4a5.

Smith, Beverly. "He's into Everything." *American Magazine*, April 1932.

Smith, Brad. "Intuit's CEO on Building a Design-Driven Company." *Harvard Business Review*, January/February 2015. https://hbr.org/2015/01/intuits
-ceo-on-building-a-design-driven-company.

Smith, Oliver. "How to Boss It Like: Justin Rosenstein, Cofounder of Asana." *Forbes*, April 26, 2018. www.forbes.com/sites/oliversmith/2018/04/26/how-
to-boss-it-like-justin-rosenstein-cofounder-of-asana/#31194at7457b.

Soboroff, Jacob, Aarne Heikkila, and Daniel Arkin. "Hawaii Management Worker Who Sent False Missile Alert: I Was '100 Percent Sure' It Was Real." NBC News, February 2, 2018. www.nbcnews.com/news/us-news/hawaii
-emergency-management-worker-who-sent-false-alert-i-was-n844286.

Spool, Jared M. "The Hawaii Missile Alert Culprit: Poorly Chosen File Names." *Medium*, January 16, 2018. https://medium.com/ux-immersion-interactions
/the-hawaii-missile-alert-culprit-poorly-chosen-file-names-d30d59ddfcf5.

Stahl, Lesley. "Slot Machines: The Big Gamble." *60 Minutes*, January 7, 2011. www.cbsnews.com/news/slot-machines-the-big-gamble-07-01-2011/.

Stangel, Luke. "Is This a Sign That Apple Is Serious About Making a Deeper Push into Original Journalism?" *Silicon Valley Business Journal*, May 9, 2018. www.bizjournals.com/sanjose/news/2018/05/09/apple-news-journalist
-hiring-subscription-service.html.

Statt, Nick. "Google Now Says Controversial AI Voice Calling System Will Identify Itself to Humans." *The Verge*, May 10, 2018. www.theverge.com/2018/5
/10/17342414/google-duplex-ai-assistant-voice-calling-identify-itself-update.

Stevens, S. S. "Machines Cannot Fight Alone." *American Scientist* 34, no. 3 (July 1946).

Stolzoff, Simone. "The Formula for Phone Addiction Might Double as a Cure." *Wired*, February 1, 2018. www.wired.com/story/phone-addiction-formula/.

Sullivan, John Jeremiah. "You Blow My Mind. Hey, Mickey!" *New York Times Magazine*, June 8, 2011. www.nytimes.com/2011/06/12/magazine/a-rough
-guide-to-disney-world.html.

Suri, Jane Fulton. "Saving Lives Through Design." *Ergonomics in Design* (Summer 2000).

Suri, Jane Fulton, and IDEO. *Thoughtless Acts?* San Francisco: Chronicle, 2005.

Taggart, Kendall. "The Truth About the Trump Data Team That People Are Freaking Out About." *BuzzFeed News*, February 16, 2017. www.buzzfeednews .com/article/kendalltaggart/the-truth-about-the-trump-data-team-that -people-are-freaking.

Taub, Amanda, and Max Fisher. "Where Countries Are Tinderboxes and Facebook Is a Match." *New York Times*, April 21, 2018. www.nytimes.com/2018 /04/21/world/asia/facebook-sri-lanka-riots.html.

Teague, Walter Dorwin. *Design This Day: The Technique of Order in the Machine Age*. New York: Harcourt, Brace, 1940.

Tenner, Edward. *Our Own Devices: The Past and Future of Body Technology*. New York: Knopf, 2003.

Trufelman, Avery. "The Finnish Experiment." *99% Invisible*, September 19, 2017. https://99percentinvisible.org/episode/the-finnish-experiment/.

Tubik Studio. "UX Design Glossary: How to Use Affordances in User Interfaces." *UX Planet*. https://uxplanet.org/ux-design-glossary-how-to-use-affordances -in-user-interfaces-393c8e9686e4.

Turkle, Sherry. *Alone Together: Why We Expect More from Technology and Less from Each Other*. New York: Basic Books, 2011.

Twenge, Jean M. "Have Smartphones Destroyed a Generation?" *The Atlantic*, September 2017. www.theatlantic.com/magazine/archive/2017/09/has-the -smartphone-destroyed-a-generation/534198/.

United States Securities and Exchange Commission. Form S-1: Registration Statement, Facebook, Inc. Washington, D.C.: SEC, February 1, 2012. Accessed July 6, 2018. www.sec.gov/Archives/edgar/data/1326801/000119 312512034517/d287954ds1.htm.

"Unlocking Mobile Money." IDEO.org. Accessed October 9, 2017. www.ideo.org /project/gates-foundation.

Vincent, James. "Google's AI Sounds Like a Human on the Phone—Should We Be Worried?" *The Verge*, May 9, 2018. www.theverge.com/2018/5/9/17334658 /google-ai-phone-call-assistant-duplex-ethical-social-implications.

Von Thienen, Julia P. A., William J. Clancey, and Christoph Meinel. "Theoretical Foundations of Design Thinking." In *Design Thinking Research*, edited by Christoph Meinel and Larry Leifer, 15. Cham, Switzerland: Springer Nature, 2019. https://books.google.com/books?id=-9hwDwAAQBAJ.

Wagner, R. Polk, and Thomas Jeitschko. "Why Amazon's '1-Click' Ordering Was a Game Changer." Knowledge@Wharton by the Wharton School of the University of Pennsylvania, September 14, 2017. http://knowledge.wharton .upenn.edu/article/amazons-1-click-goes-off-patent/.

Waldrop, M. Mitchell. *The Dream Machine: J.C.R. Licklider and the Revolution That Made Computing Personal*. New York: Viking, 2001.

Wang, Amy B. "Former Facebook VP Says Social Media Is Destroying Society with 'Dopamine-Driven Feedback Loops.'" *Washington Post*, December 12,

2017. www.washingtonpost.com/news/the-switch/wp/2017/12/12/former
-facebook-vp-says-social-media-is-destroying-society-with-dopamine-driven
-feedback-loops/.

———. "Hawaii Missile Alert: How One Employee 'Pushed the Wrong Button' and Caused a Wave of Panic." *Washington Post*, January 14, 2018. www
.washingtonpost.com/news/post-nation/wp/2018/01/14/hawaii-missile
-alert-how-one-employee-pushed-the-wrong-button-and-caused-a-wave-of
-panic/.

Weinstein, Ari, and William Mattelaer. "Introduction to Siri Shortcuts." Presentation at the Apple Worldwide Developers Conference. McEnery Convention
Center, San Jose, June 5, 2018. https://developer.apple.com/videos/play
/wwdc2018/211/.

Weiser, Mark, and John Seeley Brown. "The Coming Age of Calm Technology."
In *Beyond Calculation: The Next Fifty Years of Computing*. New York: Springer,
1997.

Wendt, Thomas. "Critique of Human-Centered Design, or Decentering Design."
Presentation at the Interaction 17 Conference, School of Visual Arts, New
York, February 7, 2017. www.slideshare.net/ThomasMWendt/critique-of
-humancentered-design-or-decentering-design.

Whyte, William, Jr. "Groupthink." *Fortune*, March 1952.

Wiener, Norbert. *The Human Use of Human Beings*. Boston: Houghton Mifflin,
1954.

Williams, Wendell. "The Problem with Personality Tests." ERE.net, July 12,
2013. www.ere.net/the-problem-with-personality-tests/.

Wilson, Mark. "The Reason Your Brain Loves Wide Design." *Fast Company*,
August 24, 2017. www.fastcompany.com/90137664/the-reason-your-brain
-loves-wide-products.

Woodhead, Lindy. *Shopping, Seduction and Mr. Selfridge*. New York: Random
House, 2013.

Wu, Tim. "The Tyranny of Convenience." *New York Times*, February 17, 2018.
www.nytimes.com/2018/02/16/opinion/sunday/tyranny-convenience.html.

XXPorcelinaX. "Skinner—Free Will." YouTube, July 13, 2012. www.youtube
.com/watch?v=ZYEpCKXTga0.

Yablonski, Jon. "Laws of UX." Accessed November 2018. https://lawsofux.
com/.

Yardley, William. "Clifford Nass, Who Warned of a Data Deluge, Dies at 55."
New York Times, November 6, 2013. www.nytimes.com/2013/11/07/busi
ness/clifford-nass-researcher-on-multitasking-dies-at-55.html.

Acknowledgments

The major effort in this book was in the reporting, and for that I owe a great debt to the many people who invited me into their lives—for hours, at least, and sometimes for years. There are too many to name here—and indeed, too many more who didn't end up being mentioned in these pages—but a few people stand out. Mladen Barbaric understood immediately what I was hoping to accomplish with this book, and over the course of three years invited me dozens of times to see his design work progress in real time, offering an unvarnished, even vulnerable look at a process that most people try to hide. In doing so, he introduced me to Bo Gillespie, who was strikingly open about his experience with his startup.

There were numerous others who typically decline to talk to reporters these days, or who, at the very least, have reason to be wary of telling their stories, given how often those stories have been misconstrued. Among the former I would count Bill Atkinson and Andy Hertzfeld, whom I was honored to have met. Among the latter I would include Erik Glaser, Brian Lathrop, and the staff at Audi's Electronics Research Laboratory, as well as Leah Pearlman and Justin Rosenstein.

There were many people who offered time and presence, expecting little in return, including the great Don Norman, who hosted me generously at the University of California, San Diego. Pragya Mishra generously translated my conversations with Renuka, and recounted the research she did on behalf of Dalberg Design. Dave Watson and Dan Formosa booted up ancient memories of designing the Ford Fusion dashboard. Nadia Walker at IDEO was indefatigable in thinking of people who might help in the reporting of this book, such as Jane Fulton Suri. August de los Reyes spent untold hours sharing his life experience with me, and his strength in finding purpose in the face of hardship was an inspiration. Emily Orr of the Cooper Hewitt design museum ferried me out to the Dreyfuss archives and helped me wade through them. The staff at Three Mile Island were essential in helping me understand how much changed there. Bob McKim waded patiently through his memories, and just the fact of our time together was an inspiration for how the strands in this book could be braided. I'd like to extend another heartfelt thanks to the researchers who generously offered their hard-won learning, such as Russell Flinchum, who devoted so many years to understanding Henry Dreyfuss; and Bill Clancey, whose work unearthing the untold particulars of John Arnold's life has been a labor of love. John Padgett put up with years of my badgering, and let me in on what he was building at Carnival; that same story led me to countless other interviews both on and off the record, and I thank those who sat for them.

There were also many people who contributed to this book in

other ways. I'm greatly thankful to my collaborator Robert Fabricant for his conviction that the world needed a book like this one, and for giving it a name—a simple thing that nonetheless pushed this book to become something concrete. I would also like to reserve a special thanks to Kyle VanHemert, whose early work doing original research for this book was not only instructive but brilliantly generative; he lit paths and forged connections that would not have been there but for his insight. Numerous friends read this book with care and dedication, offering hundreds of suggestions that made this work better than it would have been: Joe Brown, Joe Gebbia, Morgan Clendaniel, Jason Tanz, Mark Wilson, Mohan Ramaswamy, and—again—Kyle VanHemert. But my two most important readers were my agent, Zoë Pagnamenta, and my editor, Sean McDonald. Zoë shepherded this book and shaped it from the beginning; she pushed for a book that would reach beyond the confines of the design community, and saw the possibilities before anyone else. Sean was also passionate about this book from the moment the proposal landed on his desk. Over six years, Sean blended patience and steadfastness, and offered support whenever it was needed—including in ways he probably didn't realize. Without his sense of design's importance in the world of the future, this book would have never come to be. Andrea Powell was fearless, sharp-eyed, and devoted in fact-checking this book. Any errors that remain are, of course, my own.

Finally, I'd like to thank my wife, Nicole, who offered her love and support, without which I wouldn't have been able to finish. I can't wait to see the bite marks our little baby leaves on the cover when she pulls this book off the shelf.

—Cliff Kuang

First and foremost, I would like to thank Cliff for letting me rope him into this project initially even though I had *no* idea of what it would really take to bring the untold story of design to life for a broad audience. The dedication and rigor that he brought to the reporting—and his insistence on featuring compelling characters and vivid storytelling—vastly exceeded any expectations I had at the outset. I do not think there is anyone else on the planet with the background, skills, and intelligence to pull this off. Reading each draft, I was consistently struck by Cliff's ability to boil down complex concepts into simple, relatable human language. Ideas that I have long held about my work, but have struggled to communicate, would appear page by page and chapter by chapter, almost as gifts. As this book eloquently captures, the role of design has gotten much less tangible as its influence in the world has grown. That is why it was so satisfying to see this material shaped and reshaped in the hands of a master craftsman. As Joe Gebbia notes in a burb for *User Friendly*, "Rarely do I dog-ear pages or underline paragraphs as much as I did with this book." Amen.

I would also like to acknowledge the many, many fearless designers I have had the privilege to learn from over the past twenty-five years, who have shaped my belief in the untold power of design. The list is too long to recount here, so I will highlight a few principal figures: Red Burns, Gideon D'Arcangelo, Bill Drenttell, Ravi Chhatpar, and Fabio Sergio (my doppelgänger and creative soul mate). I would also like to acknowledge the generations of designers whose stories have never been told but whose contributions are still being felt today through the products and experiences they so thoughtfully created. Many more books are waiting to be written about them.

As I mentioned in the afterword, this book is a product, first and foremost, and hopefully a user-friendly one. As I learned at Frog, all products are the result of multidisciplinary collaborations. I got my start as a designer in the world of publishing (and am blessed with a supremely talented book designer for a sister), so it was fascinating to see this process from the other side. Sean McDonald is a true maestro, bringing together an unbelievably talented team and creating the space for this unique product to emerge organically. Throughout, our agent, Zoë Pagnamenta, has been the glue, supporting our unusual collaboration with deep patience and wisdom, and calling us out when necessary.

Finally, a few words for my family, starting with my father, Richard—who, at eighty-eight, is still waiting for that truly user-friendly experience—and my mother, Florence, who is the source of my creative spark, having written fourteen books . . . and counting. Most important, I offer thanks to my teenage daughters, Julia and Evie, who put up with my loud laptop pecking on evenings and weekends, and to Jill Herzig, my partner of more than thirty-four years, who sensibly warned me against embarking on this creative boondoggle but nonetheless supported me throughout. *You got my heart, you got my soul . . .*

—Robert Fabricant

Index

Donald, Arnold, 229, 231, 232, 238
dopamine, 254, 259, 263
Dreyfuss, Doris Marks, 67, 70, 94–95, 172–74
Dreyfuss, Henry, 55–59, 65–72, 87–95, 117, 154, 163–65, 177, 181, 207, 271, 273, 285–87, 290, 293, 302, 308, 310, 334, 352*n12*; Broadway work, 55–59, 66; death of, 94–95; Honeywell thermostat, 92, 93, 336, 343; industrial design and, 59, 67–68, 93; Joe and Josephine drawings, 88–89, 92, 174, 176, 178, 185, 337; Macy's and, 66–67, 165; *The Measure of Man*, 92, 337, 340, 341; RKO theater and, 55–56, 92, 173–74, 335; tank cockpit chairs, 87–88; telephone designs, 91, 93, 337, 371*n21*; Toperator washing machine, 69, 87, 335
Dropbox, 351*n32*
DVDs, 230
DVRs, 163, 321
dyslexia, 205
Dyson, James, 157, 339
Dyson vacuum cleaners, 157, 158, 339

Eames, Ray and Charles, 90
Earlham College, 280, 284
Eastman, George, 332–33
Eastman Kodak, 332–33, 336
eBay, 34–35, 249
education, 244–45
elderly, 201; suit to augment muscles of, 107–108, 340
Eliza conversational bot, 337–38
email, 199, 205, 242, 274; in-box, 134
embodied cognition, 152–54, 294, 360*n32*
emojis, 249, 260, 326–27, 342
Emotional Design (Norman), 326, 340
emotions, 155–57, 325–27, 370*n16*, 371*n20*
empathy, 163, 184–85, 190, 199, 212, 245, 257, 327; with disability, 200;

industrialized, 163–64, 170, 183, 185, 245, 273–75, 294
Engelbart, Doug, 142, 168, 243, 363*n11*; Mother of All Demos by, 187–90, 338
Enlightenment, 95
Eno (Capital One chatbot), 211–12, 259, 268
environmental concerns, 305; climate change, 34, 289
ergonomics, 86, 92, 95
Erickson, Thom, 369*n7*
errors, 86–87, 95, 173; blaming humans for, 122; designer, 83; pilot, 81, 83, 102–103, 335
Esalen, 168, 169
Esslinger, Hartmut, 326
ethnography, modern, 334
European Union (EU), 346–47
expectations, 110–11, 313
"experience," origin of word, 369*n3*
Experience and Education (Dewey), 301
Exposition International des Arts Décoratifs et Industriels Modernes, 61–62
Eyal, Nir, 258–59

Fabricant, Richard, 319–20
Fabricant, Robert, 9, 96, 130, 288, 301–30
Facebook, 118, 131, 132, 239, 243, 247–48, 250, 251, 255, 258, 259, 261, 262, 267–69, 271, 274–76, 292–95; advertising on, 267; feedback and, 35, 36; in Kenya, 147–48; Like button, 35, 36, 146, 247–49, 262, 265–66, 274, 291, 292, 342, 344; misinformation spread on, 262, 263; News Feed, 247, 248, 318; tribalism fostered by, 245, 262–64
factories, 60, 63; accidents in, 82
Fadell, Tony, 342, 344
fake news and misinformation, 262, 263, 289

McKim, Bob, 164–70, 174, 180, 181, 190
McKinsey & Company, 170
meal delivery, 316–17, 370*n8*
Measure of Man, The (Dreyfuss and Tilley), 92, 337, 341
Meikle, Jeffrey L., 69
memory: short-term, 322; sketching how something works from, 321
mental models, 31, 40–41, 105, 119, 120, 180, 288, 297, 320–22, 351*n32*; cognitive load and, 322; digital assistants and, 124; internet and, 131; metaphors and, 133
metaphors, 84, 124, 132–35, 139, 144–45, 147, 154, 155, 158, 195, 203, 295, 297, 299, 358*n22*; apps and, 149–52; brain and, 152–53; coach, 136–39; in defibrillator design, 139; desktop, 139–40, 143, 144, 146–47; dominant, in product categories, 317–18; embodied, 152–54; and Facebook in Kenya, 147–48; horse, 116, 117, 118, 126, 144; horseless carriage, 318; in-box, 134; internet and, 132, 134–35; ladder of, 147, 193, 317–19; leaf, on hybrid car dashboards, 137–39, 144; Macintosh OS and, 144; mental models and, 133; news feed, 134, 318; personal assistant, 189; personification, 155–57; time as money, 133–34, 135; visual, in Apple products, 148–49, 210
Metaphors We Live By (Lakoff and Johnson), 133, 152, 153
MetroCard, 311
Metropolis, 334–35, 362*n8*
Metropolitan Edison, 39
Metropolitan Museum of Art, 60
Mic, 260
microdermabrasion device, 328
Microsoft, 145, 191, 193–95, 199, 202, 205–206, 208, 370*n14*; Cortana, 194, 208; PowerPoint, 208–209; Visual Basic, 361*n22*; Word, Clippy in, 112; Xbox, 197, 205–206
middle class, 63, 290

Miller, George, 322, 337
mind, 95–96
Minority Report, 233, 236
Minsky, Marvin, 189–90
misinformation, 262, 263, 289
MIT, 165–67, 189, 337; Media Lab, 154, 155
Mob, the, 39
mobile phones, 368*n2*; Magic Bus Ticketing and, 283–86; *see also* smartphones
mode confusion, 144
modernism, 157, 334
Moggridge, Bill, 175–78, 180–81, 339, 361*n21*
mood boards, 155
Moore, Patricia, 200–202, 313, 340, 341
Morris, William, 332, 352*n14*
Moskovitz, Dustin, 248
Mother of All Demos, 187–90, 338
Mothersill, Philippa, 154–57
motivations, 46, 259, 344
movies, 230–31, 243, 254, 363*n11*
M-Pesa, 284, 368*n2*
Münsterberg, Hugo, 81–82
Myanmar, 263

Nadella, Satya, 202
Nairobi, 281, 283, 284, 315
Nancy, 272–73
NASA, 104, 115–16, 337
Nass, Clifford, 108–10, 112, 211, 258
National Transportation Safety Board (NTSB), 121, 122
navigability, 31
Navy, U.S., 87
Neeleman, David, 309
Nespresso, 117
Nest, 92, 336, 344–45
Netflix, 230–31, 260, 351*n33*
neural networks, 36, 44
neuroscience, 96
Newby, Paul, 342
news feeds, 134, 247, 248, 318
New York, 94
New York City Health and Hospitals Corporation, 303

Starbucks, 325
State Department, 201
Stein, Robby, 37
Stevens, S. S., 84–85, 87, 95; "Machines Cannot Fight Alone," 78–79
stores, 150–51; Selfridge, 150, 333
Story, Joseph, 129
streamlining, 70
Stumpf, Bill, 341
subway system, 311
suit to augment muscles of the elderly, 107–108, 340
Sullivan, Louis, 371n17
Swartz, Jan, 230, 239
symbols, 85
Systrom, Kevin, 259

Taming Hal (Degani), 105
tank cockpit chairs, 87–88
Tariyal, Ridhi, 183–84
task bars, 354n7
tax preparation, 325–26
Taylor, Frederick Winslow, 63–64, 333
Teague, Walter Dorwin, 58, 87, 88, 117, 164, 172, 174, 332; Polaroid camera, 117, 336
telephone, 199, 200, 205; Dreyfuss's designs for, 91, 93, 337; icon for, 91; Princess, 337, 371n21; see also smartphones
television, 230, 243, 257, 292, 321, 351n33; TiVo and, 163, 342
Tencent, 364n19
Tesla, 102, 103, 114, 119–22, 346
Tesler, Larry, 142, 144, 146
theater in Sioux City, Iowa, 55–56, 92, 173–74, 335
theme parks, 229, 254; Disneyland, 220, 336; Disney World, see Disney World
thermostats, 92, 93, 336, 343, 344–45
think-aloud, 321
Thompson, Hunter S., 168
Thoughtless Acts (Fulton Suri), 179, 297
Three Mile Island (TMI), 38–43,

351n31; accident at, 15–21, 26–32, 37, 38, 40, 42, 43, 46, 78, 83, 95, 103, 105, 338–39; control panels at, 28–31, 40–43, 105; feedback and, 28, 32, 40, 42; Norman and, 24–25, 30, 38, 338–39; PORV (pilot-operated release valve) light at, 28, 29; simulated control room at, 39–40; worker pairs at, 41–42
Tibbets, Linden, 297–98
Tilley, Alvin, 88–89, 92, 337
"time is money" metaphor, 133–34, 135
Tinder, 256
TiVo, 163, 342
toothbrushes, 163
Toperator washing machine, 69, 87, 335
touchscreens, 41, 104, 127, 145–47, 343
Toyota, 135
traffic signs, 85
Trion-Z, 217
Trump, Donald, 250, 262, 264–67
trust, 107, 119; in digital assistants, 193–94, 208; self-driving cars and, 114; social mores and, 108, 112, 114; and suit to augment muscles of the elderly, 107–108
Turri, Pellegrino, 199, 205
Tversky, Amos, 96
Twitter, 134, 255, 261, 318
2001: A Space Odyssey, Hal 9000 in, 105, 117
typewriters, 64, 199, 200, 203, 205; QWERTY keyboard for, 332

Uber, 121, 259–60, 287, 355n26
UC San Diego, 23–24
U.K. government, 345, 369n2
understanding, 113, 299; in design, 42, 56, 68, 80, 289; incomplete, 271
UNICEF, 315, 369n2
United Nations, 263, 369n2
United States, 59–63, 93
University of Texas, 244
usability research, 171